Indian Culture
and
India's Future

To
Sri Aurobindo,
who made me
understand
and love
India

INDIAN CULTURE
AND
INDIA'S FUTURE

Michel Danino

PRINTWORLD
Publishers of Indian Traditions

Cataloging in Publication Data — DK

[Courtesy: D.K. Agencies (P) Ltd. <docinfo@dkagencies.com>]

Danino, Michel, 1956-

    Indian culture and India's future / Michel Danino.

      p.   cm.

    Includes bibliographical references (p.   ) and index.

    ISBN: 9788124605653

    1. India — Civilization. 2. Civilization, Western —
Indic influences.   I. Title.

DDC 934   22

© Author

First published in India, 2011

Reprinted in 2012, 2015, 2016

Fifth impression, 2019

ISBN: 978-81-246-0565-3 (HB)

ISBN: 978-81-246-0567-7 (PB)

Printed and published by:
D.K. Printworld (P) Ltd.
Regd. office : *Vedaśrī,* F-395, Sudarshan Park
(Metro Station: ESI Hospital) New Delhi - 110015
Phones : (011) 2545 3975, 2546 6019
e-mail : indology@dkprintworld.com
Web : www.dkprintworld.com

Contents

Prologue

In the course of some 250 lectures and talks given in India over the last ten years—to students, teachers, academics, professionals and the lay public—I have found a few questions regularly thrown at me:

- What is so valuable about Indian culture? In particular, does it have any practical value in everyday life?
- We Indians may have achieved something in the spiritual field, but in the material one, don't we owe everything to the West?
- Isn't Indian culture irrelevant in our modern scientific age?
- In fact, isn't it excessive religiosity that has kept us plunged in superstition and illiteracy?
- Won't Indian culture disappear under the impact of globalization and the spread of Western culture?
- How should Indians—and Hindus more specifically—deal with the new concept of 'dialogue of civilizations'?

This book attempts to answer these questions and a few more. In doing so I will steer clear of worn-out clichés in currency at both ends of the spectrum: unthinking dismissal of India culture or its hollow glorification.

I should add that Indian culture's core values and tools have been central to my life since I decided to settle in India at the ripe old age of 21 (a decision I have never once regretted); to me they are not merely theoretical objects of academic study. I hope something of this concreteness will come through in the following pages.

A dear friend of mine once half-joked that some of my writings should be entitled 'To the Confused Indian'. If, going through this book, a few members of this ever-growing class feel some clarity, or at least some stimulation to consider new viewpoints, I will feel amply rewarded. The reader may also keep in mind that I have more often tried to ask fundamental questions than to provide facile answers; to reflect afresh on some of the big issues confronting us today is what matters.

Many Indian and non-Indian friends have helped me in my quest and work; they know how much I owe to them: generosity is indeed a cardinal Indian value; so is gratitude.

*

Notes

Some of the chapters in this book are extensively revised and enlarged versions of earlier writings, fused here with newer ones.

Detailed references for all quotations are found at the end of the book. (They are referred to in the text by Arabic numerals, while footnotes are referred to by asterisks.) My interpolations are within square brackets [ ], which means that any parentheses ( ) are those of the quoted author. Except when indicated, English translations of French texts are mine.

As full diacritical marks for Sanskrit words would be disconcerting to most readers, I have only indicated long vowels with a macron over them (such as ā or ī). Exceptions include Sanskrit words that have passed into common usage (e.g., ahimsa, ashram, avatar, Ayurveda or Vedanta), as well as names of recent persons and current geographical names.

The motif reproduced below and at the end of each chapter, is a Harappan design of 'intersecting circles'—an appropriate symbol for Indian culture.

Introduction

Is Indian Culture Obsolete?

WHEN I was a teenager in France, back in the 1970s, I stumbled on the teachings of several beings who, to my eager mind, suddenly gave a meaning to life as no Western thinker had. We call them seers, yogis, mahatmas, maharishis, but better terms would perhaps be 'explorers', 'evolvers', 'sowers', or 'builders' —although, on occasion, there is also some demolition work involved in this tortuous business of evolution. Before I set my heart on Sri Aurobindo, who eventually drew me to India, I had been deeply moved by Sri Ramakrishna, and had felt a certain shudder while reading Swami Vivekananda, perhaps the same shudder that ran through his listeners at Chicago in 1893.

Why so many such beings took birth in India is a question I will not presume to answer. But they do seem to have found (or should I say 'made'?) this land more suitable than others for the fulfilment of their action. They moved and worked within a certain worldview native to India, broadening it and renewing it when needed. What is this Indian worldview? What is so specific to it? Is it merely 'spiritual'? If not, how has it been put into practice, and with what results? Finally, does it still have something to offer to the world? Can it have some impact on the course of humanity, or are we just indulging in an academic debate over how golden and glittering our past was in contrast with the dreary present?

Swami Vivekananda confronted the question in 1894: 'India

can never be Europe until she dies. And will she die?'[1] In other words, shall we soon have to leave behind the essence of Indianness and be happy if all that is left of it is a bit of exotic local colour for foreign tourists? Sri Aurobindo was rather blunt, too:

> In the stupendous rush of change which is coming on the human world as a result of the present tornado of upheaval, ancient India's culture, attacked by European* modernism, overpowered in the material field, betrayed by the indifference of her children, may perish for ever along with the soul of the nation that holds it in its keeping.[2]

That was in 1918, and I have often had occasion to meditate on this 'betrayal by indifference'. But a more immediate question is perhaps, How would a twenty-year-old Indian today feel about 'ancient India's culture'?

The 'Angry Young Indian'

If I were to picture myself as this young Indian, my answer would likely shift the focus to the material field. Job opportunities may look better today than a decade or two ago (for how long?), but I would still ask my elders how in sixty years they managed to bring the nation to its present state. I would feel anger and contempt for the hordes of politicians and bureaucrats who have bled this country white, diverted colossal resources from their intended targets, and turned the daily life of ordinary Indians—those they ceaselessly claimed to 'uplift'—into a hopeless hell.

But I would also ask the many good, honest, capable, cultured people of this country why they have done so little to stem the rot, why they have contented themselves with throwing up their hands in despair and pleading helplessness—or, at best, with giving fine talks on every ill India is ridden with. And I may possibly be tempted to do like many of my friends: fly to some 'heaven' across the seas, where to gain admission to school or college you do not have to declare your religion in the name of

---

* Today, of course, we must read 'global' for 'European'.

God knows what 'secularism', or your caste in the name of a 'casteless society', where you do not have to pay a bribe at every step or prove that you are 'backward' before you can move forward, where your talents can be appreciated rather than stifled—in a word, where you do not have to feel ashamed of your country.

This, as I have frequently seen, is what many, if not most, young Indians carry in their hearts. It is a justified, legitimate if bitter feeling, nurtured by proof upon daily proof.

But it often goes a step or two further, and our 'angry young Indian', as I will call him or her, may voice the following feelings (I summarize here voices I have actually heard over the years):

> See how Westerners live: their cities are modern and clean, people don't dump garbage all around, trains and buses run on time, there is no corruption, no illiteracy, they are hard-working, they have discipline, a civic sense—while we Indians have none, we are lethargic, we have no courage to fight the system; hypocrites that we are, we talk about our glorious culture but dump our rubbish to the other side of the street or grease palms at the least demand, while crores of us still live in the most abject misery.
>
> All right, maybe we were great two or three or five thousand years ago, maybe our kings of old were better than the crooks and criminals who now rule us, but what good is that today? Today, it is the Westerners who are superior; they don't talk as much as we do, but they have conquered the world with their abilities and hard work. They wanted to be 'achievers' and they achieved; they hunted after success and they succeeded.
>
> And if there is any hope for this country, it is only in adopting their methods, their science and technology, their management and trade—nothing else is going to bring us prosperity, certainly not our traditions, which have degenerated into so much ignorant superstition: see the caste divisions, see the survival of *sati* or child marriage, the countless barbaric customs still prevailing in our villages,

the endless communal clashes. Who wants to waste time
glorifying all that? And what has our surfeit of religion
achieved, except to make us weak, fatalistic, always ready
to bow to everyone else? Are temples going to make the
country prosperous? Will smearing ashes or sandal paste
on our foreheads help us build the future? Let's face it:
culture is good for the elderly, the renunciate or the tourist;
it won't help us to build tomorrow's India. The sooner we
throw out those relics of the past and turn to healthy rationalism and progressive thinking, the better for all of us.

That, with endless variations, is what young Indians are fed
with more or less subtly from their schooldays, and every day
through our Westernized media. It fairly well represents current
conventional thinking, or, shall I say, the 'politically correct'
views of India aired by our amorphous intelligentsia. There is a
certain amount of truth in those statements, and we will do well
to admit it; but there is much facile thinking, too, and we will
have to confront it.

The part of truth is there for all to see. To be sure, our cities
are generally congested and unclean, because municipal officials
and clerks think their only duty is to draw a salary. True, we have
millions of illiterates, because our policy makers have failed to
make education not only compulsory and free, but also stimulating and enriching, and because our educationists think their
duty is done when they have spoken at a few seminars while the
average village school struggles along without electricity, sometimes without a roof, and quite often without teachers. Very true,
it is revolting to have to grease a palm for a mere certificate or to
pay one's way to a job, because we have come to accept that the
dharma of those in power is to live off the fat of the land even
more shamelessly than our British rulers ever did. True again, we
are generally too sluggish to protest effectively against this state
of affairs, itching to condemn it in private talk but willing to
condone it in deed. And true also, Indian tradition has often
become cluttered with meaningless minutiae or a convenient
excuse for rigid and retrograde attitudes.

Western Culture

So far so good. But there is also an ignorant part in our angry young Indian's diatribe: an idealized view of the West and a distorted notion of India's heritage. Life in many Western societies is not as rosy as all that, and it has its share of corruption, poverty and illiteracy. A degree of material success and affluence has done little to cope with central problems—otherwise, why should a growing number of Western thinkers speak with anguish of the West's decline? Why should, in particular, Western models of economic growth and development be increasingly questioned?

At a more prosaic level, why has the U.S.A., to which so many young Indians look up to, the dubious privilege of holding 25 per cent of the world's prison population?[3] Why should a fifth of U.S. high-school students go to their studies carrying a weapon?[4] Is it the West or India that invented school and college shoot-outs, manic depression, institutionalized child abuse, the psychopath and the serial killer? Why is it that few Western economies could survive without massive arms sales, most of the time to Third-World countries, feeding the hundreds of wars that ruin their economies while at the same time preaching peace and human rights? And why do many Western nations, the U.S. first among them, have to spend far more money than they really have in order to feed wasteful lifestyles, causing a worldwide vicious circle of credit crunch, the end result of which we are yet to see? Is it the West or India that has caused the planet to overheat in just two centuries, endangering its whole biosphere?

It would be easy to draw a long list of aberrations and perversions afflicting Western societies. But every society has its aberrations, you may say again, haven't we got quite a good number of them in India? We certainly do, but a better question is, Are the diseases of Western societies healing, or are they seething out of control?

Not long ago, an Indian observed the West closely and said:

[Its] institutions, systems, and everything connected with political governments have been condemned as useless; Europe is restless, does not know where to turn. The material tyranny is tremendous. The wealth and power of a country are in the hands of a few men who do not work but manipulate the work of millions of human beings. By this power they can deluge the whole earth with blood. . . . The Western world is governed by a handful of Shylocks. All those things that you hear about—constitutional government, freedom, liberty, and parliaments—are but jokes. . . . The whole of Western civilisation will crumble to pieces in the next fifty years if there is no spiritual foundation.[5]

That Indian was Swami Vivekananda, and he spoke those words in 1897, on his return from his journey to the West. In case you find him too radical, let me quote one of the Western thinkers I just alluded to, a French historian of science, Pierre Thuillier, who wrote a few years ago a penetrating analysis of the maladies afflicting the West for all its talk of 'progress', and predicted a 'great implosion' of Western society:

Westerners remain convinced that their mode of life is the privileged and definitive incarnation of 'civilization'; they are unable to understand that this 'civilization' has become as fragile as an eggshell. At the end of the twentieth century, political, economic and cultural elites behave as if the gravity of the situation eluded them. . . . Those who profess to be progressive clearly no longer know what a *culture* is; they no longer even realize that a society can continue to function more or less normally even as it has lost its soul. . . . In their eyes, a society is dead only when it is physically destroyed; they do not realize that the decay of a civilization is inner before anything else.[6]

Or what about this observation by another French thinker, André Malraux, 'I see in Europe a carefully ordered barbarism'?[7] Swami Vivekananda's statement was not that extreme, although his prediction of fifty years may have been off the mark.

Let us also remember that he criticized India's own maladies equally severely. Yet the Swami saw too deeply to fall into the common trap of throwing out the baby with the bathwater, and he kept his rock-solid faith in Indian civilization. Moreover, in America and Europe he met many dissatisfied Westerners who were anxious to understand India's message. Their numbers have been steadily growing since then, driven by a need which neither science nor Western religions have been able to meet. On a more intellectual level, some Western physicists are not shy of showing parallels between quantum mechanics and yogic knowledge. Ecologists call for a recognition of our deeper connectedness with nature, a concept inherent to the Indian worldview. A few psychologists want to learn from Indian insights into human nature. And some businessmen look up to the Gītā and its concept of dharma to work out new management strategies.

Writing in the 1950s, the U.S. historian Will Durant, who had a soft corner for India, anticipated this phenomenon when he wrote:

> It is true that, even across the Himalayan barrier, India has sent us such questionable gifts as grammar and logic, philosophy and fables, hypnotism and chess, and, above all, our numerals and our decimal system. But these are not the essence of her spirit; they are trifles compared to what we may learn from her in the future.[8]

If we want to go beyond the clichés of the day, we must allow our anger, however justified, to simmer down, and start asking a few serious questions. The first must be: Would there be in the West such a search for deeper things, however clumsy and confused, if our modern world were as perfect as we are told? Shall we still say that Indian culture is just a bundle of superstitions? In 1920, Sri Aurobindo, one of India's least understood figures of the twentieth century, summed up the whole problem in these words:

> The scientific, rationalistic, industrial, pseudo-democratic civilisation of the West is now in process of dissolution and

it would be a lunatic absurdity for us at this moment to build blindly on that sinking foundation. When the most advanced minds of the occident are beginning to turn in this red evening of the West for the hope of a new and more spiritual civilisation to the genius of Asia, it would be strange if we could think of nothing better than to cast away our own self and potentialities and put our trust in the dissolving and moribund past of Europe.[9]

The Tree of Indian Civilization

Our second question takes the form of a parable: If, in our garden, we find a huge old tree weighed down by dead branches and over-grown with creepers and thorns, shall we fell it, even as it gives us shade, cool air and fruits? Or would we not rather set to work, clear the weeds and creepers, chop off the deadwood, prune a few branches here and there, and give the tree a new youth?

The tree is Indian civilization. It asks to be cleared and pruned, not felled: it is still capable of fresh growth and new fruits. 'But is it needed at all,' you still question, 'isn't it unsuited to our modern age? If Indian culture is so great, why has it not pre-vented India's sociopolitical system from decaying? Why are we today saddled with a corrupt and inefficient administration, judiciary and political system despite advances in other fields?'

Behind this valid question lies the misconception of an 'other-worldly' Indian spirituality, soulful and even 'mind-ful', but disdainful of this coarse material creation. Take the picture one step further, and you gaze at an India steeped in religion and spirituality, but also in misery and squalor, with the underlying message that we cannot expect one without the other. Such was the colonial caricature of India, which persists in many ways despite the recent material advances. Rather than get lost in a metaphysical labyrinth, let us take a semi-historical look at the issue.

Going as far back as we can in our present state of knowledge, we have a fairly good picture of India's earliest developed society:

that of the Indus or Harappan civilization.* Archaeology has shown it to be not only the most extensive of its time (about a million square kilometres), but also one with a most efficient civic administration and a surprising degree of standardization visible in its town-planning, drainage system, brick proportions, weights and script. Remarkably, Harappan society appears to have been largely free from warfare or man-made destruction, in so far as we can judge from the material record and artistic depictions. It was devoid, too, of a glorified ruling elite, military structure, or excessively 'depressed classes'. Perhaps because this civilization did not give rise to spectacular pyramids or monumental temples, the more noteworthy achievement of a largely peaceful and prosperous society with great civic efficiency has escaped general notice. Even today, after 4,500 years, our Indian cities pale in comparison with the Harappan civic administration: it kept streets free from encroachments, constructed and maintained spacious community buildings, private and public wells, reservoirs, dams and other complex rainwater-harvesting structures, and an advanced sanitation system—enough to make us wonder at our talk of 'development' and 'progress'.

Are we then looking at just a prosperous, 'materialistic' society? No, for the Harappans are credited with evolving a form of yoga. Some of the famous Indus seals depict deities in a specific seated *āsana* (the *mūlabandhāsana*), and there are many figurines of people stretching in various postures, while the so-called (but miscalled) 'priest-king' is shown in deep contemplation. All this points to a tradition of yoga.[10] Clearly, it did not come in the way of material achievements—or did it, perhaps, aid them?

A similar though more complex picture arises from India's classical age. From Mauryan to Gupta times, from the Chalukyas to the Rashtrakutas or from the Pallavas to the Cholas and the Vijayanagara empire, we see a spiritual as well as material

---

* Also called Indus–Sarasvatī civilization, as it straddled those two great river systems. Its urban phase lasted from 2600 to 1900 BCE, although its antecedents are traceable to about 5000 BCE, even beyond in a region or two.

efflorescence on a large scale. Warring and strife were now wide-spread, though they rarely came in the way of material affluence: impressive capitals, spacious universities coexisted with a spiritually rooted artistic explosion, large Jain, Buddhist or Hindu monasteries and temple complexes, and with philosophical and devotional developments across the subcontinent. India was a pioneer in shipping, metallurgy and textile production; she had a flourishing agriculture and external trade, her own systems of medicine still alive today, and a long list of innovations in every technique from brick- to jewel-making to water management.

Where was the worldly-unworldly dichotomy on the ground? This land was then far more creative, wealthy and materially developed than Europe, as testimonies of Greek, Chinese and Arab travellers to India make clear. Two thousand years ago, her share of the world GDP is estimated to have been 33 per cent while that of Europe (including Eastern Europe) was 13 per cent.*

Repeated waves of Muslim invasions put an end to this classical age, seriously disrupting (especially in the North) delicate mechanisms of transmission of knowledge that had been honed for centuries or more; worse, they exhausted India's vitality, though without succeeding in killing it altogether. In 1750, Indian goods still stood at 25 per cent of the world production, while Europe's contribution had risen to 23 per cent.[11] Under colonial rule, however, India's share soon plummeted, as did her agricultural output. What followed was, in the words of Will Durant again, 'the most sordid and criminal exploitation of one nation by another in all recorded history'.[12] Admitting 'unaccustomed partiality and passion',[13] Durant authored in 1930 a forceful study, *The Case for India*, which might as well have been titled *J'accuse*:

> The British conquest of India was the invasion and destruction of a high civilization by a trading company utterly

---

* China's share was 26 per cent, so that India and China together contributed 59 per cent of the world's GDP. (If we extend to the whole of Asia, the figure is over 76 per cent.)

without scruple or principle, careless of art and greedy of
gain, overrunning with fire and sword a country tempo-
rarily disordered and helpless, bribing and murdering,
annexing and stealing, and beginning that career of illegal
and 'legal' plunder which has now gone on ruthlessly for
one hundred and seventy-three years. . . .[14]

England has year by year been bleeding India to the point
of death.[15] . . . The British ownership of India has been a
calamity and a crime . . . the present plunder has now gone
on beyond bearing; year by year it is destroying one of the
greatest and gentlest peoples of history.[16]

After Britain's government took over the reins from the East
India Company, another kind of destruction took shape: that
of India's native industries, crafts, administrative, educational
and medical systems. In the first decade of the twentieth century,
Sri Aurobindo, in the thick of the revolutionary movement for
India's Independence, had a first-hand experience of the actual
effects of colonial domination; a few years later, he gave this
diagnosis:

English rule . . . undermined and deprived of living strength
all the pre-existing centres and instruments of Indian social
life and by a sort of unperceived rodent process left it only
a rotting shell without expansive power or any better
defensive force than the force of inertia.[17]

'Independent' India

That, in summary, was India's condition before Independence.
But there is clearly no point blaming bygone Muslim or British
invaders when the country has had more than six decades to
rebuild and revitalize itself. Instead, 'free' India groaned under
the yoke of a Soviet-type socialistic apparatus, a monstrous
bureaucracy grafted over an already mammoth colonial administration, a rigid five-year planning with a huge and ruinous
public sector, an absurd degree of centralization and nationali-
zation, and a constant interference in every field of life which

gave people the impression that the government would do every-thing for them—which, of course, meant in practice that it did nothing except grow ever more unwieldy, inefficient, self-contained, arrogant, corrupt, unaccountable, oblivious and con-temptuous of the man-in-the-street or the man-in-the-village, its obese body gorging on the well-oiled diversion of colossal resources intended for development. Thus did Indians come to surrender to this new and perhaps worse monster all sense of initiative, all courage to protest, their proverbial tolerance stretched to the extreme, their no less proverbial lethargy remain-ing their sole refuge. Thus did the many 'good, honest, capable, cultured people' whom I mentioned at the beginning come to shun Indian politics as the dirty field it has indeed become, a *goondā-rāj*,[18] in Sri Aurobindo's own term of 1935.

Blaming India's present degradation on her ancient culture or civilization is not merely ignorant, it is dishonest. And it is plain to see that those who are fond of such self-deprecation are usually the very ones who profit from the present system. They will ridicule village superstitions but will rush to the first dubious godman. They will throw a fit at the least mention of *sati* but will not mind if thousands of schoolchildren commit suicide every year out of desperation. They will deplore the bane of poverty but not the organized looting of the country at the hands of the ruling elite. They will condemn the caste system while raising one community against another and exacerbating casteism through the system of caste-based reservations.

How is Indian culture responsible for such degeneration? Its central principle—perhaps its only principle—is dharma, which, at the plainest level, means doing one's duty sincerely and ener-getically. Ancient scriptures have thousands of pages on a ruler's duties towards his subjects—and what do our modern rulers do? Step no. 1: perversely equate dharma and religion; step no. 2: declare that secularism demands the separation of religion from politics; step no. 3: therefore, let us carefully keep dharma out of politics. Not only out of politics, but out of education and public life as well—out of our brains, out of our lives. And indeed, over the years, dharma has been uprooted from the national body, as sincere Indians painfully know.

The only way to rebuild India on sound foundations—not the transient ones of today's economic boom—is to reverse the tide and get men and women of quality to reconquer the political battlefield instead of running away from it. Quality means substance, it means 'culture' in the true sense of the term. Because Indian culture has taught that life is not as it appears, that we have a divine essence and must try to manifest it, the unique quality of India's human substance, with all its faults, remains palpable—early European travellers to India said it, Swami Vivekananda said it, Sri Aurobindo said it, and it is plain enough to the inner eye.

This was Rabindranath Tagore's advice to his fellow Indians:

> Let me state clearly that I have no distrust of any culture because of its foreign character. On the contrary, I believe that the shock of such forces is necessary for the vitality of our intellectual nature. ... What I object to is the artificial arrangement by which this foreign education tends to occupy all the space of our national mind and thus kills, or hampers, the great opportunity for the creation of a new thought power by a new combination of truths. It is this which makes me urge that all the elements in our own culture have to be strengthened, not to resist the Western culture, but truly to accept and assimilate it, and use it for our food and not as our burden. ...
>
> But before we are in a position to stand a comparison with the other cultures of the world, or truly to co-operate with them, we must base our own structure on a synthesis of all the different cultures we have. When, taking our stand at such a centre, we turn towards the West, our gaze shall no longer be timid and dazed; our heads shall remain erect, safe from insult. For then we shall be able to take our own views of Truth, from the standpoint of our own vantage ground, thus opening out a new vista of thought before the grateful world.[19]

If, therefore, we want to revitalize India, we must tap the real source of life and strength in ourselves to start with. Keep the essence of this country's long journey through time, keep the core of its experience; give it as many new forms, as many new expressions as we wish. To aspire to bring back the bygone past, glorious or not, would be foolish and fruitless. 'Our past with all its faults and defects should be sacred to us,' said Sri Aurobindo, 'but the claims of our future with its immediate possibilities should be still more sacred.'[20]

Then, if we find some aspects of Indian culture outdated, let us first understand them, then get rid of them—chop off the deadwood. If we want a prosperous country, let us tackle in earnest the cancer of corruption—remove the weeds and creepers. If we want to imitate the West, let us imitate its self-discipline, its constant search for innovation, not its greed and tragic lack of direction—do not fell the tree. Preserve it, water it, nourish it, care for it—it is a life-giving tree, and perhaps its richest fruit is yet to come.

'Out of this decay is coming the India of the future,' said Swami Vivekananda, 'it is sprouting, its first leaves are already out; and a mighty, gigantic tree is here, already beginning to appear.'[21]

Part One

A Thousand-Branched Tree

'O Lord of the Forest, evergreen, glowing, golden-hued, spreading a thousand branches....'

Rig Veda, 9.5.10

1

India's Scientific Mind

IF we are to probe the strengths of Indian civilization beyond its spiritual explorations or artistic achievements, a good field to start from is that of science and technology. While we hear every other day a call for the development of a 'scientific temper' in modern India—generally by people who have no understanding of science—there is little inquiry into India's early steps in the field, much less into the nature of the Indian scientific mind, admittedly one of the most creative in the ancient world. Whether we deal with the size and age of the universe, huge or infinitesimal time scales, numbers from zero to infinity, the notion of evolution, cosmic dimensions underlying the construction of altars and temples, we find not only a familiarity with concepts that would appear only centuries later in the West, but an obsession with the infinite that allows no dogmatic limit and encourages the most daring conceptualizations.

Fascinating examples of this Indian approach to scientific knowledge systems are best drawn from mathematics and astronomy (inseparable in early times) and architecture, but more could be produced from fields ranging from poetics to music. It is another cruel irony that none of our Indian universities should find it worthwhile to offer a course in this rich aspect of our heritage, as though 'history' should be restricted to meaningless series of dates, dynasties and wars.

A Cosmic Temper

We first return to the Harappan world, where, despite the absence of written records, we find evidence of elaborate systems of units of length and weight showing a rudimentary decimal system, a knowledge of geometry reflected in a sophisticated town-planning, and some evidence of basic astronomical observations. A millennium later, the *Vedānga Jyotisha*, India's most ancient extant scientific text (dated to about 1400 BCE*), spells out the notion of calendar, seasons, equinoxes and solstices, and discusses the 27 *nakshatra*s or lunar mansions; a little later, the *Shulba Sūtra*s describe elaborate geometrical constructions of Vedic fire altars, spell out the so-called 'Pythagorean theorem' and yield precise values for the square roots of 2 or 3. The *Vaisheshika Sūtra*s indulge in bold speculations on time and space and are the first Indian texts to discuss the concept of atoms. The daring speculations of Buddhist and Jain mathematicians follow: the Jaina cosmology, for instance, involved a time scale of 2^{588} years (that is, 2 multiplied by itself 587 times!) and was at ease with the notion of infinity.

Because many ancient texts disappeared forever, important gaps remain in our understanding of the transition towards the Siddhāntic period—the golden era of Indian mathematics and astronomy, from the fifth century CE. (A *siddhānta* is a conclusion and, by extension, a technical treatise.) A simple way to gauge the creativity of those times is to list a few achievements of the celebrated Āryabhata, born in 476 CE, who in fact ushered in the Siddhāntic School. Most of his contributions come to us from his *Āryabhatīya*, a concise, sometimes cryptic, text of 121 verses which yields, among other advances:

♦ a proposed value of π equal to 62832/20000 or 3.1416 (correct to the fourth decimal), and a surprisingly perceptive explanation that this value is only 'approximate';[1]

---

* In this book I use the now standard CE ('Common Era') and BCE ('Before Common Era') instead of the older AD and BC.

♦ an ingenious method for the extraction of square and cube roots;[2]

♦ a succinct and precise table of sines (or *jyā*), in the form of just two lines of coded syllables giving sine values of angles up to 90° (in twelve increments of 3°45'), with all values correct to three or four significant figures;[3]

♦ a statement that the earth is a sphere with a diameter of 1,050 *yojana*s, which comes fairly close to the actual figure;[4]

♦ a prescient assertion that the earth's rotation is what causes the fixed stars to appear to move.[5] Unfortunately, some of his successors, notably the great savant Brahmagupta (born *c.* 598 CE), could not accept this view of a rotating earth and sought to retain a stationary one, thereby probably hindering the progress of Indian astronomy;

♦ observations of the planets' orbits, recorded with 'astonishing precision',[6] in the words of the French scholar Roger Billard, who did an advanced statistical study of Āryabhata's table, proving it to be based on actual observations;

♦ a correct understanding of the basic mechanism of solar and lunar eclipses, which he attributed to the moon's disc and the earth's shadow respectively;[7]

♦ remarkably accurate estimates for the sidereal day and year;[8]

♦ a notion that the moon and planets are not self-luminous but actually reflect sunlight.[9]

Āryabhata also worked out a conceptual framework of *yuga*s —the four ages of Hindu mythology. Even though it was not free of errors as far as planetary positions were concerned, the concept of endless *yuga*s and a pulsating, ceaselessly destroyed and re-created universe, led to a contemplation of the infinite which was a hallmark of Indian savants: 'Time is without beginning or end,' said Āryabhata.[10] From this 'contemplation' flowed insights which our rational mind can only regard as 'coincidences': the value of a 'day of Brahmā', 4.32 billion years, 'happens' to be almost exactly the age of the earth. Or, as the well-known American astronomer Carl Sagan noted:

The Hindu religion is the only one of the world's great faiths dedicated to the idea that the Cosmos itself undergoes an immense, indeed an infinite, number of deaths and rebirths. It is the only religion in which the time scales correspond, no doubt by accident, to those of modern scientific cosmology. Its cycles run from our ordinary day and night to a day and night of Brahma, 8.64 billion years long. Longer than the age of the Earth or the Sun and about half the time since the Big Bang. And there are much longer time scales still.

... A millennium before Europeans were willing to divest themselves of the Biblical idea that the world was a few thousand years old, the Mayans were thinking of millions, and the Indians of billions.[11]

Such is India's native framework, a worldview that dislikes limits, since the inner Reality can essentially have none. For Āryabhata, the ultimate objective of astronomy appears to have been spiritual: 'One attains the supreme *brahman* after piercing through the orbits of the planets and stars.'[12] The physical and the spiritual infinites could only be the same.

Occasionally, early Indian mathematicians and astronomers fell victims to the broader mythological framework, trying for instance to impose a perfect conjunction of all the planets at the start of every day of Brahmā or *kalpa*, which does not work in practice, or taking the Purānas' metaphorical geography too literally. But at least, their minds dared to toy with the infinite, and a cosmic space-time was their daily enjoyment.

Mathematics : The Joy of Infinity

Every culture gave names to numbers. In India, significantly, smaller numbers bore numerous names each, most of them derived from philosophical and spiritual concepts. A few examples will illustrate the point:

♦ *Shūnya* (or *kha*) for zero is a well-known case, but other terms for it, such as *ākāsha, ambara, vyoman* (all meaning 'sky'), *ananta* ('infinite'), *pūrna* ('full'), imply totality and wholeness rather than void, suggesting that the two concepts are simply two aspects of the same truth.

♦ Number **1**, *eka*, suggests the notion of indivisibility: other names for it therefore include *ātman, brahman* (the soul and Self), *sūrya* (the sun), *ādi* (the beginning), *akshara* (the syllable Aum), the moon (*soma, indu*), the earth and its many names, and many more symbols of unity.

♦ Number **2**, *dvi*, is also named after the Ashvins, the twice-born, *Yama* (as the primordial couple of the Rig Veda), the two eyes, and other symbols of duality.

♦ Number **3**, *tri*, after the three Vedas, Shiva's three eyes, his trident (*trishūla*), the three worlds, the three *gunas*, the triple Agni and so on.

♦ Number **4**, *chatur*, after the four *āshrama*s or stages of human life, the four ages (*yuga*s), the four Vedas, Vishnu's arms or Brahmā's four faces.

♦ Number **5**, *pañcha*, after the five elements, the Pāndavas or Rudra's five faces.

♦ Number **6**, *shat*, after the six *rāga*s, the six classical systems of philosophy (*darshana*s), Kārttikeya's six faces.

♦ Number **7**, *sapta*, after the seven Buddhas, the seven oceans (*sāgara*s) and islands (*dvīpa*s), the seven seers (*rishi*s), divine Mothers, rivers, days of the week, horses of Sūrya, etc.

♦ Number **8**, *ashta*, after the eight points of the compass or the eight mythical elephants upholding the world.

♦ Number **9**, *nava*, after the planets, the traditional nine jewels (*ratna*), the body's orifices, or Durgā (celebrated during the nine nights of the *Navarātri* festival).

♦ Number **10**, *dasha*, after Vishnu's ten avatars, the Buddha's ten powers and stages, or Rāvana's ten heads.

The list goes on with **12** Ādityas, **25** *tattva*s, **27** *nakshatra*s, **33** *deva*s, **49** Vāyus . . . and for larger numbers such terms would be attached together, leading to long words devoid of any meaning except the mathematical.

This device fell into disuse with the spread of the much more efficient decimal numeral system, but the association of spiritual and philosophical concepts with number names illustrates the absence of a rigid boundary between science and spirituality in the minds of Indian mathematicians. Perhaps that is why we find many of them reaching out to the infinite: long before Rama-nujan, Indian savants showed 'a "mania" for large numbers', as French historian of number systems Georges Ifrah puts it in his monumental *Universal History of Numbers*.[13] The Rig Veda makes frequent mention of 100,000 (foes, gifts, cattle heads...), while the Yajur Veda goes up to a million million (10^{12}), a number it calls *parārdha*.[14] This grew by leaps and bounds in Jaina literature (such as the *Anuyogadvāra Sūtra*), in which con-templation of an infinite and eternal universe led to numbers exceeding 10^{250} (in other words, 1 followed by 250 zeros, although this notation did not exist then). In the *Lalitavistara Sūtra*, the Bodhisattva reels off endless series of multiples of 10, naming them up to 10^{145} and eventually conjuring up a number equivalent to 10^{421}!

Several texts propose different values for one of those colossal numbers, named *asamkhyeya*—or 'innumerable', which cannot be counted; the *Lalitavistara Sūtra,* again, adds this poetic defi-nition: it is the number of raindrops falling on all the worlds for ten thousand years!

Let us remember, by contrast, that the highest named number in ancient China and ancient Greece was 10,000 (the 'myriad' in Greek); Arab names did not go beyond 1,000; and Europe had to wait until the thirteenth century before the French introduced the 'million': only in the seventeenth century were the billion, trillion and quadrillion conceived of. Ifrah repeatedly states his admiration for this specific achievement of the Indian mind:

> We have here, if need be, one more proof of the very clear Indian intellectual lead over all contemporary Western thought, and one more testimony to the great fertility of the Indian savants' minds.[15] ... [Moreover,] the Sanskrit numeral notation carried within itself the very seed of

the discovery of the principle of the decimal place-value notation.[16]

While reaching out to the infinite, some of India's common symbols of infinity were put to good use: numbers such as 10^9, 10^{14}, 10^{21}, 10^{25}, 10^{27}, 10^{29}, 10^{105}, 10^{112}, 10^{119} were named after the lotus (*padma, utpala, kumud* ...), others after the ocean, the earth, and of course *ananta,* the infinite itself.

Ultimately, mathematical infinity got a name of its own, *khachheda* or *khahara. Khachheda* means 'divided by *kha*', *kha* being 'space' or 'void', one of the names for 'zero'. 'Division by zero' gives an intuitive definition of infinity:* any fraction increases in value as its denominator is reduced; as the latter tends towards zero, the fraction tends towards infinity. The term *khachheda* was introduced by the great mathematician Brahma-gupta in his *Brāhmasphuta Siddhānta* (628 CE); *khahara,* with a similar meaning, was used later by another celebrated scientist, Bhāskara II or Bhāskarāchārya (twelfth century).

Infinity is not found only at the colossal end of things: it also takes us to the infinitesimal. Thus the *paramānu,* or 'supreme atom', corresponded either to a length of about 0.3 nanometre or to a weight of 0.614 microgram![17] We find the same phenom-enon when we explore the mysteries of Time: we are familiar with the infinite scale of *yugas,* but at the other end of it, in his *Siddhānta Shiromani,* Bhāskarāchārya defined the *nimesha* (literally, the blink of an eye) as one 972,000th of a day, or about 89 milliseconds, and went on dividing it further and further till he reached the *truti,* a unit of time equal to one 2,916,000,000th of a day—or about 30 microseconds![18] Of what earthly use could such unearthly units of time and length have been to the ancients? Or did they conceive of them just for the joy of it?

India's fascination with huge numbers is well illustrated by the legend of *chaturanga,* India's early version of chess,[19] a legend conveyed by Arabic sources. Sessa, a clever Brāhmana, once

---

* This definition is not rigorous, however, and modern mathematics uses more elaborate ones (they were fine-tuned only in the nineteenth century).

demonstrated this new game to a king, who was so pleased that he told him to ask for any reward. Sessa humbly requested one grain of wheat on the first square of the board, two on the second, four on the third, eight on the fourth, and so on, doubling the number of grains on every square right up to the sixty-fourth. The king thought the request was ridiculously modest and insisted on a more substantial one, but Sessa declined. The royal mathematicians set about calculating the amount, but after great labour could not proceed beyond a few squares. Embarrassed, the king had mathematicians called from a neighbouring kingdom, who were familiar with the new decimal place-value system and at home with large numbers. They soon worked out the desired number of grains: $2^{64} - 1$, a number that requires twenty digits to be written out in the conventional way. The savants explained to the king that even if the whole earth were sown with wheat, it would take over seventy harvests to get the desired quantity! To save the royal face, a wily minister suggested that he should open his granary to the Brāhmana and ask him to start counting the grains himself, never stopping till he reached the correct number. Sessa got the message and was never heard of again.

Leaving calculations aside, we find astonishing mathematical concepts forming the canvas of 'mythological' stories. The Buddhist text *Avatamshaka Sūtra* (often rendered as the 'The Flower Ornament Sutra') depicts a network of pearls placed in heavens by Indra in such a way that 'in each pearl one can see the reflections of all the others, as well as the reflections within the reflections and so on.'[20] This might appear as mere poetic fancy and a practical impossibility, but three U.S. mathematicians took it up as a challenge. What they found was a mathematical validation of the Buddhist image: Indra's pearls precisely followed the arrangement of circles in a mathematical entity called a Schottky group, and they worked out several actual designs of pearls fulfilling the text's apparently impossible conditions.[21] But what is it that drove its authors to dictate them? Intuition? Or perhaps simply a poetic approach to mathematical truths, like the raindrops falling on all the worlds that defined the infinite.

It is fascinating to note that in 1957, the American physicist David Bohm, who was obsessed with unveiling the deeper reality of matter (we will meet him again in the next chapter), had a 'vision' almost identical to that of the *Avatamshaka Sūtra.* 'The vision came to him,' writes his biographer F. David Peat, 'in the form of a large number of highly silvered spherical mirrors that reflected each other. The universe was composed of this infinity of reflections, and of reflections of reflections. Every atom was reflecting in this way, and the infinity of these reflections was reflected in each thing; each was an infinite reflection of the whole.'[22] An eloquent reminder that a mystical perception of reality is not India's monopoly: it is a capacity inherent in human consciousness.

Astronomy: The Mystery of Infinity

To early Indian astronomers, the universe was the most immediate illustration or manifestation of the infinite. We are familiar with the classical time scales of *yugas, mahāyugas, manvantaras* (each equal to 71 *mahāyugas*) and *kalpas* (each equal to 14 *manvantaras*), tending towards limitless time scales. But the term *yuga* or 'age' once had a very different value. In the ancient *Vedānga Jyotisha,* a *yuga* referred to a cycle of five years. Much later, Āryabhata's cosmology was based on a *mahāyuga* of 4,320,000 years consisting of four equal ages of 1,080,000 years each. Later astronomers kept the same value for the *mahāyuga,* but with the durations of the four ages following a decreasing series in ratios of 4:3:2:1, probably to reflect the Purānic concept of a progressive decrease of the truth: from the age of truth, *Satyayuga* or *Kritayuga,* to our current *Kaliyuga,* the numbers of years are now 1,728,000, 1,296,000, 864,000 and 432,000 (thus a *mahāyuga* became ten times as long as a *Kaliyuga*). A 'day of Brahmā' was equal to 1,000 *mahāyugas,* that is, 4,320,000,000 or 4.32 billion years; adding a night of equal duration, we reach 8.64 billion years, the number that so fascinated Carl Sagan because its scale is comparable to the age of our universe.

The concept of cyclic dissolutions (*pralaya*) and new creations is also reminiscent of the 'pulsating universe' today's astronomers sometimes speak of. As regards the 'much longer time scales' Carl Sagan spoke of, Brahmā's entire life adds up to 311,040 billion human years, which yet represents 'no more than zero in the stream of infinity'.[23] Indeed, 'time is without beginning and end,' as Āryabhata put it.

It would be an error to take such figures literally: as their perfect ratios show, they are meant to be symbolic. With modern humans hardly more than 100,000 years old, we will be hard put to match India's extraordinary cosmogony with the physical reality as we know it. So once again, we may ask what was the use of it all. One simple answer is, to keep minds open.

Let us compare with Judeo-Christian Europe's belief that the creation came into existence just a few thousand years ago, for the first and last time: that was in *anno mundi*, the 'year of the world' 3761 BCE, according to rabbinical calculations prevalent from the tenth century onward. In the seventeenth century, Archbishop James Ussher revised those calculations and proposed that the universe had been created in 4004 BCE, a belief which prevailed until Darwin (and still prevails among a few fundamentalist Christian sects). Clearly, when we compare with the Indian concepts, we are dealing not only with different time scales, but with different *mind scales*.

As far as the dimensions of the universe are concerned, Āryabhata provides us with an intriguing statement. According to him, the precise dimension for the 'circumference of the sky' is 12,474,720,576,000 *yojana*s.[24] This works out to a sphere over 4,600 times the size of our solar system[25]—not by any means a small place. But what does this 'orbit of the sky' actually mean? One of Āryabhata's commentators, Bhāskara I, explains:

> For us, the sky extends to as far as it is illumined by the rays of the Sun. Beyond that, the sky is immeasurable. . . . The sky is beyond limit; it is impossible to state its measure.[26]

Now, astronomers tell us that the Sun has a magnitude of 4.7 at a distance of 10 parsecs,[27] or about 30 10^{13} km; this is approximately the smallest magnitude perceivable to the human eye, and therefore the distance 'illumined by the rays of the sun' for a human observer. Oddly, Āryabhata's value is about one fifth of this distance, and therefore, in astronomical terms, of the same order of magnitude—a coincidence, no doubt, but one that shows again that our savants' mind scale was broadly in tune with the universe.

Sāyana and the Speed of Light

Another enduring riddle in the history of Indian science has been widely circulated in recent years: could it be that ancient Indians somehow figured out the velocity of light?[28] As far as we know, it was measured for the first time by the Danish astronomer Ole Roemer in 1675, with an error of about 25 per cent, and more precisely in the nineteenth century. But there is a curious comment by the fourteenth-century Vedic commentator Sāyana on a hymn of the Rig Veda[29] addressed to Sūrya, the sun-god. Sāyana records a tradition associated with Sūrya:

> Thus it is remembered:
> [O Sūrya] you who traverse 2,202 *yojana*s in half a *nimesha*.

In much of the ancient literature, the *yojana* is equated to 8,000 human heights, or 13.6 km taking an average height of 1.70 m (there are variants for the *yojana*'s value, but this is the most common[30]). And the *nimesha*'s value is generally 16/75th of a second.[31] With these values, Sāyana's statement yields a speed of 280,755 km/s, remarkably close to the known velocity of light (299,792 km/s, thus some 6 per cent too small).

Is this just another coincidence? But if it is, what could be the intended meaning in making the sun race madly through the heavens, when Indian astronomers had long known that it does no such thing? And if it is not a coincidence, how did the unknown authors of the 'remembrance' Sāyana refers to figure out such a figure for the speed of light, when Western science could only measure it three centuries later? Roemer's method of measurement was based on observations of the eclipses of Jupiter's moons, and therefore on the telescope, an instrument unknown to Sāyana and his predecessors; any method based on naked-eye observations, if at all it were possible, would prove very approximate, and there is no trace of it in what we know of India's scientific literature. Or did some seer develop other ways of gaining this sort of knowledge?

The riddle will remain one until more explicit references to this tradition come to light.

Microcosm and Macrocosm

What is in the mind soon finds its expression outside; the microcosm reflects and symbolizes the macrocosm. This fundamental equation runs through every aspect of Indian civilization.

As elsewhere, astronomy in India developed partly to keep calendars, fix the dates of seasonal sacrifices or predict the occurrences of eclipses. The Rig Veda is replete with cosmic references, such as the marriage of Earth and Heaven, hymns to the Dawn, to the three worlds, eclipses and meteors. In addition, there seems to be a deliberate astronomical code embedded in the ordering and numbers of its hymns: according to its discoverer, the Vedic scholar and physicist Subhash Kak, totalling up the number of hymns in each book of the Rig Veda in various combinations yields the synodic periods of the five planets, and much more astronomical symbolism.[32]

The *Shulba Sūtras* are treatises of sacred geometry usually dated between the eighth and the sixth centuries BCE; only four of them are extant. As instruction manuals for the construction of Vedic altars (variously called *yajña bhūmikā, agni, citi* or *vedī*), they prescribe complex geometrical constructions with bricks of various sizes and shapes—square, rectangular, triangular, rhomboid, pentagonal. The bricks are to be laid in five layers, each of them usually made of 200 bricks (so 1,000 bricks in all). But as we might expect, there was a whole cosmogony behind the altar: the first layer symbolizes the earth, the last the highest heaven, so that the entire altar is a representation of the universe with its various intermediary worlds.

The surface area of a particular altar is regarded as inalterable, but its shape can be changed. This leads to transformations based on complex geometric operations. Let us mention the construction of a square of given dimensions, its transformation into a rectangle, the doubling of the area of a given square (an exercise that led those early geometers to give √2 the value 577/408 or 1.414215, correct to the fifth decimal; a similar result was obtained for √3), or the perennial problem of the geometrical squaring of a circle, that is, the construction with nothing but a compass and a ruler of a square having the same area as a given circle (the reverse problem, the circling of a square, was also dealt with). Another result was a clear formulation of the so-called Pythagorean theorem (in reality expressed by Euclid). In addition, the *Shulba Sūtra*s appear to have had an astronomical backdrop: thus, a deliberate dissymmetry in the chariot-wheel altar has been interpreted by Subhash Kak as representing the eccentricity of the orbit of the sun.[33]

The science of architecture, or *Vāstu-Shāstra*, stemmed from a similar conceptual framework: temples were essentially seen as representations of the cosmos, often centred on Mount Meru, or else representations of the cosmic being symbolized by a human body. Cosmogony was also interwoven in rituals: the primary function of salutations to the cardinal points, observance of seasons and eclipses, the worship of the planets (*navagraha*) and astrology as a whole (regardless of its predictive value), were all meant to connect the individual to the universe—a connection of no value for our modern, 'rational' persons, but of vital importance for ancients, and still to some extent for Hindus rooted in their traditions, even if the meaning of such rituals has often faded.

But cosmic designs were not limited to temples. Beginning with the impressive Harappan cities (*c.* 2600 BCE), we find a careful orientation of streets along the cardinal directions, grid plans, enclosing fortifications, etc. In the case of Mohenjo-daro, however, the German archaeologist Holger Wanzke[34] observed that the alignment of Mohenjo-daro's upper city has a 1° to 2° clockwise divergence from the cardinal directions and in fact points to an east-west alignment along the Pleiades star cluster (*Krittikā*), which rose due east and set due west during the mature Harappan phase at the vernal equinox (because of the precession of the equinoxes, it no longer does so). The *Shatapatha Brāhmana* (2.1.2.3) indeed refers to a time when the Pleiades, then the first of the 27 *nakshatras*, 'does not swerve from the east,' which is precisely the mature Harappan period. There is also convincing evidence that small holes drilled into massive ring stones found at Mohenjo-daro were intended to mark the position of sunrise through the year, either for ritual or for agricultural purposes—or both, more likely.[35]

Recent research into the astronomical backdrop of the layout of many Indian cities of historical times has documented fascinating lost traditions. U.S. astrophysicist J. McKim Malville and his team surveyed a few such cities, convinced that ancient Indians were keen to embed cosmic designs into the urban plan.[36] At Chitrakut, for instance, straddling the Uttar Pradesh–Madhya Pradesh border, shrines and places of pilgrimage were found arrayed in arrow-like designs reminiscent of Rāma (his symbol is the bow and arrow) and precisely oriented to the sunrise and the sunset on the summer solstice, June 21–22. In Benares (ancient Kāshi), shrines to the fourteen Ādityas were carefully located throughout the city; some of them were quite small, tucked away in the corner of a wall, and had been all but forgotten. However, once mapped, these shrines were found to form an array of sunbeam-like alignments precisely pointing to the rising sun at the start of every Hindu month and on a few special dates.

Apart from giving us a fine illustration of how modern lines of scientific inquiry can sometimes retrieve long-forgotten traditions, McKim Malville's work highlights the sacred backdrop of even supposedly 'secular' architecture and town planning: ancient

Indians—and, generally, ancient people—needed everything around them to remind them of their bond with the cosmos; perhaps, ultimately, of their identity with it.

Life Sciences

If, then, the human body is a representation of the cosmic being, the *purusha*, we should be able to turn this knowledge to a method of healing. Indeed, this is one of the foundations of Ayurveda, which aims at harmonizing the human body with cosmic elements and forces. It is also in tune with the yogic knowledge of *prāna* and its circulation through the subtle body.

More unexpected is the notion of invisible creatures, perhaps a prescience of microbes and germs. Thus the *Ashtāngahridaya-samhita* refers to blood corpuscles that are 'circular, legless, invisible, and coppery in colour'[37]—strangely reminiscent of red blood cells, even though the authors of this fundamental text of Ayurveda had no microscope at their disposal. 'The earth and the air all swarm with living organisms,'[38] says the Mahābhārata in the same vein. Incidents strangely evocative of genetic manipulations appear in the same epic and other texts, for instance the splitting of Gāndhārī's embryo into a hundred, which were to give birth to the Kauravas. Such insights (they cannot have been actual practices) remain unexplained, except by the all-weather term of 'intuition', or, more profoundly, by the Upanishadic dictum, *yasmin vijñāte sarvam idam vijñātam*: that which being known, all is known.[39]

But the most striking 'intuition' in the field is perhaps the representation of the *Dashāvatāra*, the ten incarnations of Lord Vishnu upon earth, with its series of the fish, the tortoise (reptile), the mammal (boar), the half-animal half man (Narasimha), the dwarf and finally the human. Traditionalists who object to the parallel with Darwinian evolution, miss the point: it would certainly be wrong to claim that ancient Indians 'discovered' Darwinian evolution, but they clearly perceived the principle of the evolution of forms supporting an evolution of consciousness.

That may indeed be the whole meaning of evolution, as Sri Aurobindo proposed. We must salute the depth of perception of the *rishi*s who saw the purpose behind this long journey of increasingly complex bodies: the progressive embodiment of a higher and higher consciousness. No other culture gave us so striking an allegory.

Beyond the Mind

The quest for the infinite was by no means exclusive to ancient India; rooted deep down in the human being, it has surfaced in every civilization. But nowhere was it so systematic, daring, methodical, all-embracing.

The desire to see universal mechanisms conform to cosmogonic concepts did lead to errors at times. For instance, like many of his successors, Āryabhata thought that on 18 February 3102 BCE, at the start of the *Kaliyuga*, the sun, the moon and the five planets were all in conjunction; this was not quite correct, as those seven bodies were actually spread over some 50°; also, his theory imposed a fixed number of revolutions of the sun, the moon and the planets over a *yuga*, which again did not match reality. Or, as I mentioned earlier, we find Brahmagupta taking Āryabhata to task for his concept of a rotating earth.

Despite such shortcomings, the overall assessment of mathematical and astronomical advances remains highly flattering, and Indian savants of the Siddhāntic period were centuries ahead of their Western counterparts. Their advances helped the growth of 'modern' science through the agency of the Arabs, possibly too through early European travellers to India. Even 'modern' scientists such as J.C. Bose or S. Ramanujan were, to some extent, imbued with the perspective of their predecessors. This worldview could still act as a foundation for an Indian 'scientific temper' and give Indian science the fillip it has been vainly looking for elsewhere.

But the Indian worldview will not be scientific to the exclusion of the spiritual or the poetic. The Indian scientific mind is a mind in love with infinity and eternity; it is conscious of being a mere 'boat on the sea of true and false knowledge',[40] as Āryabhata beautifully put it in his penultimate verse. Like Bhāskarācārya's daughter, Līlāvatī, waiting in vain for her *ghatī yantra* to fill up, it loses the sense of time and drifts into a contemplation of this mysterious universe.*

---

* As the Persian legend goes, Bhāskarācārya had calculated an auspicious time for the wedding of his daughter, and warned her that there was only one such time. On the appointed day, along with her bridegroom, she sat staring at a *ghatī yantra* floating on water: this bowl of bronze with a tiny hole at the bottom, a traditional Indian water clock, will sink in exactly 24 minutes (a *ghatī*). Unknown to her, however, a pearl from her necklace got loose and, falling into the bowl, blocked its hole: the auspicious moment passed, and she could no longer get married. To console her, Bhāskarācārya composed *Līlāvatī*, a book of mathematical puzzles which enjoyed a considerable popularity. (Bhāskarācārya himself says nothing of the legend, however, and we do not know whether the Līlāvatī he mentions in his book was his wife, his daughter, or some imaginary lady.)

2

India's Gifts to the World

CIVILIZATIONS never live in isolation. In antiquity, through land as well as sea routes, India had considerable exchanges with Mesopotamia, Elam, Dilmun and Magan (the four Bronze Age civilizations of the Persian Gulf), Bactria and Margiana in Central Asia, Egypt, Greece and the Roman Empire, China, Tibet, Southeast and Far East Asia. A prodigiously creative civilization, she left footprints abroad in the fields of spirituality, religion, philosophy, language, scripts, literature, art, architecture, mathematics, astronomy, medicine, and technologies from metallurgy to shipping. This outflow was not confined to the remote past; it continued through Arab and European travellers, and entered a new phase in colonial times, impacting Western literatures and philosophies, and in our times leading to widespread practices of yoga and meditation.

Incomprehensibly, today's average Indian student, whether at school or at college, hardly learns anything of this massive contribution of India to world culture and civilization. There must be a serious defect in our educational system, for no other world culture has such qualms about highlighting its share in humanity's advances. In India, despite many gaps, much lost literature, numerous destroyed centres of learning, we still have a good deal of material to go by, supplied by archaeological, epigraphic and literary evidence. But this material has mostly remained confined to scholarly circles, hardly ever reaching the student or the layman, even though its significance has long been known. In 1918, for instance, Sri Aurobindo wrote of India:

> She expands too outside her borders; her ships cross the ocean and the fine superfluity of her wealth brims over to Judea and Egypt and Rome; her colonies spread her arts and epics and creeds in the Archipelago;* her traces are found in the sands of Mesopotamia; her religions conquer China and Japan and spread westward as far as Palestine and Alexandria, and the figures of the Upanishads and the sayings of the Buddhists are re-echoed on the lips of Christ. Everywhere, as on her soil, so in her works there is the teeming of a super-abundant energy of life.[1]

When they are unbiased, standard Indological studies by Western scholars readily acknowledge the West's debt to India, in certain fields at least. The highest tribute we come across is probably the one paid by Will Durant:

> India was the motherland of our race and Sanskrit the mother of Europe's languages; she was the mother of our philosophy, mother, through the Arabs, of much of our mathematics; mother, through Buddha, of the ideals embodied in Christianity; mother, through the village community, of self-government and democracy. Mother India is, in many ways, the mother of us all.[2]

French Indologist Sylvain Lévi's appreciation was no less generous, but geographically more circumscribed:

> From Persia to the Chinese Sea, from the icy regions of Siberia to the islands of Java and Borneo, from Oceania to Socotra, India has propagated her beliefs, her tales and her civilization. She has left indelible imprints on one-fourth of the human race in the course of a long succession of centuries. She has the right to reclaim in universal history the rank that ignorance has refused her for a long

---

* The Malay Archipelago, which includes Indonesia and the Philippines.

time and to hold her place amongst the great nations summarising and symbolising the spirit of Humanity.[3]

An 'ignorance' which another class of Western scholars, operating consciously or not within a Eurocentric worldview, have too often tried to perpetuate, reducing India's achievements to mere footnotes of the Mesopotamian and Greek civilizations. Some Indian historians, too, have toed that line, becoming in this respect inheritors of the colonial view of Indian civilization. Credit has been denied where credit was due.

In reality, the world's debt to India is, if anything, likely to be larger than previously assessed, although, for three reasons at least, we may never be able to quantify it with any degree of precision:

1. The loss of much material in every field of knowledge. Most great Indian intellectual works, whether Pāṇini's *Ashtādhyāyī* (his celebrated grammar), the *Charaka Samhitā* (a major treatise of Ayurveda), Kautilya's *Arthashāstra* or the Tamil grammar *Tolkāppiyam*, include long lists of more ancient but lost treatises: we may never be able to re-create the precise history of ideas and discoveries in India.

2. Difficulties with Indian chronology: the dates of most Indian works are the object of ceaseless debates, with at times well over a millennium between the earliest and latest proposed dates!

3. Wide gaps in our knowledge of the mechanism of transmission of ideas, concepts and techniques out of India. As we now know, ancient civilizations had more extensive exchanges and ideas travelled farther and faster than our notion of 'antiquity' had earlier assumed. In India's case, only a small part of those interactions is properly documented.

Despite such limitations, the overall picture is striking. I will only attempt here the briefest overview of India's major contributions, with some emphasis on lesser known areas. (Although

I will examine cultural fields separately, we should not lose sight of the fact that they were actually inseparable travel companions.)

Early Outreach

Right from the Indus–Sarasvatī civilization, we note an eagerness to reach out: Harappans built ships and sailed all the way to Mesopotamia (though archaeologists are still debating what they gained in exchange for their exports of ornaments, timber and other items). They established outposts in Bahrain, Oman and perhaps Mesopotamia, also as far as Shortughai in northern Afghanistan, near the Amu Darya river. Intensive trade exchanges went on for centuries and continued well into historical times. Land routes to Central Asia, Tibet or China, including the spice roads and silk roads (through Gilgit), became widely travelled.

So too, the sea routes to Egypt and other parts of Africa, thanks to an early knowledge of monsoon winds; cowrie shells originating from India or the Maldives were used as currency in Kenya and Egypt in the third millennium BCE. Much later, considerable trade exchanges took place with the Roman Empire, especially from south India, which is dotted with troves of Roman coins. Indeed, south India exported so much wealth in terms of gems that it has been called 'the treasure chest of the ancient world'.[4] In 77 CE, Roman historian Pliny the Elder made this sarcastic remark on the depletion of the Roman treasury:

> By the lowest reckoning India, China and the Arab peninsula draw from our empire 100 million sesterces every year, that is the sum which our luxuries and our women cost us. ... In no year does India absorb less than 50 million sesterces of our empire's wealth, sending back merchandise to be sold with us at a hundred times its prime cost.[5]

The figures appear too round to be true, but the imbalance of trade favouring India is undeniable. Pliny, who never married, put the blame squarely on luxury-loving Roman women, but Indian pepper (used not just as a condiment but also for embalming), silk and medicinal plants were certainly prized by both sexes, and the Roman navy was particularly fond of Indian teakwood.

Indonesia and beyond was reached from Bengal, Andhra and Tamil Nadu. Excavations of India's partly submerged port cities along its eastern and western shores are gradually bringing to light more extensive contacts than previously thought. There may also have been ancient exchanges, direct or indirect, with pre-Columbian America, especially the Mayan civilization: similar cultural features have long been pointed out, for instance the concept of four *yuga*s, parallels in calendars (the starting point of the Mayan calendar is 3114 BCE, almost the same as that of India's Kali era in 3102 BCE), in astronomy and astrology, artistic and architectural motifs—elephants, for instance, animals unknown to America, are depicted in some Mayan monuments.[6] Be that as it may, ancient India was very much a maritime civilization: the Rig Veda refers to oceans and shipping, while the *Jātaka* tales, Buddhist texts and the *Arthashāstra* mention ports and sea voyages, and the Mauryan kings had a full-fledged navy.

Of course, culture travelled out of India equally well through foreign travellers, traders, pilgrims and invaders. Phoenician ships probably sailed to India's western shores (not far from Mumbai) by 975 BCE, taking ivory, apes and peacock back to King Solomon. In 510 BCE, Darius the Great, king of Persia, reached the headwaters of the Indus; his Greek mercenary Scylax sailed down to the sea and back home by the Red Sea, reaching Suez after two and a half years. As a matter of fact, for some time Persia acted as a bridge between India and Greece: 'Indian troops took part in the invasion of Greece [by Persia] in 480 BC, while Greek officials and mercenaries served in various parts of the [Persian] Empire, including India.'[7]

The exchanges that followed Alexander's incursion (326 BCE) are fairly well documented, in particular the presence of Greek envoys in the Mauryan court. Although Greek travellers to India were not always very reliable in their records, they did build cultural bridges; thanks to them, we know that Alexander learned a lesson or two in humility from the 'gymnophysts' or yogis.

Chinese Buddhist pilgrims, such as Fa-Hsien in the fifth century CE, Sung-Yun in the sixth and Hsuan-Tsang in the seventh, were more painstaking in recording their travels through this vast land, leaving invaluable testimonies. Soon, it was the turn of the Arabs, whose interaction with India proved crucial in bringing Indian sciences to Europe's shores. In 868 CE, the Arab philosopher Abu Umar Jahiz of Basra waxed eloquent over India's achievements:

> I have found the Indian people extremely advanced in *jyotisha* and mathematics (*hisab*). They have got a particular type of Hindi script. They occupy a very prominent position in the field of medical sciences and possess such secret knowledge that they can cure serious incurable diseases. They are excellent in carving stone statues, making coloured paintings on the niches of the buildings. They are the inventors of the *shatrang* [chess] which is one of the best intellectual games. Their swords are extremely fine. They are fond of swordsmanship and are masters of this art. They can neutralize the effect of poison by their mantras. Their music is attractive. ... There are many types of Indian dances which are very popular.[8]

Islam's encounter with a Hindu, Buddhist and Jain India, brutal as it was, was not without rich intellectual dialogues, and we will see the example of al-Bīrūnī a little later. Eventually, the steady influx of European travellers before and during colonial times resulted in a massive export of Indian culture, directly this time, which was to make a profound impact on Europe and America—a generally untold fallout of the colonial rule in India.

India's Gift of Spirituality and Thought

India's most durable and better-known contributions may well be in the field of spirituality, religion and philosophy.[9]

Egyptian mythology shares some traits with India's: Hathor, the heavenly cow, is rather like Kāmadhenu, while the terrible goddess Sekhmet evokes Kālī or Durgā; the worship of sun-gods

(Amon-Re and Aton) was as central to Egyptian religion as that of Sūrya to India's; and the myth of Isis bringing Osiris back to life reads like an echo of the tale of Sāvitrī. More significantly, the concept (and goddess) of *Ma'at*, the cosmic and social order, strongly parallels the Indian dharma. Claiming a direct Indian influence as the cause of such parallels would be perilous, however: universal features of pre-Christian mythologies are clearly at play, but possibly also indirect contacts with Vedic concepts and themes conveyed through the Mittanis.[10] From about 1600 to 1300 BCE, their kingdom extended from northern Mesopotamia to Syria and had undeniable Indic roots: the Mittanis kings often bore Sanskritic names (Sutarna, Paratarna, Parashukshatra, Saukshatra, Dasharatha ...), and in their Bogazköy treaty with the Hittites, they invoked Vedic gods: Mitra, Varuna, Indra and Nāsatya (another name for the Ashvins). The Mittanis were connected by marriage to Egypt's eighteenth dynasty to which Akhenaton, the illustrious 'Sun King', belonged, leading Subhash Kak to conjecture that his exclusive cult of Aton, the Sun god, might derive from the Vedic concept of the One reality.[11]

Bridges between India and Mesopotamia existed since Harappan times. The Greek Vedic scholar Nicholas Kazanas, studying the myth of the Great Flood, concluded that the Mesopotamian Deluge is likely to have Vedic origins,[12] and we know how it was repeated in the Bible and other traditions. The U.S. scholar S.H. Levitt boldly paralleled the Rig Veda with the Mesopotamian religion of the third millennium BCE, and asserted:

> We can date the early Indic tradition on the basis of comparable points in ancient Mesopotamia. By this, the Rigveda would date back to the beginning of the 3rd millennium BC, with some of the earliest hymns perhaps even dating to the end of the fourth millennium BC.[13]

I will leave aside here the thorny issue of the Rig Veda's date, as Levitt's chronological implications clash with the mainstream view; the cultural bridges he highlights are more important for the moment.

Scholars[14] have also cited a series of such bridges between Vedic
and Celtic cultures. Common examples include the Druids' concept of reincarnation, of a mother-goddess and a 'divine couple',
tree worship, the eight types of marriages in Celtic society (and
the exalted position of woman in it), its calendar, and the orality
of Druidic tradition. Peter B. Ellis, in his wide-ranging study, *The
Druids*, writes of

> the extraordinary parallels and similarities between the
> Celtic and Hindu cultures, occurring in the areas of lan-
> guage, law, religious attitudes and mythology, music and
> caste.[15]

Ellis reproduces a striking enamel depicting a Celtic deity seated
in *padmāsana*, with a pattern of four swastikas on his chest.
Although we can only speculate on the origin of those parallels,
they are too many and run too deep to be put down to 'coincidences'.

Close similarities between the Rig Veda and the *Zend-Avesta*
have long been stressed, with deities such as Mitra, Varuna,
Aryaman common to both, as well as the worship of fire. There
are also obvious linguistic connections between the languages of
the two texts, Vedic Sanskrit and Avestan. This has generally been
explained within the framework of the theory of a migration by
so-called Aryans (or Indo-Aryans) from somewhere in Central
Asia: one branch is said to have entered India and another Iran,
or, in a variation, Aryans entered India directly from Iran. This
Aryan invasion theory, however, now stands discredited on
archaeological, anthropological, literary and cultural grounds;
in fact, archaeologists agree that there is no trace of such a
migration—neither into India nor into Iran—and the Rig Veda
preserved no memory of it.[16] Alternative theories of a migration
out of India (the 'Out of India Theory' or OIT school) have been
formulated in recent years,[17] but they are still far from gaining a
wide acceptance. Besides, interactions over long periods, rather
than outright migrations, provide an equally valid model.

We stand on surer ground when we come to the historical

period. It is tempting to see Indian myths and concepts echoed in ancient Greece. Obvious parallels between Zeus and Indra, Gaia and Bhū, Uranus and Varuna, Aurora and Usha, Helios and Sūrya, Athena and Durgā, Aphrodite and Lakshmī, among others, have often been highlighted and cannot be the result of mere chance. Equally fascinating is the Orphic legend of how 'the universe was formed in the body of Zeus, after he had swallowed Phanes, the offspring of the great "World Egg", in whom all the seeds of things are present. Thus the world is the body of God,'[18] which is also the Indian conception. We must note the identity between ambrosia, the food of the gods (from a Greek word meaning 'immortal'), and the Indian *amrita*.[19] Greek gods are engaged in endless fights with Titans, much as *deva*s with *asura*s (although the Greek myths tend to exhibit more violence and cruelty than their Indian counterparts). Another important Indian notion is reflected in the story of Virgo, the embodiment of Justice, who in the course of four ages—gold, silver, bronze and iron—is compelled to gradually retreat from humanity, finally to fly away once weapons are used in the iron age to kill cows; echoes of the Indian *yuga*s or four ages are unmistakable.

Mythology apart, the two Greek epics attributed to Homer and the two Indian epics share certain motifs—especially the *Iliad* and the Mahābhārata, both of which narrate a great war that engulfs many great heroes. In the philosophical realm, Greek philosophers often echo Indian concepts. In the sixth century BCE, Pythagoras taught the 'transmigration of the soul' from body to body, respect for all life forms and vegetarianism, much of which was new to Hellenic traditions. Pythagoras and Empedocles claimed they could remember their former lives, and Empedocles's thought has been compared to India's Sāmkhya system of philosophy. Plato's philosophy also gives considerable space to rebirth and karma, and, more importantly, his thoughts and concepts often parallel Upanishadic ones.[20]

Here, too, the precise chain of transmission is a matter of debate. According to the Neoplatonist philosopher Iamblichus, Pythagoras had travelled to Egypt, Assyria and India; in the last country, he discoursed with Brahmans* and learned from them. Several Enlightenment thinkers, such as the French philosopher Voltaire, never tired of stressing this point which, to them, showed India's greater antiquity and that the Brahmans had been 'the first teachers of humankind'.[21] But Iamblichus lived more than eight centuries after Pythagoras, and we have no contemporary evidence for the story. Even if it is no more than a legend, its evocation of substantial exchanges between Greece and India is correct. Thus the fourth-century Neoplatonist philosopher Eusebius conveyed a tradition according to which 'certain learned Indians actually visited Athens and conversed with Socrates.'[22] H.G. Rawlinson narrates the encounter as conveyed by Eusebius:

> They asked him to explain the object of his philosophy, and when he replied, 'an inquiry into human affairs', one of the Indians burst out laughing. 'How', he asked, 'could a man grasp human things without first mastering the Divine?'

There is a definite Indian ring to the story. To Rawlinson,

> It is more likely that Pythagoras was influenced by India than by Egypt. Almost all the theories, religious, philosophical, and mathematical, taught by the Pythagoreans, were known in India in the sixth century BC.[23]

As regards Plato, T. Lomperis's conclusion to an insightful study entitled *Hindu Influence on Greek Philosophy* is worth noting:

> Plato, through the Pythagoreans and also the Orphics, was subjected to the influence of Hindu thought, but he may not have been aware of it as coming from India.[24]

Such a current of thought and belief from India to Greece would account for the numerous parallels that the Greek geographer

---

* I prefer this spelling (Sanskrit *brāhmaṇa*) to the more common 'Brahmin', which is a phonetic distortion. (As always, spellings in quotations are left unchanged.)

and historian Strabo of the first century BCE found between the two cultures. But while he marvelled at them, he could not explain them:

> On many points, their [the Brahmans'] opinions coincide with those of the Greeks, for the Brahmans say with them that the world was created, and is liable to destruction, that it is of a spheroidal figure, and that the Deity that made and governs it is diffused through all its parts. . . . Concerning generation, the nature of the soul, and many other subjects, they express views similar to those of the Greeks. They wrap up their doctrines about the immortality of the soul and judgment in Hades [the home of the dead in Greek mythology] in fables after the manner of Plato.[25]

The westward spread of Buddhism out of India built partly on those earlier channels of communication. We do not have much information on the earliest ambassadors of Buddha's teachings, but we do know that Ashoka's emissaries reached Alexandria in Egypt (as his thirteenth edict indicates) and that Buddhism travelled early to the Middle East. Recent excavations at the Egyptian Red Sea port of Berenike have confirmed that an extensive sea trade existed between India and the Middle East from the third century BCE onward, and elements of Indian thought and religion must have travelled along with mundane goods such as textiles and spices.

In a phenomenon of peaceful acculturation unparalleled in the history of religion, Buddhism spread through Afghanistan to the Parthians and various Central Asian peoples before the Christian era; through the fabled Silk Road, Buddhist teachers travelled from India into China from the first century CE (although some Buddhist texts had preceded them by a century or two). China responded with great enthusiasm to the new teachings; Buddhism often blended with both Confucianism and Taoism, and the Buddha was sometimes portrayed as a reincarnation of Laotzu, the legendary founder of Taoism (who, curiously, is dated to the sixth century BCE, along with Confucius, Buddha,

Mahāvīra, Zoroaster and Pythagoras!). Through China, the wave rolled on to Mongolia. In stages, from India this unparalleled cultural 'conquest' reached Sri Lanka, Myanmar, Thailand (ancient Siam), Malaysia, Indonesia. Contact with this last region, made both by land and sea, was recorded not only in a large number of inscriptions, but also in Buddhist texts and in Purānas. They generally refer to the region as 'Suvarnadvīpa' or 'Suvarnabhūmī', the golden island or land. Cambodia (Khmer), Laos, Vietnam (Champa), Korea, and finally Japan were the next destinations. Tibet seems to have long had its own independent contacts with India, and from the sixth century CE onward, evidence shows the growing presence of Buddhism there (although it may well have started earlier). By then, the face of Asia had completely changed.

On the ground, Hinduism and Buddhism were not as compartmentalized as they are often made out to be, and it is no surprise to see Hindu gods travel along with the Buddha, sometimes as part of the Buddhist pantheon: thus we find Ganesha from Afghanistan to China; Sūrya, Shiva, Brahmā, Skanda appear in Afghanistan and other parts of Central Asia from the second century BCE. In Turkestan, we come across representations of Buddha with some of Vishnu's attributes (such as the *shrīvatsa*); elsewhere in Central Asia, there is evidence of amalgamation of Shaivism and Buddhism (as happened later in Indonesia). Vishnu and his avatars, Shiva, Ganesha and many other deities are found all over Southeast Asia; Ganesha, Indra, Agni, Yama, Sarasvatī, Varuna, Brahmā, Prithivī, Sūrya and Chandra are all present in Japanese pantheons. Gods apart, *rishi*s are also occasionally revered, such as Agastya in Thailand and Indonesia.

One firm evidence for the spread of Hinduism comes to us from Armenia in the second century BCE. This region then included a part of Turkey and a part of Iran, and two Indian princes had travelled there from Kannauj, bringing with them a cult of Krishna and founding a city called Veeshap. They were killed in some quarrel, but their descendants erected two temples, as the Syrian historian Zenob Glak recorded some 500 years later in his *History of Taron*. The temples, which contained two brass statues about five and seven metres high of a god called 'Kissaneh' (Krishna, obviously), were destroyed about 301 CE by 'Saint' Gregory the Illuminator, amidst the slaughter of over 1,000 resisting Hindus, including the temple priests; the survivors were forcibly baptized.[26] A new kind of 'dialogue of civilizations' had begun.

And yet, Hinduism and Buddhism left a definite impact on Christianity, though exactly how much has been a subject of intense discussion. What is certain is that Indic ideas had long been present in the Near East, brought there by traders from India as well as Buddhist missionaries. Indeed, as soon as Europeans discovered Indian culture, they were struck by a number of uncanny similarities. In the eighteenth century, for instance, Voltaire pointed out that the Christian use of holy water had its origin in the sanctity attached to Ganga water.[27] Jesus has often been compared both to Buddha and to Krishna, for their miraculous births as much as for their teachings. Indeed, Jesus' teaching of non-violence or the notion of a divine incarnation are strikingly non-Judaic concepts. Roy Amore, a scholar of Buddhism, traced many parables and events in the New Testament to Buddhist stories and found 'numerous similarities in the lives of the two masters',[28] Buddha and Jesus. In his conclusion, Amore suggested that

> The two masters' teachings ... share a common message. ... The Christians may have borrowed from the Buddhists, who were spreading their religion towards the West in the first Christian century. Thus, Christians may have been exposed to Buddhist art and literature, to modes of dress, to wisdom sayings as well as monastic practices. ...
>
> There are several indications that Luke and Matthew were drawing upon a source or sources that in addition to sayings about the end of an era also contained sayings that were in effect Jewish-Christian versions of Buddhist teachings. The Sermon on the Mount has the highest concentration of these Buddhistic sayings, but they are also found in

quantity in later chapters of Luke and Matthew. Luke alone has the very Buddhistic account of the birth of Jesus, and the greatest number of Buddhistic passages is in Luke.

Jesus drew upon Buddhist as well as Jewish concepts and images in presenting his own teaching, which was not identical with traditional Judaism or with Buddhism. By this means the Buddhist ideal of nonviolence, the concept of treasures in heaven, the quest for a pure mind, and other Buddhist teachings came into the Christian tradition. The Buddhist presence continued after Jesus' death and influenced some of the early Christian communities to interpret the career of Jesus along the lines of a god-come-down (avatar). The doctrines of the preexistence of Jesus, the stories about his birth and infancy, and the belief in his return to heaven followed the Buddhist model.[29]

Indeed, Amore goes as far as to suggest that Christianity's appropriation and adaptation of the avatar concept is what 'enabled Christianity to supplant the old Iranian religions and ironically, to block the rapid westward expansion of Buddhism itself.'[30]

Besides borrowing concepts and belief systems, Christianity's use of the rosary, incense, candles, bells, the worship of relics, monasticism and the organization of monasteries can all be paralleled with Buddhist and Hindu traditions and customs, and probably drew on them. Art historian Rikki Scollard[31] points to further parallels between the angels and the *apsara*s, catacombs and cave temples, cathedrals and *chaitya*s, Jesus' and Buddha's 'temptations', the practice of circumambulation, and more. Again, mere chance cannot explain such a body of shared beliefs and practices.

Less well known but equally distinct is the Vedantic ring in the Gnostic Gospels.[32] Their non-dogmatic, non-sectarian outlook brought about their near destruction at the hands of rising Christianity; fortunately, most of them were rediscovered at Nag-Hammadi in Upper Egypt in 1945. The emphasis was not on any particular belief, much less dogma, but on inner and spiritual experience. Any Hindu or Buddhist would feel perfectly at ease with passages such as this one:

> Abandon the search for God and the creation and other matters of a similar sort. Look for him by taking yourself as the starting point. Learn who it is within you who makes everything his own and says, 'My God, my mind, my thought, my soul, my body.' Learn the sources of sorrow, joy, love, hate. . . . If you carefully investigate these matters, you will find him *in yourself*.[33]

Buddhism also greatly influenced the vanished but important Manichean religion. A Manichean text, written in the form of Buddhist sūtras, speaks of its founder, Mani, as the Tathāgata (in Buddhism one of the titles of the Buddha), and mentions both Buddha and the Bodhisattva.

Clearly, Indic thought and spirituality travelled far and wide and left deeper footprints than Eurocentric perspectives have so far acknowledged.

Language, Script and Literature

The question of the origin of Indo-European languages remains mired in controversy, again because of the Aryan Invasion theory. Let me just state here that Sanskrit is too refined and complex to be their original common ancestor, the hypothetical Proto-Indo-European (PIE); yet the latter, if it did exist in the form reconstructed by linguists (and some of them are careful to stress that this is by no means certain) could still have originated in India, contrary to conventional linguistics which insists on a 'homeland' outside India, although with strong and persisting disagreement as to its precise location. Whether or not the Indian subcontinent was the homeland of PIE, as the Belgian Indologist Koenraad Elst and Nicholas Kazanas have argued,[34] among other scholars, perhaps an acceptable decipherment of the Indus script would alone tell us. When we will come to see this highly desirable development, Sarasvatī alone knows.

Be that as it may, Europe's discovery of Sanskrit became a central pillar of the young discipline of comparative philology, from Schlegel to Max Müller to Bopp. Later in the nineteenth century, the Swiss linguist Ferdinand de Saussure, an expert in Pānini and in Sanskrit grammar, developed in the course of his teaching in Paris and Geneva the foundations of modern linguistics, basing himself partly on Pānini's concept of language.

When we come to historical times, we can follow the spread of Sanskrit to Central Asia, China, Tibet and the Southeast, while Pāli travelled from Myanmar to Vietnam. Large collections of manuscripts in Sanskrit but also Prakrit have been found in most of those regions, all the way to Mongolia. Indeed, until the Chinese destruction of Tibetan monasteries from the 1950s onward, Tibet was a repository of Sanskrit texts (mostly in Tibetan translation), some of which had actually disappeared from India. Sanskrit inscriptions are common in many countries of Southeast Asia, and numerous place names are plainly Sanskritic: Srikshetra, Hamsavati, Ramyanagara, Ramapura (in Myanmar), Ayuthya, Srivijayavajrapuri (Thailand), Bhadrapattana, Vikramaditya, Jyeshtapura (Cambodia), Vijaya, Champa and Amaravati (Vietnam). . . . . Bali, where Hinduism has so far survived, has preserved river names such as Ganga, Sindhu, Yamuna, Kaveri, Sarayu and Narmada! To an even greater extent, royal figures in the region often took pride in adopting Sanskritic personal names, from Vikrama Varman (in Vietnam) or Shrī Sūryavamsha (Thailand) to Jayadevī (Cambodia) and Shri Lokapāla (Indonesia). . . .[35]

Not surprisingly, then, Asian scripts were directly derived from Brāhmī, India's first script in the historical period: the Burmese, Tibetan, ancient Cambodian (the Cham script), Malayan, Javanese, Sumatran and Philippine (the Tagalog script), to name a few. The Kharosthi script, whose origin remains uncertain, was extensively used in northwest India, Central Asia and parts of Iran in the early centuries CE.

Language and script dig a channel for literature to flow in. Apart from the Hindu-Buddhist teachings, the Rāmāyana and the Mahābhārata are present through large parts of Asia, from

China to Cambodia. The Rāmāyana's presence in today's Thailand, Malaysia, Laos,[36] Indonesia[37] and other parts of Asia[38] remains vibrant. The *Pañchatantra* and Somadeva's *Kathāsaritsāgara* (the 'Ocean of Stories') travelled widely too, westward through the Arabs, spawning many collections of stories on the way, from the *Arabian Nights* to La Fontaine's *Fables*.

The start of European studies of India, in the closing years of the eighteenth century, opened her treasures of Sanskrit literature to Europe, later to America. England took the lead (with William Jones and the Asiatic Society of Bengal), France and Germany followed. The impact was profound and lasting. The two Epics again, and a few literary pieces such as Kālidāsa's *Abhijñānashakuntalā*, enthralled generations of poets and writers, beginning with Goethe, who in 1792 enshrined Shakuntalā in a poem. Philosophers were struck by the Gītā and the Upanishads, and often more so by Buddha's thought. Major nineteenth-century literary movements from Romanticism to Symbolism owed a debt to the 'new' ideas flowing from the 'Orient': India, and to some extent China, opened radically new horizons, as those civilizations turned out to be more ancient than the Greek and the Judeo-Christian, and to be treasure houses of wisdom and spirituality.

We can gauge India's impact on the West's nineteenth-century intelligentsia by listening to a few of its great literary figures. (Because India's influence on France—then Europe's intellectual and cultural centre—remains poorly known, I will devote the next chapter to French writers and thinkers).

The German philosopher Arthur Schopenhauer was deeply struck by some of the Upanishads:

> From every sentence, deep, original and sublime thoughts arise, and the whole is pervaded by a high and holy and earnest spirit. ... In the whole world there is no study so beneficial and so elevating as that of the Upanishads. It is destined sooner or later to become the faith of the people. ... The study of the Upanishads has been the solace of my life, it will be the solace of my death.[39]

On the U.S. philosopher and poet Ralph Waldo Emerson, it was the Gītā that had a similar impact:

> I owed a magnificent day to the Bhagavad-Gita. It was as if an empire spoke to us, nothing small or unworthy, but large, serene, consistent, the voice of an old intelligence which in another age and climate had pondered and thus disposed of the same questions which exercise us. ... It [Vedic thought] is sublime as night and a breathless ocean. It contains every religious sentiment, all the grand ethics which visit in turn each noble poetic mind.[40]

Emerson's disciple, Henry David Thoreau, spoke no less highly of Hindu thought:

> In the morning I bathe my intellect in the stupendous and cosmogonal philosophy of the Bhagavad Gita in comparison with which our modern world and its literature seems puny.[41]

Another American, the well-known novelist Mark Twain travelled around the globe and left a charming account of his visit to India in his *Following the Equator*. His generous impression of this land has often been quoted:

> So far as I am able to judge, nothing has been left undone, either by man or nature, to make India the most extraordinary country that the sun visits on his rounds. Nothing seems to have been forgotten, nothing overlooked. ... Land of religions, cradle of human race, birthplace of human speech, grandmother of legend, great grandmother of tradition. The land that all men desire to see and having seen once even by a glimpse, would not give that glimpse for the shows of the rest of the globe combined.[42]

Art and Architecture

Philosophy and religion apart, India's best-known contributions are in the field of art, perhaps because they remain conspicuous, despite considerable losses here too. In Afghanistan, right from their first explorations in the nineteenth century, archaeologists brought to light much Indian art of great value. Buddhist murals and rock-cut caves spread there from India on their way to China. Gandhāra art had its impact on the whole region, as did the Mathurā school of Kushāna art; the colossal Bamyan Buddhas, sculpted under its influence, sadly no longer require any introduction.

India's massive impact on Southeast Asian art has survived better on the whole. The simple Buddhist *stūpa* rose into pagodas from Myanmar to Japan. Hindu and Buddhist temples still dot Myanmar and Thailand, while Java's Borobudur—the largest Buddhist *stūpa* in the world—or Cambodia's Angkor-Vat temple —the largest Hindu temple in the world—count among the marvels of this world—architecturally, but also because of their cosmic conceptions. Stories of Buddha, Rāma, Krishna, Vishnu or Shiva adorn their walls, along with important myths such as that of the *samudramathana*—the churning of the ocean. Temple art apart, heroic tales from the Rāmāyana and the Mahābhārata are enacted in traditional Javanese-Balinese theatre, dance, shadow plays and puppet shows. Of course, regional cultural developments and other influences (e.g., China's on Korea) often mingled with the Indian inputs, creating varied styles across the whole region. Despite such variety, something distinctly 'Indian' emerges: Indian art grew from sacred roots, and its branches reflect this essential orientation.

Indeed, Western scholars often used to call the whole Southeast Asian cultural sphere 'Greater India', and the acculturation process 'Indianization', or even 'Hinduization'. Thus the French Indologist George Cœdès's landmark work was titled *Hinduized States of Indochina and Indonesia*.[43] Whatever the term, the fact is an integrated cultural sphere looking up to India as its fountainhead.

Governance

An often overlooked field in which India made great advances is governance. Some form of semi-democratic rule certainly existed in proto-historical India, perhaps as early as the Indus–Sarasvatī civilization, where the ruling class is conspicuous by its complete absence from artefacts as well as architectural forms. This has led several archaeologists, such as B.B. Lal, J.M. Kenoyer or Gregory Possehl, to describe Harappan governance as a sort of confederacy of regional powers, perhaps the prototype for the historical *mahājanapada*s of the Ganges plains. About the latter, the Canadian historian Steve Muhlberger writes in a stimulating paper:

> The experience of Ancient India with republicanism, if better known, would by itself make democracy seem less of a freakish development, and help dispel the common idea that the very concept of democracy is specifically 'Western.' ... It is especially remarkable that, during the near-millennium between 500 B.C. and 400 A.D., we find republics almost anywhere in India that our sources allow us to examine society in any detail. ... The republics of India were very likely more extensive and populous than the *poleis* of the Greeks. The existence of Indian republicanism is a discovery of the twentieth century. The implications of this phenomenon have yet to be fully digested. ... Historians [may] find, in the Indian past as elsewhere, plenty of raw material for a new history of the development of human government.[44]

In the present state of our knowledge, it may be too much to claim that India's experiments with democracy and republicanism served as models elsewhere. However, again, as anthropologists and historians increasingly acknowledge, ideas travel more easily and farther afield than our models can explain. Only further research on ancient contacts between India and the Western world could throw light on this intriguing possibility.

Science

In the previous chapter, we had a few glimpses of India's contributions in the scientific field. However, it is not always easy to decide which of them migrated out of India. The *Shulba Sūtras* (p. 36) are a case in point. The U.S. historian of mathematics A. Seidenberg established that the mathematical knowledge contained in these four ancient Indian treatises of geometry did not derive from Old-Babylonian mathematics (of 1700 BCE); instead, in his opinion, both Pythagorean and Old-Babylonian mathematics had a common origin in a still older source going back to the second millennium BCE, but, as he demonstrated, a common source 'very much like what we see in the *Shulbasūtras*'.[45] Since these four Sanskrit texts are conventionally dated in the first millennium BCE, Seidenberg hesitated to identify the *Shulba Sūtras* with that source. But the texts make it clear in several places that their 'mathematical rules must have been developed in India many centuries before [their] composition,'[46] as S. Balachandra Rao puts it. How many centuries is the question. If the *Shulba Sūtras* were a codification of more ancient traditions practised 'during long preceding ages',[47] those traditions might have formed a common fund with Old-Babylonian mathematics, or perhaps even given rise to it. In the present state of knowledge, we simply cannot conclude.

We are on firmer ground when we deal with India's signal contributions to world mathematics: the decimal place-value system of numeral notation which we use daily in noting numbers—one of the greatest scientific advances of all time. The 594 CE inscription from Sankheda (near Baroda) is the oldest dated Indian document containing a number written in the place-value form. In India, the zero is represented with place value in the well-known 876 CE inscription of Bhojadeva at Gwalior, although there are several earlier candidates between 681 and 702 CE.[48] At any rate, the zero appears in a Khmer inscription (at Trapeang Prei, province of Sambor) of 683 CE, where the year 605 (of the Shaka era) is engraved in stone, and in another the same year in Sumatra (Palembang).[49] Zero with place value must therefore have been in use somewhat earlier in India, and we may yet find inscriptions to fill the gap. This is also confirmed by a Jain text, the *Lokavibhāga*, precisely dated 458 CE, which uses the place-value zero (with numbers represented by words rather than numerals). Writing in 499 CE at the age of 23, Āryabhata knew this system, as his *Āryabhatīya* explains calculations that would be impossible without it—for example the extraction of square and cube roots.

Even before the decimal place-value system was fully worked out, Indian savants conceived very large numbers, as we saw earlier. A quotation from Georges Ifrah gives a fair idea of India's contribution in the field:

> The Indian mind has always had for calculations and the handling of numbers an extraordinary inclination, ease and power, such as no other civilization in history ever possessed to the same degree. So much so that Indian culture regarded the science of numbers as the noblest of its arts. ... A thousand years ahead of Europeans, Indian savants knew that the zero and infinity were mutually inverse notions.[50]

According to the Webster's Dictionary, an alternative designation for the so-called 'Arab numerals' is 'Hindu–Arabic numerals'. Regrettably, the term is rarely used (and never in India!); but a still better term would be 'Indic numerals', since they evolved from the Brāhmī script. (They had no place value at first, as we can see them on Ashoka's edicts, for instance.) That origin is no longer in dispute: Arab savants themselves acknowledged it, and more recently Georges Ifrah[51] put the last nail in the coffin of alternative theories.

India's knowledge of astronomy and geography probably aided the Arabs' progress in navigation and maritime trade. We know of the visit to the Baghdad court of the Caliph al-Mansūr (in the second half of the eighth century) by an Indian astronomer, 'who brought with him ... planetary tables, texts for the calculations of eclipses, ascension of signs and other matters of astronomical import.'[52] Al-Mansūr soon ordered two major works of Brahmagupta to be translated into Arabic (Hindu pandits assisted Arab scholars in this considerable task). A few years later, in 803 CE, astronomers from India were on record for helping set up observatories at Baghdad and Damascus.[53]

In the early ninth century, the Caliph al-Mamūn established in Baghdad the famous 'House of Wisdom'; functioning as a 'translation bureau',[54] it employed scholars from various parts of Europe and Asia to translate scientific texts, Greek and Indian ones especially, into Arabic. The translators were paid handsomely —the weight of the manuscript in gold! At least two Indian savants worked on the highly prized Indian manuscripts from various branches of knowledge.

This was also the time when the Persian mathematician and astronomer al-Khwārizmī, working at the same House of Wisdom, wrote several treatises, some of them compiled from Indian texts. He wrote in particular on the Indian decimal numeral system and on algebraic algorithms elaborated by Indian mathematicians. Translated into Latin, al-Khwārizmī's works relayed some of India's advances to Europe. Amusingly, his own Latinized name, *algoritmi*, became the origin of the word 'algorithm'; the term thus has an indirect Indian connection. Following the same channels, the Arabic translation of Āryabhata's *Āryabhatīya* was in turn translated into Latin[55] in the thirteenth century: Āryabhata was known as 'Arjabhad' in the Arab world and as 'Ardubarius' in medieval Europe.[56]

Two centuries after al-Khwārizmī, the Persian scholar and scientist al-Bīrūnī travelled to India as part of Mahmūd of Ghazni's entourage and authored in 1030 a comprehensive study of Indian customs and sciences with, in particular, lengthy discussions on Indian astronomy, his favourite field of research. Al-Bīrūnī collected Sanskrit manuscripts and translated texts by Brahmagupta and Varāhamihira into Arabic or Persian.[57] A staunch Muslim, he was nonetheless fascinated by Indian philosophy and attempted to give a fair account of it, although he found Hindus 'niggardly in communicating that which they know'. In fact, he attributed to the Hindus' 'haughtiness' their belief that 'there is no country but theirs, no nation like theirs, no kings like theirs, no religion like theirs, no science like theirs.' Al-Bīrūnī's own comments suggest an explanation for this attitude: 'Mahmûd utterly ruined the prosperity of the country, and performed there wonderful exploits, by which the Hindus became like atoms of dust scattered in all directions. ... Their scattered remains cherish, of course, the most inveterate aversion towards all Muslims.' Of special relevance to our story is his following remark: 'This is the reason, too, why Indian sciences have retired far away from those parts of the country conquered by us, and have fled to places which our hand cannot yet reach. ...'[58]

Although pockets of scholarship persisted in the North, the networks of knowledge unravelled in stages, announcing a general southward trend. A highly creative school of astronomy and mathematics took root in Kerala and flourished there till the seventeenth century or so.[59] Topics of mathematics were as diverse as sine tables, algebraic notation, indeterminate equations of first, second and third degrees, permutations and combinations, infinite series and power expansions of trigonometric functions. As the British mathematician Ian Pearce writes:

> The works that have so far been analysed are of such a high level that it is thought there may be missing links between the 'classical period' and the medieval period of Kerala. There is also interest in the claims that European scholars may have had first-hand knowledge of some Kerala mathematics, as the area was a focal point for trading with many parts of the world, including Europe. ... If indeed it is true that transmission of ideas and results between Europe and Kerala occurred, then the 'role' of later Indian mathematics is even more important than previously thought. ... The work of Indian mathematicians has been severely neglected by Western historians.[60]

And, worse, by most Indian historians! The last point about a possible transmission of Kerala mathematics to Europe has received some attention from Indian scholars in recent years,[61] although caution remains in order.

Another case of neglect was pointed out by the indefatigable scholar K.V. Sarma. Shortly before his death in 2005, he published a list of 3,473 science texts compiled from 12,244 science manuscripts found in 400 repositories in Kerala and Tamil Nadu. Of those 3,473 texts, no more than 7 per cent are available in print. Historians of science, wrote Sarma, know nothing of the remaining 93 per cent and thus regard this 7 per cent 'as the whole and sole of the contribution of India to science. This is a sorry situation from which Indian science has to be rescued and resurrected.'[62] We may legitimately expect to find important scientific and technological advances in the thousands of manuscripts still awaiting study.

Medicine

India's achievements in the field of medicine, including early surgery and Ayurveda, are fairly well documented. What is not so well known is that they crossed India's borders in several directions. The Greeks, according to the French Indologist Jean Filliozat,[63] probably took their notion of *pneuma* (breath) from that of *prāna*, which appears as early as the Atharva Veda. Plato in his *Timaeus* provides a theory of three elements in balance or association in the body, which is somewhat similar to the *tridosha* principle of Ayurveda. The Hippocratic Collection makes several references to the borrowing of some Indian drugs and medical formulas. 'Indian herbals were sought after in the Roman world.'[64] Later, the Greek physician Galen (130–200 CE) who spent many years in Rome, acknowledged some borrowings from Indian sources.

Ayurvedic medicine followed India's cultural expansion into Central Asia and China. It became very popular in Tibet in particular, where, fusing with local health traditions, it gradually evolved into what is now known as Tibetan medicine. Manuscripts were recovered from Central Asia of medical texts in Sanskrit (or translated into the local language). A number of Indian drugs were preserved in the Japanese Imperial Treasury from the eight century onward, and we find Sushruta, one of the founders of Ayurveda, mentioned in Sanskrit inscriptions in Cambodia. Equally noteworthy is the story of an Ayurvedic physician who migrated to Baghdad in the ninth century CE, became the physician-in-chief there after 'successfully curing his royal patient of a long-standing stomach trouble', and went on to translate *Sushruta Samhitā* into Arabic and Persian ('Sushruta' was Arabized into 'Susrud'). *Charaka Samhitā*, another major text of Ayurveda, followed, translated by an Arab scholar.[65] The two texts were also among 'medical, pharmacological and toxicological texts in Sanskrit'.[66]

Two lines of evidence suggest the possibility of acupuncture originating in India. One is the traditional form of acupressure still practised in Kerala and Tamil Nadu, based on the *marma* points. The other is the existence of Chinese and Korean traditions to that effect: Korean experts, for instance, opined that those who taught acupuncture to China's Yellow Emperor must have come from India.[67] This evidence, of course, remains circumstantial.

Technology and Craft

How much the ancient world owed to India in matters of shipping and sailing is also open to discussion, but it has been suggested that both the Romans and the Arabs may have gained their knowledge of monsoon winds from India. Later, in 1498, when Vasco da Gama had sailed to Malindi (on Kenya's Indian Ocean coast), looking for a sea route to India, he hired there an Indian sailor from Gujarat, whose knowledge of the monsoon winds guided da Gama's expedition to Calicut (Kozhikode).

There are stray references to show that technological know-how or products travelled out of India from ancient times. From about 500 BCE, the celebrated 'wootz' steel produced in south India was exported to the Middle East and Europe; it was called 'Damascus steel' as it was there that it was made into sharp swords. Roman historian Quintus Curtius narrates how Alexander the Great received from Porus of Taxila 100 talents, or about 3 tons, of Indian steel as a gift, rather than gold or silver. Whether this can be accepted as factual or not, it anyhow testifies to the reputation of Indian steel in the Mediterranean world.[68]

We saw earlier how another Roman historian complained about the considerable imports from India. It is a fact that the Roman Empire opened a highway of trade ending all along India's western and eastern shores: Bharuch, Kanmer, Mangalore, Muziris, Pattanam, Korkai, Kaveripattinam, Arikamedu are just a few of the many ports mentioned in Roman literature or where archaeological findings have confirmed Roman contacts. Roman as well as Indian sources (such as the early Tamil literature) document the import by Romans of Indian pearls, beryls, ginger, pepper, but also Indian teakwood which helped build their navy, indirectly contributing to the Roman expansion. The ancient Iranian port city of Siraf (modern Taheri) was entirely built with Indian teakwood. Blackwood from Punjab was also prized. Later, the Arab world helped introduce Indian goods into Europe and northern Africa (Ethiopia, for instance). Among India's significant exports, cotton and sugar cane stand out, but we also have evidence of export of silk, precious stones, amber, corals, glass, gold, rugs, spices, perfumes, swords, iron, ivory. . . . At the top of the Persian Gulf, Basra was sometimes called the 'gateway of India', and such commerce led Indians to settle in Arabia in both pre- and post-Islamic times. It bears repetition that India was a major production centre and her exports exceeded imports by far.

In the course of those sustained exchanges, some of India's technological advances with regard to cast iron, zinc and its alloys, dyeing, tanning, soap or glass making, were closely studied by her trading partners.

Joseph Needham, the well-known historian of science in China, who also investigated some of India's contributions in the field, made this prescient remark a few decades ago:

Future research on the history of science and technology in Asia will in fact reveal that the achievements of these peoples contributed far more in all pre-Renaissance periods to the development of world science than has yet been realized.[69]

And Today?

There is a tendency to think that India's outward flow of contributions gradually dried up during the medieval period. It did slow down, only to resume in full swing under the British colonial rule: that was perhaps the greatest benefit of that age, but it was the West more than India that benefited from the inevitable exchange. We have seen how Sanskrit literature spread like wildfire in Western intellectual circles. That churning prepared the ground for Swami Vivekananda's living teaching of Vedanta. A few decades later, it was Sri Aurobindo's turn when a few of his works, in particular *The Life Divine,* were published in the U.S.A.; his vision of an evolutionary purpose in the material creation appealed to Western minds, as did his method of integral yoga aimed at the total transformation of human nature.

We can discern another sort of influence in the dramatic changes physics underwent in the twentieth century, revolutionizing our perception of the material universe. Swami Vivekananda, again, played an initial part in this, albeit a modest one. Nikola Tesla, the Serbian-American scientist and irrepressible inventor who pioneered the use of alternating current motors, met him in New York in 1896. Let us hear a brief account of the conversation in Vivekananda's own words:

> [Mr. Tesla] was charmed to hear about the Vedantic Prâna and Âkâsha and the Kalpas, which according to him are the only theories modern science can entertain. Now both Akasha and Prana again are produced from the cosmic Mahat, the Universal Mind, the Brahmâ or Ishvara. Mr. Tesla thinks he can demonstrate mathematically that force

and matter are reducible to potential energy. I am to go and see him next week, to get this new mathematical demonstration. In that case, the Vedantic cosmology will be placed on the surest of foundations.[70]

Tesla, for all his bold intuition, could not work out this equivalence between matter and energy—that, of course, would be Einstein's great breakthrough a few years later. But Vivekananda's thought was certainly in tune with the new frontiers of science. He also met Kelvin and Helmholtz, two other great scientists of the time, but we do not have records of their conversations.

Three decades later, quantum physics saw great advances with the work of the Austrian Erwin Schrödinger. Steeped in the study of Indian philosophy and Vedanta in particular, he counted the Bhagavad-Gītā and the Upanishads among his favourite readings (and named his dog 'Atman'!). Schrödinger's equation is well known to students of quantum physics, but not so his inner equation between the microcosm and the macrocosm:

> This life of yours which you are living is not merely a piece of this entire existence, but in a certain sense the whole; only this whole is not so constituted that it can be surveyed in one single glance. This, as we know, is what the Brahmins express in that sacred, mystic formula which is yet really so simple and so clear: *tat tvam asi*, this is you. Or, again, in such words as 'I am in the east and the west, I am above and below, I am this entire world.'[71]

This perspective was not solely philosophical; in the feverish quest of reality that quantum physics had unleashed, it helped Schrödinger to give shape to new concepts, such as his wave theory of matter. According to a biographer of his, 'The unity and continuity of Vedanta are reflected in the unity and continuity of wave mechanics. ... This new view would be entirely consistent with the Vedantic concept of All in One.'[72]

Another pioneer of the discipline was the German Werner Heisenberg, creator of the revolutionary uncertainty principle which shook the Newtonian conceit about the ultimate knowability of things. As it happened, Heisenberg travelled to India in 1929, invited by Tagore, 'with whom he had long conversations about science and Indian philosophy. This introduction to Indian thought brought Heisenberg great comfort.'[73] This is reported by Fritjof Capra, who interviewed Heisenberg in 1972 and recorded his sustained interest in Eastern concepts.

Capra developed in his works his own conviction that science and other frontiers of knowledge are moving towards a non-Newtonian, non-Cartesian paradigm founded on certain truths that Eastern mysticism had long discerned and expressed—truths such as the interconnectedness and interdependence of all phenomena. Capra, however, did not limit himself to such static concepts; he studied Hinduism and Buddhism deeply enough to grasp their dynamic side. In his widely read *Tao of Physics*, here is how he views the symbolism of Shiva's dance:

> For the modern physicists, then, Shiva's dance is the dance of subatomic matter. As in Hindu mythology, it is a continual dance of creation and destruction involving the whole cosmos; the basis of all existence and of all natural phenomena. Hundreds of years ago, Indian artists created visual images of dancing Shivas in a beautiful series of bronzes. In our time, physicists have used the most advanced technology to portray the patterns of the cosmic dance. . . . The metaphor of the cosmic dance thus unifies ancient mythology, religious art, and modern physics.[74]

In an apt illustration of this metaphor, a statue of Shiva–Natarāja, the lord of dance, was installed in June 2004 at the CERN, Europe's Centre for Research in Particle Physics which straddles the Franco-Swiss border. The beautiful two-metre tall statue was a gift from the Indian government; on its plaque is inscribed the above quotation from Capra, preceded by this comment by the distinguished art critic Ananda K. Coomaraswamy in his *Dance of Shiva*: 'It is the clearest image of the activity of God which any art or religion can boast of.' Important experiments are right now under preparation at the CERN'S Large

Hadron Collider, which may eventually identify the elusive Higgs boson, popularly known as the 'God particle'. If it is indeed found there (there are rival accelerators elsewhere), I hope it will be named the 'Shiva particle'!

I cannot leave the field of physics without mentioning the American David Bohm, who made significant contributions to quantum physics from the 1940s. A relentless seeker and explorer, Bohm had a close relationship with J. Krishnamurti (with whom he coauthored a book), studied Buddhist philosophy and exchanged with the Dalai Lama, who once joked that Bohm had become his physics teacher, but that 'when the lesson is over I forget everything'. In attempting to uncover the deeper reality tantalizingly hinted at by the great paradoxes of quantum physics, Bohm developed a worldview that rejected chance and separation, and stressed the 'unbroken wholeness' and 'implicate order' of the universe—an order that makes the whole contained, or enfolded, in every part. He spoke of

> an invisible but pervasive energy, to which the manifest world of the finite responds. This energy, or spirit, infuses all living beings, and without it any organism must fall apart into its constituent elements. That which is truly alive in the living beings is this energy of spirit, and this is never born and never dies.[75]

I am not suggesting that Indic philosophies propelled the great scientific advances of the early twentieth century. What it did was to help a few of the great innovators towards a new intellectual frame of reference amidst the crumbling old order; in a more diffuse manner, it catalyzed the search for new worldviews. That much is a significant contribution. There is still scope, in my opinion, for Indic notions and metaphors to inspire new scientific explorations, especially where the concept of consciousness is brought into play—a concept explored in India in greater depth than anywhere else.

In another field, India's perspectives on nature and the restrained use of natural resources got reflected in a new school of economics spearheaded in the 1960s by E.F. Schumacher, the author of the ground-breaking *Small Is Beautiful* (published in 1973). During a stay in Myanmar where he had studied economic problems of the Third World, Schumacher had come into contact with Buddhism and realized the extent to which current economics had pushed aside the human dimension. In 'Buddhist economics', as he called his system, 'since consumption is merely a means to human well-being, the aim should be to obtain the maximum of well-being with the minimum of consumption. . . . The less toil there is, the more time and strength is left for artistic creativity. Modern economics, on the other hand, considers consumption to be the sole end and purpose of all economic activity.'[76] Although his advocacy of a non-capital-intensive, non-energy-intensive, low-consumption society was, expectedly, ignored by mainstream economists, his challenge to the triumphalist notion of ever-increasing growth is gaining relevance from year to year, as the unsustainability of our financial systems based on the myth of growth stares us in the face. Ironically, India, which should have been at the forefront of such a 'new economics', Buddhist or not, is under the spell of runaway growth and high consumption—with all the dehumanizing loss of culture and identity that this entails.

The influential Swiss psychiatrist and thinker, Carl Jung, also turned to Eastern explorations (and visited India in 1937). His conception of a 'collective unconscious' and its 'archetypes' would make much sense to a Vedantin, but what Jung perhaps appreciated most in Hinduism and Buddhism was the manner in which they make us responsible for our own destinies and our future development. To him, 'modern man was in search of a soul,' to paraphrase the title of one of his books, and he did not shy from integrating a spiritual dimension in his theory of human psychology (something Freud would not accept). Jung's interest in Indic traditions, and in rebirth and yoga in particular, was complex and not always favourable,[77] but in trying to build a broad synthesis that integrated other traditions (such as Christianity, Taoism, Gnosticism, alchemy, Kabbala . . .), he reached conclusions that sometimes echo Sri Aurobindo's view of the close relationship between matter and spirit:

> If we can reconcile ourselves with the mysterious truth that spirit is the living body seen from within, and the body the outer manifestation of the living spirit—the two being really one—then we can understand why it is that the attempt to transcend the present level of consciousness must give its due to the body. We shall also see that belief in the body cannot tolerate an outlook that denies the body in the name of the spirit.[78]

In a profound insight, Jung also wrote, 'We have never yet hit upon the thought that while we are overpowering the Orient from without, it may be fastening its hold upon us from within.'[79]

Indeed, India's living presence in the West has been felt more in the field of yoga and meditation: with yoga teachers found at almost every street corner, there are about fifteen million practitioners in the U.S. alone. Notions of rebirth and karma were discreet engines of the 'New Age' movement. Words like 'guru', 'pandit', 'karma' or 'mantra' are now commonplace, even if they have often acquired new shades. In the 1990s, official statistics revealed that Buddhism was then the fastest-growing religion in France and Australia, with Buddhist meditation centres mushrooming in those countries.[80] Such a phenomenon reflects a need for deeper values, which Western belief systems, from Christianity to atheism, have been sorely unable to fulfil. India remains a reference point for those seekers who cannot be satisfied by dogmatic systems. Sri Aurobindo foresaw this as early as in 1908, when he called India 'the distinct physician of Europe's maladies'.[81]

When all is said and done, India's greatest gift to the world will prove to be the experiential and verifiable method of self-exploration and self-fulfilment called 'yoga'. It is her most ancient gift, too—we have evidence of its practice in the Indus–Sarasvatī civilization—and it holds as much potential in our troubled times as it did 4,500 years ago.

A Civilizing Force

India's cultural expansion has had a peculiarity: it stamped out no pre-existing regional cultures. The spread of Buddhism and Hinduism did not spell the end of Confucianism or Taoism in China, or of Shinto in Japan. The resulting impact was certainly deeper and longer-lasting than that of a brutal military conquest. As Hu Shih, Chinese thinker and ambassador to the U.S. in the 1940s, wrote of China's case:

> India conquered and dominated China culturally for 2,000 years without ever having to send a single soldier across her border. ... Never before had China seen a religion so rich in imagery, so beautiful and captivating in ritualism and so bold in cosmological and metaphysical speculations. Like a poor beggar suddenly halting before a magnificent storehouse of precious stones of dazzling brilliancy and splendour, China was overwhelmed, baffled and overjoyed. She begged and borrowed freely from this munificent giver.[82]

The Indian scholar and historian D.P. Singhal told that story in his monumental *India and World Civilization,* and concluded:

> India never imposed her ideas or culture on any nation by military force, not even on the small countries in her neighbourhood, and, in the case of China, it would have been virtually impossible to do so since China has usually been the more powerful of the two. So the expansion of Indian culture into China is a monument to human understanding and cultural co-operation—the outcome of a voluntary quest for learning.[83]

India's overall impact is summed up in these words by the art expert Philip Rawson:

> The culture of India has been one of the world's most powerful civilizing forces. Countries of the Far East, including China, Korea, Japan, Tibet and Mongolia owe much of what is best in their own cultures to the inspiration of ideas

imported from India. The West, too, has its own debts. But the members of that circle of civilizations beyond Burma scattered around the Gulf of Siam and the Java Sea, virtually owe their very existence to the creative influence of Indian ideas. . . . No conquest or invasion, no forced conversion imposed them. They were adopted because people saw that they were good and that they could use them.[84]

If India's civilizing influence on the world has been considerable, it is yet to be properly assessed in quality, extent and durability. An important field of serious research, it remains inexplicably neglected in India, partly because of the persistence of historical models derived from or subtly imbued with colonial and Eurocentric views of Indian civilization, which have tended to project the West as the source of all useful knowledge, all real progress and civilization. We have, however, seen here a number of Western scholars who have shaken off this bias; paradoxically, it is often in India that we find it most entrenched.

Indeed, India's educational system fails to recognize that the field deserves to be treated as a full-fledged discipline: we need schools of Indic studies in our Indian universities and research institutions, which generally display a supreme ignorance of all things Indian. Only then will Indian students be encouraged to research, document and explore further their country's contributions to world culture. A proper perspective of India's heritage and a legitimate pride in belonging to this stream of civilization would follow as a matter of course—not a hollow, romantic or chauvinistic pride, but one based on sound critical knowledge.

The assertion of some early European Indologists and travellers to India that she was the 'cradle of civilization' was doubtless overenthusiastic—world civilization had many cradles, not one—but they were right in the sense that India has not merely been a tireless creator in every field: she has also been an unsparing giver.

3

India in France

IN any colonial domination, the conqueror is often more profoundly influenced by the conquered than he could have anticipated. India's impact on British, American, German philosophers, writers, poets and artists was considerable and has been fairly well documented. But it is often overlooked that for much of the eighteenth and nineteenth centuries, India was an object of fascination and at times reverence in Europe's cultural centre —France. There are several reasons for this lack of awareness: the language barrier, France's limited physical presence in India during the colonial era, and also, in the twentieth century, what Roger-Pol Droit called 'the oblivion of India'[1]—a phase now clearly over in our twenty-first century.

With hindsight, we can learn much from a survey of the main channels of India's influence on French literature and thought— all the more so as this influence has shown signs of revival in recent times.[2]

The Pioneers

Before the mid-eighteenth century, contacts between France and India were few and far between, and most accounts of the Indian subcontinent were rather fanciful. *Les Indes* ('Indias', in the plural) were synonymous with a mysterious, ill-defined remote region full of half-monstrous creatures at worst, crude savages on the whole, and enigmatic naked 'gymnosophists' at best—the perfect antithesis of Europe. In the literary field, the chief discernible Indian undercurrent of that period, albeit through Arab and Greek intermediaries, was that of the *Pañchatantra* on La Fontaine's celebrated *Fables*, which also made use of animal characters to draw lessons on human nature and behaviour. La Fontaine, in fact, expressly stated in his preface his debt to 'Pilpay, the Indian sage'.

The interplay between India and Europe moved to a different level as the colonial race warmed up. Travellers became more frequent, less inventive, and brought back more and more reliable material—including, in 1731, the first complete manuscript of the Rig Veda (in Grantha script), deposited with the Royal Library in Paris. However this treasure would not be recognized for decades, as no one in Europe could read Sanskrit till the 1780s.

Thus the first serious French writers on India had to sift through travellers' accounts and build on scraps and pieces—sometimes on forgeries too. Such was the well-known case of Voltaire, who was convinced that the *Ezour-Vedam* brought to him in 1760 by a traveller was the genuine Veda: in reality, it was a crude fabrication by French Jesuits in Puduchery, made with a view to denigrating Indian 'idolatry' and indirectly establishing the superiority of Christianity. But nothing was to deter Voltaire in his enthusiasm for most things Indian and his abhorrence of all things Judeo-Christian: he managed to use the *Ezour-Vedam* to prove the superiority of Indian wisdom! In fact, it is surprising how, with so little genuine material on his hands, he intuitively perceived India's contributions to civilization:

> I am convinced that everything has come down to us from the banks of the Ganges, astronomy, astrology, metempsychosis, etc.[3] ... The Greeks, in their mythology, were merely disciples of India and of Egypt.[4]

Voltaire's fascination led him to write in 1773 a now forgotten essay, *Historical Fragments on India*,[5] which, although limited in its sources, is strewn with brilliant insights; he also devoted to India two chapters of his influential *Essai sur les mœurs et l'esprit des nations* (sometimes rendered as 'Essay on Universal History'), where we read this unexpected thought:

> If India, whom the whole earth needs, and who alone needs no one, must by that very fact be the most anciently civilized land, she must therefore have had the most ancient form of religion.[6]

Well ahead of his times, Voltaire harboured no illusions about Europe's real motives for the colonization under way:

> We have shown how much we surpass the Indians in courage and wickedness, and how inferior to them we are in wisdom. Our European nations have mutually destroyed themselves in this land where we only go in search of money, while the first Greeks travelled to the same land only to instruct themselves.[7]

In many ways, Voltaire the sceptic, the champion of reason, opened in France a first door to India. Among others, Diderot, the pillar of the epoch-making *Encyclopédie*, included in it a few serious and sympathetic articles about Indian religion and wisdom. To the Encyclopaedists, the discovery of India had two great advantages: her ancient civilization offered an alternative, however hazy at first, to the biblical worldview (and a chance to cock a snook at the Church), and it demonstrated that Greco-Roman, Judeo-Christian Europe did not have the monopoly of wisdom or civilization—or even antiquity. India thus provided such vanguard thinkers with ammunition and nurtured the new currents of thought that were going to upset the neoclassical, but still deeply Christian order.

An Oriental Renaissance

In the second half of the eighteenth century, French travellers to India—savants and adventurers alike—left important and wide-ranging testimonies: Jean-Baptiste Gentil, A. Anquetil-Duperron, A. de Polier, Pierre Sonnerat among others,[8] most of whom, like their British counterparts, saw in India the cradle of humanity, and in Indians the 'gentlest of people'. Anquetil-Duperron published in 1801 a Latin translation of fifty Upanishads; it was translated not from the Sanskrit but from a Persian version prepared under the direction of Dara Shikoh, and for decades it remained the only one available in Europe—indeed, it was the one that so impressed Schopenhauer.

British and German scholars were the first to unlock the secrets of Sanskrit. But in 1814, it was France that created Europe's first chair of Sanskrit at the *Collège de France*, and the *Société asiatique de Paris* was born in 1821 (two years before London's). Eminent Orientalists such as Eugène Burnouf, de Chézy, Langlois or Barthélémy-Saint-Hilaire dipped into the numerous Indian manuscripts accumulated at the *Bibliothèque nationale* (the National Library, formerly Royal Library), and founded the French school of Indology that was to continue in the twentieth century with the likes of Sylvain Lévi, Louis Renou,[9] Jean Filliozat, Olivier Lacombe, Jean Varenne and many others.[10]

But more than the Vedas, Pāṇini, the Laws of Manu or Buddhist texts, it was the first translations of the two great Indian epics and of Kālidāsa's works (especially his *Abhijñāna-shakuntalā*), also the Gītā and a few Upanishads, that kindled the imagination of nineteenth-century France's intelligentsia, especially the Romantics. Those texts were widely read, feverishly exchanged, avidly commented upon.

Victor Hugo, half attracted, half repelled by Asia, perhaps more at home in an Arabian Orient, dotted his vast work with Indian themes and gods, composed a whole poem ('Suprématie') based on the episode of the *Kena Upanishad* that sees Agni and Vāyu failing to conquer a blade of grass, and declared:

Oriental studies have never been so intensive. ... In the century of Louis XIV one was a Hellenist, today one is an Orientalist. ... The Orient has become a sort of general preoccupation. ... We shall see great things. The old Asiatic barbarism may not be as devoid of higher men as our civilization would like to believe.[11]

Edgar Quinet, a strongly anticlerical historian, venerated India:

India made, more loudly than anyone, what we might call the 'declaration of the rights of the Being'. There, in this divine self, in this society of the infinite with itself, lies clearly the foundation, the root of all life and all history.[12]

In Quinet's daring vision, Europe would soon experience an 'Oriental Renaissance', which was to have a greater impact than that of the sixteenth century. This was in 1842. His more renowned friend Michelet, the humanist and prolific chronicler of France's history, exemplified this prophecy when he sought to unveil 'the soul of India, secret and concealed, and, within that soul, a talisman which India herself is not too keen to see.'[13] In Michelet's perception, India was the ancient mother of us all:

India, closer than us to the creation, has better preserved the tradition of universal brotherhood. She inscribed it at the beginning and at the end of her two great sacred poems, the *Ramayan* and the *Mahabharat*, gigantic pyramids before which all our small occidental works must stand humbly and respectfully. When you grow tired of this quarrelsome West, please indulge in the sweet return to your mother, to that majestic antiquity so noble and tender. Love, humility, grandeur, you will find it all gathered there, and with such simple feelings, so detached of all miserable pride, that humility never even needs a mention.[14]

Michelet was particularly moved by 'a colossus five hundred times taller than the Pyramids, a monument as living as they are dead and mute—India's gigantic flower, the divine Ramayana.'[15]

His impassioned outburst in his *Bible of Humankind* deserves to be quoted at some length:

> The year 1863 will remain cherished and blessed. It was the first time I could read India's great sacred poem, the divine *Ramayana*. ... This great stream of poetry carries away the bitter leaven left behind by time and purifies us. Whoever has his heart dried up, let him drench it in the *Ramayana*. Whoever has lost and wept, let him find in it a soothing softness and Nature's compassion. Whoever has done too much, willed too hard, let him drink a long draught of life and youth from this deep chalice. ... Everything is narrow in the Occident. Greece is small—I stifle. Judea is dry—I pant. Let me look a little towards lofty Asia, towards the deep Orient. There I find my immense poem, vast as India's seas, blessed and made golden by the sun, a book of divine harmony in which nothing jars. There reigns a lovable peace, and even in the midst of battle, an infinite softness, an unbounded fraternity extending to all that lives, a bottomless and shoreless ocean of love, piety, clemency. I have found what I was looking for: the bible of goodness. Great poem, receive me! ... Let me plunge into it! It is the sea of milk.[16]

Other great figures of the Romantic movement—poets de Vigny, Lamartine, Leconte de l'Isle, among others—drank at India's fountain, some to the point of inebriation. Lamartine, for instance, said of Hindu philosophy, 'It is the Ocean, we are but its clouds. ... The key to everything is in India.'[17]

The Symbolists also found their inspiration stimulated and expanded by the new world India offered them: Baudelaire, Mallarmé, Verlaine (who wrote a poem titled 'Çavitri'), Rimbaud, or the 'accursed poets' such as Nerval or Lautréamont. Some of France's best-known novelists followed suit, from Balzac to Jules Verne (who located a whole novel in India: *La Maison à vapeur* or 'The Steam House'). The famed sculptor Rodin lavished praise on bronzes of Shiva's dance.

The mood was decidedly oriental and the nineteenth century

saw a strong presence of India in France's creative life and imagination.

The Twentieth Century

Despite this enthusiasm, France's exploration of India did not cross the threshold. It displayed a generous adhesion of the heart, the emotions and the aesthetical sense, but also a lack of intellectual moorings that might have lessened the risk of drifting on the 'Indian Ocean'. There had been the philosopher and statesman Victor Cousin, who in 1828 placed India at the start of his course on the history of philosophy:

> When we read with attention the poetical and philosophical monuments of the East, above all those of India, which are beginning to spread in Europe, we discover there many a truth and truths so profound, which make such contrast with the meanness of the results at which European genius has sometimes stopped, that we are constrained to kneel before Oriental philosophy, and to see in this cradle of the human race the birthplace of the highest philosophy.[18]

But Cousin's respect for India remained an exception, followed a few decades later by Charles Renouvier or the influential thinker and historian Hippolyte Taine.[19] Other French philosophers largely ignored the Indian wave; Hindu and Buddhist thought and message did not appear to mesh well with the French taste for cold rationalism. The two World Wars further pushed utilitarian and materialistic trends to the front. India lost her sheen and receded into the background.

Nevertheless, her indirect influence could be felt in Surrealism's search for a reality behind the surface and its rejection of blind chance. And she still had spokesmen of varying talent in Romain Rolland (whose lives of Ramakrishna and Vivekananda met with acclaim), Maurice Magre or René Guénon. René Daumal, author of the novel *Mount Analogue*—a metaphor for Mount Meru—went deeper than many, studied Sanskrit and mastered it to the point of writing a grammar of the language; his plans to translate large portions of Sanskrit literature were cut short by his premature death in 1944, at the age of 36, but he still left penetrating essays on Indian drama, music and poetry.[20] Henri Michaux put India's inner quest at the centre of his poetry. André Gide translated Tagore's *Gitanjali* into French. André Malraux visited India several times, was fascinated by her art, and probably understood her central message better than his contemporaries (with the exception of Daumal); he read the Gītā in the original and referred to it in passages such as this:

> The deepest opposition [between the West and India] rests on the fact that the fundamental evidence of the West, whether Christian or atheist, is death, whatever meaning the West gives to it, whereas India's fundamental evidence is the infinity of life in the infinity of time: 'Who could kill immortality?'*[21]

Indeed, Malraux's conversations with Nehru, whom he would meet several times until the 1960s, and his almost naïve but vain attempts to persuade him of the relevance of India's spirituality in today's world, make poignant reading.[22]

Despite such great names coming to her rescue, India's slide into oblivion continued in the French mind, even as some of her thoughts were so internalized as to become unrecognizable. Her epics or sacred texts were no longer in fashion with French students, and French Indologists became an isolated circle on the margins of the academic mainstream. Materialism reigned supreme, with a tinge of Christianity here and a dash of Marxism there; it had no further use for a dubious 'mysticism', especially of the Oriental kind. 'The whole earth' no longer needed India, at least France did not. Non-European cultures were, once again, regarded as unworthy of study, except at best to satisfy a momentary curiosity. Even today, the French educational system, moulded in that attitude, gives them virtually no place. Roger-Pol Droit

---

* A reference to Bhagavad-Gītā, 2.17.

eloquently showed[23] how a French teacher or professor of philosophy will more often than not be perfectly ignorant of thought systems originating from India; to them, ancient Greece is the sole reference. The great scholar Georges Dumézil's extensive studies of Vedic gods focused primarily on the structures of Indo-European mythologies, not on any substantial teaching from the Vedas.

Something of a reaction took place after the Second World War, perhaps precisely because it confronted Europe with a radical failure of her ideals of humanism and pacifism, and with the acute void left by uncompromising materialism. French lovers of India now had a better chance of being heard: Arnaud Desjardins, Alain Daniélou, Alexandra David-Neel, Jean Herbert or Jean Biès deserve mention, among many others. From the epics or Kālidāsa, the vogue now turned to the words and writings of India's living yogis, among them Sri Ramakrishna, Swami Vivekananda, Sri Aurobindo, Ramana Maharshi, Swami Ramdas and Ma Anandamayi.

Right from 1914, when he published his monthly *Arya* in both English and French editions, Sri Aurobindo was a crucial, if discreet, bridge between India and France, and probably the only Indian seer ever to have been formally honoured at the Sorbonne.[24] His vision of spiritual evolution and his method of integral yoga appealed not only to the aspiring heart but to the intellect weary of the shallowness of Western psychology or the brilliant but ephemeral edifices of existentialism, structuralism, poststructuralism, modernism, postmodernism, deconstructionism, and the endless sequence of isms and post-isms built upon each other's ruins. At this juncture, Sri Aurobindo helped prepare the ground for a renewed acceptance of non-Western thought; Mother, his French-born companion, kept the stream living.[25]

All these undercurrents resurfaced powerfully in the New Age movement of the 1960s, which in France represented a determined challenge to the rule of Cartesianism. As a popular movement, it chafed at the inadequacies of Western ideas, ideals, culture and society, and once again looked eastward. Hatha yoga and various meditation techniques spread, so did Buddhism whether Tibetan or Zen. (Although Buddhism became France's 'fastest-growing religion' in the 1990s, its followers there generally do not view it as a formal religion, rather as a practical method for self-discovery.) A whole literature appeared on the scene (pioneered in part by the avant-garde magazine of the 1960s, *Planète*), producing a cocktail of yoga, esotericism, health techniques or search for past lives.

A good deal of distortion, appropriation and misappropriation followed, but that was unavoidable, especially when France's academic and scholarly milieu was so unmindful of India, and when in addition Indian intellectuals interacting with France often appeared tied to the apron strings of a Sartre, a Lacan, a Foucault or a fashionable Derrida.

Today ... and Tomorrow?

In the last two or three decades, a number of fresh studies of India have appeared in France. Some of the old misconceptions or preconceptions cling on, although less stained with a sense of European superiority than in the nineteenth century, more imbued with a sincere effort to understand this world apparently so different, yet so intimate at times. At the very least, it means that the old fascination with India's heritage is not dead; it is reviving with fresh vigour and finding new voices.

If, in these times of monocultural magma, a nation still symbolizes a specific aspect of the human spirit, then France represents the higher intellectual quest and a certain élan in the adventure of self-discovery. That is what makes her encounter with India so pregnant with possibilities: Is the human mind doomed to forever turn in the same circles, catching no more than one new glimmer of the Truth at every turn? Or can it muster enough humility to acknowledge its intrinsic incompleteness and the need for a higher consciousness beyond this stumbling from semi-error to semi-truth, beyond its irremediable incapacity to fulfil our potential? Can it finally open itself so much as to grasp what exceeds it—a vaster, more essential quest that India symbolizes? That, beyond all Indological learning, is the question raised by France's encounter with India; it is the question that impelled a Voltaire, a Michelet or a Malraux. The bridge will have to be strengthened and broadened if the common deeper roots of India and Europe are to be nourished, and if the West is to rediscover a durable foundation for its culture.

India can choose to help in the process: the timeless creator and tireless giver that she is should shed her passivity and effectively project all that is precious in her heritage; when her own intelligentsia has failed to rise to the challenge, it is not just 'the whole earth that needs India', but also India that does need some fraternal comprehension from other shores, because her central preoccupation was always the very essence of what culture is about.

4

For the Love of Nature

A STRONGLY marked aspect of that culture, and one that offers a rich field of investigation, is India's ancient love story with nature. A story that all the more calls for our attention as we do not yet know whether it will have a happy ending.

Nature as the Divine

Looking back as far as we can see, in the Rig Veda we find Earth and Heaven often addressed in union as a single being (*dyāvā-prithivī*) and honoured together; they are 'parents of the gods' (7.53), 'father and mother' but also the 'twins' (1.159); together they 'keep all creatures safe' (1.160). From the beginning, our planet is imbued with divinity, as is the rest of the creation: the biblical gulf between the creator and the created finds no place here.

Further proof of the earth's divinity is that she holds in her depths the hidden sun, Mārtanda, and the divine Fire, Agni, another name for whom is Vanaspati, the tree-lord of the forest:

> O Agni, that splendour of yours which is in heaven and in the earth and its growths and its waters. (3.22.2)
> He is the child of the waters, the child of the forests, the child of things stable and the child of things that move. Even in the stone he is there. (1.70.2)

In a pregnant image, the Rig Veda sees the cosmos as a thousand-branched tree (3.8.11, 9.5.10). Turning this image upside down to remind us of the source of this manifestation, the Gītā (15.1) speaks of cosmic *ashvattha* (the pipal or holy fig tree, *Ficus religiosa*) with its roots above and branches below. Elsewhere in the Mahābhārata, he who worships the *ashvattha* is said to worship the universe: such is the often forgotten concept behind the worship of sacred trees in India, particularly in temples— once again, the universal at the centre of daily life.[1] In the same line, the *kalpavriksha* or *kalpataru*, the heavenly tree, grants our every desire, since there is nothing the universe cannot give us.

The Atharva Veda movingly sings our planet's beauties and bounties in its 'hymn to the Earth', *Bhūmi sūkta* (12.1). Indeed, the Vedas are replete with images drawn from nature—from mighty mountains, impetuous rivers and oceans, to majestic trees such as the pipal or the banyan. Some hymns ask not only the gods but the waters, trees and other plants to accept the bard's prayer; the Black Yajur Veda (4.2.6) even invokes plants as 'goddesses'. India's ancient medical system, Ayurveda, which makes use of thousands of medicinal plants, is rooted in this attitude; a branch of it, *vrikshāyurveda*, is entirely dedicated to the treatment of trees, plants and seeds.

Of course, this closeness to nature was not confined to the Scriptures. We find representations of trees (especially the pipal, again) on artefacts of the Indus–Sarasvatī civilization. There is also an intriguing seal depicting a supine woman from whose womb a plant emerges. As in many prehistoric (but not necessarily 'primitive') societies, a mother-goddess cult seems to have been closely associated with nature. In historical times, art forms whether Hindu, Buddhist or Jain made generous use of trees, plants and birds, and literature was pervaded with nature's many charms—who has not thrilled at Kālidāsa's exquisite descriptions of forest ashrams or mountain ranges? Who has not marvelled at the boldness with which the Sangam poets of the Tamil land made use of hills, forests and rivers or the ocean to convey their heroes' moods and weave the cosmic into the human? For generations children, too, have been entertained by the *Pañchatantra*'s irresistible animal fables.

For animals were revered, at least as symbols. Indus seals frequently depict the bull, the tiger, the elephant, the rhinoceros or the buffalo, although their precise significances remain a matter of speculation. Later, at some point of time, the cow takes pre-eminence. Aditi, the mother of the gods in the Rig Veda, is often called 'the divine Cow'. Ushas or the Dawn comes drawn by horses or by cows, or both. Indra, Sūrya and other gods are addressed as the 'Bull'. Even the humble dog finds its exalted representation in Saramā. Animals act as *vāhanas*, vehicles for many of the gods, occasionally lending them an elephant's head or even their whole bodies, as with Lord Vishnu's first avatars. Even when they are not deified, animals are objects of affection; we know how lovingly the Rāmāyana describes the brave vulture or the monkeys, or how the *Bhāgavatam* evokes the child Krishna's devotion to his cows, which they more than reciprocate. As we saw in the previous chapter, this concern for the lowest creatures is what so moved Michelet in the nineteenth century, for he could find no equivalent of it in European culture.

But there is always, lurking behind, a symbol: Krishna (the supreme divinity) and the cows (the creation) are nothing but a pictorial representation of the Rig Veda's initial identity between earth and heaven.

Sanctuaries

In ancient India animals were, no doubt, harnessed, but also cared for. Shāstras proscribed their unnecessary killing, perhaps taking their cue from Ashoka, who in his edicts prohibited hunting and cruelty to animals. Ashoka went further, declaring many species to be protected and stipulating medical treatment to them when necessary. Kautilya's *Arthashāstra* (2.26) describes forest sanctuaries where wildlife was protected from slaughter. Ancient kingdoms often adopted animals for their emblems, ranging from the elephant (for the Gangas), the lion (the Kadambas) or the tiger (the Cholas) down to the humble fish (the Pāndyas).

Realizing the essential role of water, India lavished attention on water harvesting and water management structures. I briefly referred earlier to those of the Indus civilization: some 4,500 years ago, the fascinating city of Dholavira, in Gujarat's forbiddingly arid Rann of Kachchh, dedicated a third of its surface or about 17 hectares to huge and often interconnected reservoirs, some of them cut in sheer rock. Monumental waterworks continue into the early historical era, as excavations at Sringaverapura (in Uttar Pradesh, about 200 BCE) revealed.[2] Later, we find across India a great variety of reservoirs, spectacular stepped wells, dams, water-diverting devices (such as the 1,800-year-old Grand Anicut on the Kaveri in Tamil Nadu), canals, all the way down to the humble village pond—but such ponds often formed part of elaborate networks.[3]

Folk and Tribal Heritage

But why keep to the past? Even to this day many patches of the country's forest cover exist thanks to the ancient tradition of 'sacred groves'. Named *kovilkādu* in Tamil Nadu, *kāvu* in Kerala, *nandavana* or *deivavana* in Karnataka and Andhra Pradesh, *deorai* in Maharashtra, they can be found in many parts of India, on the outskirts of the villages that protect them from hunting and tree cutting. Some contain hero stones or a small shrine surrounded by large terracotta figures, especially of horses. In the South, terracotta figures are often ritually broken and made anew every year in a symbolic evocation of nature's yearly death and rebirth. Part of an endangered tradition, sacred groves have been vanishing; the few that remain well protected are host to a remarkable biodiversity.

So too, India's numerous rural communities and tribes, many living off the forest, knew how to protect it—Bishnois, Bhils, Warlis, Santhals and Todas, or the Chipko movement have provided fine illustrations of this mindset. And it is not 'secular': temples generally have at least one sacred tree (*sthalavriksha*), and the greater its age, the greater its sacredness. Kanchipuram's Ekambareshwar temple boasts a venerable mango tree of impressive size and contorted appearance, which according to tradition is a few thousand years old; its four massive branches are said to represent the four Vedas (interestingly, the temple's presiding deity is the *prithivīlinga*: the 'earth *linga*'). In fact, in rural and tribal India, trees have long played an important part in rituals and festivals associated with moments of life such as puberty, marriage, praying for a child, praying for rain, and so on; in some parts, boys and girls used to be married to a tree before their actual weddings. In the *Vata Sāvitrī pūjā* still in vogue in Maharashtra, which enacts the tale of Sāvitrī and Satyavan, women tie a thin thread around a pipal; the longer the thread, the longer the husband's life will be.

Let us also stress that most rituals make use of one or several specific plants—*bilva*, sandalwood, neem or *tulasī*. . . . The plant provides a channel for the worshipper to attune to the universe. Since the rituals depended on them, such sacred plants had to be preserved. This is true not only of Hindu rituals, but also of many tribal ones: the Todas of the Nilgiris, for instance, depend on a number of rare species for their complex rituals, which have to be abandoned if any of the plants involved comes to disappear.

From the sacredness of trees and other plants derives the sacredness of food, food-giving and food-sharing, one of the high traditions of India running through scriptures as well as historical records. The recipient of Bhīshma's monumental discourse on dharma and the duties of a king, Yudhishthira asked Krishna to summarize that teaching. Krishna's answer is unexpected:

> The world, both animate and inanimate, is sustained by food. . . . The giver of food is the giver of life and indeed of everything else. Therefore, one who is desirous of well-being in this world and beyond should make special endeavour to give food.[4]

Then and Now

It would be easy to dilate on this ancient love story. But what happened? Does it end in some heartbreak? Why do we see so few traces in 'modern' India of this reverence for our mother? Torn landscapes, ugly buildings, dirty surroundings, ravaged forests, denuded hills, filthy or dying rivers meet our weary eyes everywhere. Village ponds fill up with garbage, streams dry up, cows turn into scavengers, cattle is cruelly treated from birth to slaughter. Dams kill rivers and submerge pristine forests, thermal and nuclear plants rival with each other in the extent and persistence of the pollution they inflict on the planet. All this to grant us the refined privilege of 'modern living' in cacophonous cities choked by noxious fumes and crammed with cardboard buildings—paradises of garbage, heavens of squalor. The triumph of technology, the proof of progress.

What went wrong?

Our first answer must be the direction India thoughtlessly adopted after Independence. A freak hybrid of Western utilitarianism and Stalinist industrialization; wasteful five-year plans; huge dams, huge nuclear plants, huge factories, all functioning under a huge bureaucratic structure—an unwieldy, ineffectual, incompetent and corrupt machinery. Forest departments became the first destroyers of the environment, uprooting native forests to make way for commercial crops, looking the other way as mafias log or mine 'protected' areas or encroach upon tribal land, failing to provide villagers with alternative fuels, and spending far more funds on their multiplying officers and staff than on protecting shrinking forests. Agriculture became the graveyard of millions of tons of fertilizers and pesticides, without a thought for tomorrow, and is now a field for experiments with genetically modified crops, the long-term effects of which are unknown and unpredictable. Our policy-makers disregarded the enormous potential of alternative energy sources a country like India is so profusely blessed with, and blindly promoted their narrow idea of 'modern technology'. Industries were bound with a thousand useless rules, but hardly one or two to compel them to effectively limit pollution or process toxic waste.

The so-called 'natural resources' were no longer a gift to be wisely used, but the object of our greed, to be grabbed and exploited. For our petty needs and pettier pleasures, we think nothing of endangering a whole planet with all its species. Global warming is only one manifestation of this phenomenon; there are others: expanding dead zones in the oceans, clouds of pollution covering whole continents, massive destruction of tropical forest and grassland, and extinction of animal and plant species on an unprecedented scale: 20,000 of them every year, according to current estimates. 'Overall the world is using 50 per cent more of the planet's resources than the world can supply,' says a recent report of World Wildlife Fund.[5]

It boggles the mind how our puny species could wreak havoc with the planet's environment in a little over two centuries of 'Industrial Revolution'—the mere blink of an eye if we compare with the earth's geological scales: four and a half billion years of slow and painful evolution now threatened by the 'crown of the creation'—you and me. In this sense, our species' distinctive trait is not intelligence, but self-destructive blindness; with all our mighty means, we cannot even ensure that our children will inherit a liveable environment!

Sons of the Earth

So where is the solution? In a return to the past, with idyllic and thrifty lifestyles? But we can never go back, for better or worse. The first step is to become aware. Aware that what we call 'progress' is not true progress, because it turns us into slaves, not masters. Aware that there are workable alternatives: cleaner energy, cleaner industries, less wasteful living habits. Aware also that the core engine of our present course remains greed—clothed in elegant labels such as 'development', 'free-market economy', 'globalization'—and until this greed goes, there is little hope for real change. Aware, finally, that it will certainly not go on its own, entrenched as it is in our unregenerate nature. Should we entertain any vain hopes, let us just take a straight look at the cynical attitude of most nations, including the U.S.A., India and China, on issues of global warming, at Brazil's unrepentant destruction of the Amazonian forest, at Norway's and Japan's insistence on their 'right' to slaughter whales to extinction, at French hunters' insistence on their 'right' to shoot down migratory birds for the fun of it, and at a thousand more sinister proofs of our 'bestiality'—but beasts are not 'bestial', we alone are.

It is likely therefore that we will have to be faced with stark consequences of our folly before we finally consent to alter our chosen course. Desertification, disappearance of glaciers and rivers, famine, poisoning of the air, water and soil, multiplication of diseases, mass extinction of species—none of this is enough, none of this will open our eyes. Our feverish hyperactivity is heating up the whole planet to no purpose, and is triggering uncontrolled changes possibly of an apocalyptic nature. Except that they are not 'apocalyptic': they are caused by our blindness, not by some god's wrath. Here and there, the growing voice of those who have long realized the dangers ahead is being heard—but is it acted upon fast enough to change course?

In the meantime, the best we can do is to add to that growing voice and growing action—to learn to speak up, and to work in the field. For too long, average Indians have been divested of their responsibility towards the environment they live in; let us shake off this lethargy and stop waiting for a corrupt and remiss government to lead the way. In the West, movements for the environment have gained strength and have had some real impact, however insufficient. They have at least helped people realize that technology will always create more problems than it can solve; they have sent millions in search of 'alternative lifestyles'. In India, drunk with the wine of 'economic growth', we lag behind and stubbornly go on brandishing discarded panaceas. If we want awareness to reach the masses, it must be not only on the basis of modern ecology, but also through the ancient worldview that sees this earth as sacred. The modern Indian rarely has any intimate relationship with nature: it is not enough to watch birds or have a walk in a forest; only when one perceives nature as a being, a presence, can one recapture something of the ancient spirit.

But let also every one of us phase out plastic bags, use water and other resources sparingly and cut down on our consumption. Let us adopt a pocket of forest, a grassland, a river or a hillside, visit it regularly, watch its progress or degradation, try and interest a few local students in its fate. Let us put this vision into practice instead of merely criticizing the official machinery. This much is in our power.

Let us become 'Nature worshippers', in the old Vedic sense of the term. Sings the Atharva Veda in its *Bhūmi sūkta*:

> I am a son of Earth, the soil is my mother. ...
> O Earth, may your snowy peaks and your forests be kind to us! ...
> May we speak your beauty, O Earth, that is in your villages and forests and assemblies and war and battles. ...
> Upon the immutable, vast earth supported by the law, the universal mother of the plants, peaceful and kind, may we walk for ever!

Indian and Western Traditions

I lived in the Nilgiri Hills of western Tamil Nadu for over two decades, and as a beautiful tropical rainforest—a Shola, as it is called—was getting ruthlessly destroyed at our doorstep, I could not help getting dragged into forest conservation. The unrelenting sound of machetes and axes chopping down young trees while the appointed 'guards' were busy collecting bribes was not something I was capable of putting up with. As a result, in the early 1980s I launched into a sustained campaign, first applying considerable pressure on a Forest Department unwilling to act, unwilling even to acknowledge that the situation was serious. The pressure grew to such heights that when a sincere officer happened to be in charge of our area—a white sheep among the black—a lot could be achieved in a short time, including the creation of a 'watchdog committee' made up of local citizens, to whom the charge of protecting the forest was promptly devolved.*

Our motivation made up for our lack of resources, and in a few years we had spread awareness among the local communities to an extent we could only have dreamed of earlier. This success story, which no official organ ever highlighted, as it sprang from a severe critique of the Forest Department's policies and disabilities, got diluted when newer officials silently resisted our work, forcing me to resign in protest—a classic tale in India's official mythology. Shortly afterwards, in 2003, I left the Nilgiris to settle in the plains, and the watchdog committee survived in name only.

While it was active, we used to be sent high officials so we would show them around the forest and explain our work to them. I invariably observed how most of them were unaware of what constitutes a forest, even though they were supposed to have some academic learning and a considerable field experience; if they saw tall standing trees and some greenery around, they decided that the forest was in good shape. No one noticed the wide gaps in the canopy, the missing generations of younger adult trees, or the rapid spread of exotic weeds in the undergrowth. This inability to grasp reality is probably the privilege of every bureaucracy on the planet, but it is particularly acute in India.

Sometime in the late 1990s, it was the turn of a retired Principal Chief Conservator of Forests of the Tamil Nadu government, on a private visit to 'our' forest. While a few of us walked him around the main bridle path (no such visitor ever asked to be taken deeper inside the forest), we engaged in a conversation about forest preservation, in the course of which he made a few startling statements. 'Overprotection', as he called it, could be undesirable, and some degree of woodcutting was not necessarily bad; also, forests sometimes needed fires to induce regeneration, sprouting of new

---

* The Longwood Shola Watchdog Committee (Kotagiri), created in 1998, was the first of its kind in Tamil Nadu.

seeds, clearing of undergrowth, etc. When I politely expressed scepticism, he revealed the source of his information: he had seen this explained in a programme of Discovery Channel.

This calls for two kinds of comment.

The first is that the programme the retired PCCF had watched must have been referring to coniferous forests such as those of North America's west coast, which are dominated by pine, fir, spruce, etc. In the course of ages, those forests have adapted to natural fires caused by lightning (although not to the now far more frequent and destructive man-made fires). However, that has no bearing on tropical evergreen rainforests such as those of the Western Ghats, which thrive in a perpetually moist milieu (provided their canopy is in good shape); here, any forest fire would be irreversibly destructive. As for 'overprotection', anyone familiar with forest conservation in India will be hard put to show where that is taking place. Was the retired PCCF sending us a not-so-subtle message that we were not really needed? However that may be, the fact is that rainforests of the Western Ghats, including the Shola forests of the Nilgiris, have evolved over millions of years, and till the last century or so, had to suffer almost no human interference—which is the same as absolute protection. It would be standing reality on its head to assert that illicit cutting, the kind of which has led many of our forests to their present degraded condition, especially near densely populated areas, has done them any good.

Discovery or Rediscovery?

My second reflection is of a deeper nature. No one will deny the quality of some programmes on Discovery or other such channels, the beauty of the images, their informative and educational value. But no amount of such programmes will help us cultivate a real contact with nature: you cannot 'learn' nature the way you learn English or science or the latest news. Moreover, such programmes can only, at best, reflect the minds of Western environmentalists of scientific bent. They have no doubt done a remarkable and often courageous work in the last few decades, but they do not have the monopoly of an understanding of nature. In fact, they often forget that science is not necessarily the best tool to understand nature—if it were, why should it have brought this planet to the brink of irremediable degradation in such a short span of time?

If we are to understand the roots of this phenomenon, we must probe how the Judeo-Christian tradition broke away from nature and began regarding her as so much inanimate matter to be exploited (a polite word for plunder). That unfortunate attitude, which has resulted in much of the ruthless abuse we see all over the world, can be traced to the Old Testament, and to Genesis in particular. On that fateful sixth day, Jehovah (or Yahweh) proclaims, 'Let us make man in our image, in our likeness, and let him rule over the fish of the sea and the birds of the air, over the livestock, over all the earth, and over all the creatures that move along the ground.' And he said to newborn man, 'Fill the earth and subdue it'.[6] Jehovah does not stop there; inexplicably, he seems to hold the earth responsible for man's sins. After generously cursing various nations through a succession of fire-spewing prophets, he turns his wrath to our poor planet: 'I will make the land of Egypt a ruin and a desolate waste among devastated lands.'[7] 'See, the Lord is going to lay waste the earth and devastate it; he will ruin its face and scatter its inhabitants. . . . The earth will be completely laid waste and totally plundered.'[8] 'Cursed is the ground because of you.'[9] And so on, Book after ranting Book.

The contrast with the ancient Indian attitude is as stark as could be. Indian tradition regards the earth as a goddess, Bhūdevī; her consort, Vishnu, the supreme divinity, incarnates from age to age to relieve her of the burden of demonic forces—sometimes of humanity itself. This he does out of love for the earth, his companion. Sītā, his wife when he is Rāma, means 'furrow', and in the end she returned to the earth whence she had come. Shiva, too, is bound to the earth through Pārvatī, daughter of Himavat or the Himalayas. Earth and Heaven are therefore inseparable: 'Heaven is my father; my mother is this vast earth, my close kin,' says the Rig Veda.[10] Earth is as sacred as Heaven, since she is our mother—not a dead heap of 'natural resources'. Nature, rather than an adversary to be conquered and despoiled, is our best defence: 'Blue water, open space, hills and thick forests constitute a fortress,' proclaims Valluvar in the *Kural* (742). Rivers from Gangā to Sarasvatī and Kāverī are goddesses (the Brahmaputra, of course, is a rare god among them), mountains from the Himalayas to the Vindhyas are gods. The whole of nature is felt to be pervaded with the divine Spirit.

Such was, of course, the view of most of the ancient world, from the Greeks (for whom the earth was Gaia and Demeter) to the Norsemen, the Mayas and Aztecs, and the Amerindians. But all those cultures were wiped out by the steamroller of the Christian advance, to which any worship of nature was 'Pagan idolatry' (which is also the attitude of Islam).

Strangely, even in India the sages of old had foreseen a waning of this communion with nature. During the *Kaliyuga*, our present Dark Age, one of the many signs of growing chaos, according to the *Shiva Purāna*, is that the merchant class 'have abandoned holy rites such as digging wells and tanks, and planting trees and parks.'[11] Note how such simple acts of nature conservation were regarded as a 'holy rite', a sacred activity. The new religion of utilitarianism is the cause of this steep decline, yet we can see something of that reverence subsist in some aspects of Indian life, from the sacred groves to the *bhūmi pūjā* conducted at the start of any construction. Even borewell contractors often perform a brief ceremony or prayer before drilling the earth (though they perhaps pray for their money not to go waste).

So if to Westerners nature is a 'discovery', we Indians only need to *re*discover and revive the old spirit and infuse it into modern methods, including scientific ones. In doing so, we should remember that science is no more than a tool, and a dangerous one when its awesome power is harnessed to our endless greed. We will be able to use it rightly only if we keep alive in our hearts and minds our true relationship with our material mother. And if we must certainly take a leaf out of Western ecologists' book as regards their sense of commitment and their effectiveness in getting a

number of measures adopted, on the other hand, they could also
—and a few do—imbibe with benefit something of the ancient
Indian approach. The two together would work wonders.

Subduing the Earth

Jehovah's fury at the earth, which he claims to be his own creation, is, as I said, inexplicable. Those who try to rationalize it
often repeat the old story of the original sin: man's rebellion
against Jehovah fully justified the latter's divine 'wrath'. But why
should poor Earth suffer for man's supposed sins? Moreover, the
very notion of original sin admits of a gulf between the creator
and the creation. In the Indian Vedic conception, which is older
than the Bible even by the most conservative estimate, there is no
'original sin', no fall, no rebellion against the creator, no cursing
of humanity or of the earth; there is only one divine universe:
'Truth is the base that bears the Earth,' says the Rig Veda.[12]

Enlightened Western thinkers have condemned this notion of
a fatal divorce brought about by the Bible between God on one
side and his creation on the other, pointing out that no such
divorce existed in 'Pagan' or pre-Christian conceptions. Let me
quote Pierre Thuillier, who wrote in 1995:

> In Paganism, natural realities were perceived to be living,
> inhabited by 'souls'.... A spring (or a tree) was not reduced
> to a physical reality, a material reality. It was something
> more, an entity with a life of its own. It was therefore per-
> fectly natural for a spring to be respected and even revered.
> It was seen as a marvellous manifestation of Nature, her-
> self regarded as living. The Earth, let us recall, was also
> perceived as one great organism; the Greeks called her
> 'Mother Earth'. Even minerals appeared endowed with a
> certain life, and all individual existences mysteriously
> associated with one another amidst the Whole, of which
> humanity itself was but one fragment.
>
> With Christianity, a supposedly 'superior' religion, that
> attitude towards nature was totally disqualified. Henceforth,

it was forbidden to revere springs as if they had a dignity of their own. People's whole adoration had to be turned to the Christian God and to him alone. ... It is true that nature, created by God, retained a certain spiritual value. But a radical transformation had taken place: earth, air, water and fire, now theologically stripped of all 'soul', were no more than objects which *Homo technicus* was free to manipulate as he wished. ... Through its doctrine, the Judeo-Christian tradition somehow legitimized officially the most daring technical enterprises.[13]

Another recent example is Edward Goldsmith, founder-editor of the pioneering magazine *The Ecologist*. In an interview, he explained:

The Bible makes man the centre of the universe, since it assigns to him the role of 'subduing' the Earth. ... The religions of the Book went astray the moment they allowed a bipolar relationship to be established between God and men, then between men and nature. ... I believe we should go back to forms of cosmic religiosity as they existed before the advent of the great monotheistic religions.[14]

Indeed, we shall not find in the Bible or the Koran a single passage echoing the pre-Christian world's reverence for the Earth as our divine mother. Moving away from India, let us turn to the Native Americans, with a few sentences from Chief Seattle's 1855 speech to a White governor who had come to 'purchase' (in reality to grab) huge tracts of his clan's lands:

What is it that the White Man wants to buy, my people will ask. It is difficult for us to understand.

How can one buy or sell the air, the warmth of the land?

That is difficult for us to imagine. If we don't own the sweet air and the bubbling water, how can you buy it from us? Each pine tree shining in the sun, each sandy beach, the mist hanging in the dark woods, every space, each humming bee is holy in the thoughts and memory of our people.

... Every part of this soil is sacred in the estimation of my people. ...

We are part of the earth, and the earth is part of us. The fragrant flowers are our sisters, the reindeer, the horse, the great eagle our brothers. ...

We know that the White Man does not understand our way of life. To him, one piece of land is much like the other. He is a stranger coming in the night taking from the land what he needs. The earth is not his brother but his enemy, and when he has conquered it, he moves on. ... He treats his mother the Earth and his Brother the sky like merchandise. His hunger will eat the earth bare and leave only a desert. ...

Your God is not our God! ... Our people are ebbing away like a rapidly receding tide that will never return. The White Man's God cannot love our people, or he would protect them. ...

But why should I mourn at the untimely fate of my people? Tribe follows tribe, and nation follows nation, like the waves of the sea. It is the order of Nature, and regret is useless. Your time of decay may be distant, but it will certainly come, for even the White Man ... cannot be exempt from the common destiny.

We may be brothers after all. We will see.[15]

'Your God is not our God' is a statement that calls for deep reflection. Should we invoke an earth-cursing, self-confessed jealous and angry god, or an earth-loving and earth-saving one? For the moment, let us pray that Mother Earth will not, in turn, curse us too harshly, deserved though her curse would be.

Part Two

Indian Culture
at the Crossroads

5

The Colonized Indian Mind

SO far, we have surveyed a few bright achievements of Indian culture, not without encountering problematic realities. But problems are, in the last analysis, a touchstone, and no culture worth the name will shun the test.

One of the biggest challenges to Indian culture was undoubtedly the shock of the colonial adventure—a shock whose ripples continue to be felt today. Having suffered the burden of two centuries of British occupation, India has, since Independence, tried to come to terms with the impact of that exotic presence perhaps diametrically opposed to her own temperament and culture. Should the nation's immune system eject the antigenic intruder? Does it have the vigour to do it at all? If anything, this introspection has only intensified in recent decades, as Western lifestyles aggressively spread around the globe. But it stands to reason that for an effective 'decolonization' to take place—or to find out whether and how far it is desirable—we should first take a closer look at the effects of this colonization, what traces it has left on the Indian mind and psyche, and how deep.

Historical Background

First, an aside. I have only referred to the British occupation, not to the Muslim invasions, though they stretched over a much longer span of time and violently collided with Indian civilization. Yet, strangely, in spite of their ruthlessness, their proud use of violence to coerce or convert, India's Islamic rulers rarely attempted to take possession of the Indian mind: a few, in faithful obedience to Koranic injunctions, simply tried to stamp it out; that they did not succeed is another story.

The British, too, dreamed of stamping it out, but not through sheer brute force or coercion. As we know, besides their primary object of plunder, they viewed—or perhaps justified—their presence in India as a 'divinely ordained' civilizing mission. They spoke of Britain as 'the most enlightened and philanthropic nation in the world'[1] and of 'the justifiable pride which the cultivated members of a civilised community feel in the beneficent exercise of dominion and in the performance by their nation of the noble task of spreading the highest kind of civilisation.'[2] Such rhetoric was constantly poured out to the Britons at home so as to give them a good conscience, while atrocities perpetrated on Indians were discreetly hidden from sight.

To achieve their aim, the British rulers followed two lines: on the one hand, they encouraged an English and Christianized education in accordance with the well-known Macaulay doctrine, which projected Europe as enlightened and progressive, and on the other hand, they pursued a systematic denigration of Indian culture, scriptures, knowledge systems, customs, traditions, crafts, cottage industries, social institutions and educational system, taking full advantage of the stagnant character of Hindu society at the time. There were, of course, notable exceptions among British individuals, from John Woodroffe to Sister Nivedita or Annie Besant—but almost none to be found among the ruling class. Let us recall how, in his 1835 Minute, Thomas B. Macaulay asserted that Indian culture was based on 'a literature . . . that inculcates the most serious errors on the most important subjects . . . hardly reconcilable with reason, with morality . . . fruitful of monstrous superstitions.' Hindus, he confidently declared, had nothing to show except a 'false history, false astronomy, false medicine . . . in company with a false religion.'[3]

Indians were perhaps too innocent to see through the cunning with which their colonial masters set about their task. In the middle of the 1857 uprising, the Governor-General Lord Canning wrote to a British official:

> As we must rule 150 millions of people by a handful (more or less small) of Englishmen, let us do it in the manner best calculated to leave them divided (as in religion and national feeling they already are) and to inspire them with the greatest possible awe of our power and with the least possible suspicion of our motives.[4]

Even a 'liberal' governor such as Mountstuart Elphinstone wrote in 1859, '*Divide et impera* [divide and rule] was the old Roman motto and it should be ours.'[5]

In this clash of two civilizations—for it was undoubtedly one—the European, younger, dynamic, hungry for space and riches, appeared far better fitted than the Indian, half decrepit, half dormant after long centuries of internal strife and repeated onslaught. The contrast was so severe that no one doubted the outcome—the rapid conquest of the Indian mind and life. That was what Macaulay, again, epitomized when he proudly wrote to his father in 1836:

> Our English schools are flourishing wonderfully. ... The effect of this education on the Hindoos is prodigious. No Hindoo, who has received an English education, ever remains sincerely attached to his religion. ... It is my firm belief that, if our plans of education are followed up, there will not be a single idolater among the respectable classes in Bengal thirty years hence. ... I heartily rejoice in the prospect.[6]

Macaulay's projected statistics failed to materialize; he thought the roots of Hinduism to be shallow, but they quietly held fast. However, this educational strategy did succeed in creating a fairly large 'educated' class, anglicized and partially Christianized (often atheicized), which looked up to its European model and ideal, and formed the actual base of the Empire in India.

Came Independence. If India did achieve political independence—at the cost of amputating a few limbs of her body—she hardly achieved independence in the field of thought. Nor did she try: the country's so-called elite, whose mind had been shaped and hypnotized by their colonial masters, always assumed that in order to reach all-round fulfilment, India merely had to follow European thought, science, medicine, industry and sociopolitical institutions.

The Symptoms

Six decades later, at least, we begin to see how gratuitous those assumptions were. Yet the colonial imprint remains present at many levels. At a very basic one, it is amusing to note that Pune is sometimes called 'the Oxford of the East', while Ahmedabad is 'the Manchester of India'—and since Coimbatore is often dubbed 'the Manchester of south India', we have at least out-Manchestered England herself. The Nilgiris of Tamil Nadu are flatteringly compared to Scotland (never mind that Kotagiri is called 'a second Switzerland'), and tourist guides refer to Kerala's Alappuzha as 'the Venice of the East'. Also with a view to tickling potential visitors, Puduchery calls itself 'India's Little France' or 'the French Riviera of the East'. India's map seems dotted with European places, if slightly jumbled. Things get more troublesome when Kālidāsa is labelled 'the Shakespeare of India', when Bankim Chatterji needs to be compared to Walter Scott or Tagore to Shelley, and Kautilya becomes India's very own Machiavelli. Undoubtedly, our compass is set due west. Would the British call Shakespeare 'England's Kālidāsa', let alone Manchester 'the Coimbatore of northwest England'?

But I think the most disturbing signs of the colonization of the Indian mind are found in the field of education. Take the English nursery rhymes taught to many of our little children, as if, before knowing anything about India, they needed to know about Humpty-Dumpty or the sheep that went to London to see the Queen. More seriously, the teaching is almost entirely based on Western inputs, as though India never produced any knowledge of her own: I am not aware of a single Indian contribution to science, technology, urbanization, polity or philosophy, being taught to Indian schoolchildren. The blanking out of India's pursuit for knowledge in every field of life is complete.

Higher education is hardly different. Students will study mathematics, physics or medicine without having the least idea of what ancient India achieved in those fields. I have never been able to understand why, for instance, they should not be made aware that the decimal place-value system of numeral notation they use daily is of Indian origin; that the so-called Gregory series, Pell's equation or the fundamentals of combinatorics were anticipated by several centuries by Indian mathematicians of the Siddhāntic period; or that Indian astronomers of the same era had developed powerful algorithms that enabled them to calculate planetary positions and the occurrences of eclipses with an excellent degree of precision. It is equally hard to accept that medical students should know nothing of Indian systems of medicine such as Ayurveda or Siddha, of proven efficacy for a wide range of disorders and even serious diseases. If the topic is psychology, the Western variety alone will be taken up, completely eclipsing the far deeper psychological system offered by yoga. Water harvesting is taught as if it were a new contribution from the West, even if it was widely practised from Harappan times onward. I could go on with metallurgy, chemistry, textiles, transport and a host of other technologies.

Our educational policies systematically discourage the teaching of Sanskrit, and one wonders again whether that is in deference to Macaulay, who found that great language to be 'barren of useful knowledge' (though he confessed he knew none of it!). It is symptomatic that in the 1980s, a controversy arose as to whether the teaching of Sanskrit was 'secular' or not. The Central Board of Secondary Education (CBSE) attempted to wriggle out of it by arguing before the Supreme Court in 1994 that if Sanskrit was taught, then should not Arabic, Persian, French or German, too, be taught? The Supreme Court bench, directed by a Sikh judge, threw the argument out and reminded us of a simple truth: 'Without the learning of Sanskrit it is not possible to decipher the Indian philosophy on which our culture and heritage are based. ... [The] teaching of Sanskrit alone as an elective subject can in no way be regarded as against secularism.'[7]

In the same vein, the Upanishads or the two epics stand no chance, and students will almost never hear about them at school. Indian languages (still called 'vernacular', a word whose root meaning is 'belonging to native slaves'[8]) are plainly given a lower status than English, with the result that many profound scholars or writers who chose their mother-tongue as their medium of expression remain totally unknown beyond their state, while textbooks are crowded with second-rate thinkers who happened to write in English.

If you take a look at the teaching of history, the situation is equally troubling. Almost all Indian history taught today in our schools and universities has been written by 'native historians who [have] taken over the views of the colonial masters,'[9] as the historian of religion Klaus Klostermaier put it. India's historical traditions are brushed aside as so much fancy to satisfy the dictum that 'Indians have no sense of history.' Indian tradition never said anything about mysterious 'Aryans' invading the country from the Northwest, but since nineteenth-century European scholars decided so, our children continue to learn by rote this theory now rejected by most archaeologists. South Indian literature remembered nothing about 'Dravidians' being driven southward by the naughty Aryans, but this continues to be stuffed into young brains to satisfy political ideologies. Saint Thomas never came to south India, as historical sources make amply clear, but let us perpetuate the myth to create an imagined early Christian foothold in India. The real facts of the destruction wreaked in India by Islamic invaders and by some Christian missionaries must be kept outside school curricula, since they contradict the 'tolerant' and 'liberating' image that Islam and Christianity have been projecting for themselves. Even the freedom movement is not spared: as the distinguished historian R.C. Majumdar and others have shown, no objective critique of Mahatma Gandhi or the Indian National Congress is allowed, and the role of other important leaders is belittled or erased. I will enlarge upon these issues a little later (in Chapter 8).

Nothing illustrates the bankruptcy of our education better than the manner in which, twelve years ago, State education ministers raised an uproar at an attempt to discuss the introduction of the merest smattering of Indian culture into the curriculum, and at the singing of the *Sarasvatī Vandanā*, a customary homage to the goddess of Knowledge.* The message they actually conveyed was that no Indian element is acceptable in education, while they are satisfied with an education which, a century ago, Sri Aurobindo called 'soulless and mercenary',[10] and which has since degenerated further into a stultifying, mechanical routine that kills our children's natural intelligence. They find nothing wrong with maiming young brains and hearts, but will be up in arms if we speak of bringing in a few time-tested elements of India's heritage. They will lament at the all-round loss of values and harangue us about 'value-based education', while refusing to make use of what was for ages the source of the best Indian values.

Swami Vivekananda put it in his typical forthright style:

> The child is taken to school, and the first thing he learns is that his father is a fool, the second thing that his grand-father is a lunatic, the third thing that all his teachers are hypocrites, the fourth, that all the sacred books are lies! By the time he is sixteen he is a mass of negation, lifeless and boneless. And the result is that fifty years of such education has not produced one original man in the three presidencies. ... We have learnt only weakness.[11]

---

* In the words of Tavleen Singh (by no means a 'Hindutva' journalist): 'A country which has education ministers who jeer at a hymn which says of learning (as Saraswati) that she is the goddess before whom even Brahma, Vishnu and Mahesh bow probably deserves to be illiterate.' *India Today*, 9 November 1998.

Ananda Coomaraswamy, who wrote at length on Indian education at the beginning of the twentieth century, gave this stark diagnosis:

> It is hard to realize how completely the continuity of Indian life has been severed. A single generation of English education suffices to break the threads of tradition and to create a nondescript and superficial being deprived of all roots—a sort of intellectual pariah who does not belong to the East or the West, the past or the future. The greatest danger for India is the loss of her spiritual integrity. Of all Indian problems the educational is the most difficult and most tragic.[12]

The child becomes a recording machine stuffed with a jarring assortment of meaningless bits and snippets. The only product of this denationalizing education has been the creation of a modern, Westernized 'elite' with little or no contact with the sources of Indian culture, and with nothing of India's ancient worldview except for a few platitudes to be flaunted at public functions or cocktail parties. Browsing through any English-language daily or magazine is enough to see how we revel in the sonorous clang of hollow clichés. If Western intellectuals come up with some new 'ism', you are sure to find it echoed all over the Indian press in a matter of weeks; it was amusing to see, a few years ago, how the visit to India of a French philosopher and champion of 'deconstructionism' sent the cream of our intellectuals raving wild for weeks, while they remained crassly ignorant of far deeper thinkers next door. Or if some Western painters or sculptors come up with some new-fangled cult of ugliness, their Indian counterparts will not lag far behind.* And let some Western nations make a new religion of 'human rights' (with intensive bombing campaigns to enforce them if necessary),

---

* I am not, of course, suggesting that all Western artists revel in ugliness ; I only refer to the second-rate among them who do, no doubt as a shortcut to celebrity : in the present death-worshipping atmosphere, they are sure to garner much more attention from the media than genuine creators.

and you will hear a number of Indians clamouring for them parrot-like, unable to realize that even though the primary focus of Indian society was functions and duties rather than rights, it had enough democratic mechanisms to provide for redress in case of abuse.

The list is endless, in every field of life, and if India had been living in her intellect alone, one would have to conclude that she has ceased to exist—or will do so after one or two more generations of this senseless de-Indianizing.

Maladies of the Mind

The root of the problem is that we have ceased to think by ourselves. We are spoon-fed and often force-fed almost every one of our thoughts, or what masquerades as thought. Independent reflection is discouraged at every step, starting at school.

Yet it is not my point that English education in India has been an unmitigated evil. It was a necessary, probably an unavoidable evil. India had to be shaken from her lethargy, to open up to the world and face its challenges, and that was the fastest way to compel her to do so. There is also no doubt that this opening to dynamic currents of thought from the West contributed in no small measure to the quest for independence, as has often been pointed out. Sometimes indeed, one poison is needed to cure another. But to continue taking poison after the cure is over is inexcusable. India's failure to boldly formulate and implement her own system of education after Independence—a system rooted in the best the past can offer but turned resolutely to the future— must rank as her most ruinous error.

But intellectual subjection does more than simply impoverish the Indian mind or wean it away from its roots. It also introduces serious distortions into its thinking processes. With their clear and bold thought, Western thinkers since the eighteenth century no doubt did much to pull Europe out of the Dark Ages brought about by Christianity. But they had to take shortcuts in the process: they needed sharp intellectual weapons and had no time to develop the qualities of pluralism, universality, integrality native to the Indian mind and nurtured over thousands of years. Their thought was essentially divisive and exclusive: God was on one side and the creation on another; an abyss separated matter from spirit; one was either a believer or an atheist, either a Christian or a Pagan, either ancient or modern, determinist or indeterminist, empiricist or rationalist, rightist or leftist. Whether one was an adept of idealism, realism, positivism, existentialism or any of the thousand isms the Western intellect keeps building and demolishing, Truth was parcelled out into small, hardened, watertight bits, each no wider than one line of thought or one philosophical system, each neatly labelled and set in contrast or opposition with the other.

The result of this Western obsession with divisiveness has been disastrous in India's context. Her inhabitants had never known themselves to be 'Aryans' or 'Dravidians' in the racial sense, yet they became thus segregated; they had never labelled their worldview a 'religion' (a word with no exact equivalent in Indian languages), but it had to become one. Nor was one label sufficient: India recognized and respected the endless multiplicity of approaches to the Truth (what is commonly, but incorrectly, called 'tolerance'), but under the Western spotlight those approaches became so many 'sects' almost rivalling each other (perhaps like Catholics and Protestants). Hinduism was thus cut up into convenient bits—Vedism, Brāhmanism, Vaishnavism, Shaivism, Shaktism, Tantrism, etc.—which Indians themselves had not isolated in this rigid, cut-and-dried fashion. As for Buddhism, Jainism and Sikhism, which had simply been regarded in India as new paths, initially at least, they were arbitrarily stuck with a label of 'separate religions'. Similarly, thousands of semi-fluid communities were duly catalogued by the British rulers as so many cast-iron castes.[13]

Unfortunately, this itemizing and labelling of their heritage became an undisputed fact in the subconscious mind of Indians: looking at themselves through Western eyes, they passively accepted being defined and dissected by their colonial masters. The Indian mind had become too feeble to take the trouble of assimilating the positive elements of Western thought and rejecting the negative or unsuitable ones: it swallowed but could not digest. Even some of the early attempts to lay new foundations—the Brahmo Samaj and many other 'reformist' movements in particular—were, despite their usefulness as a ferment, conceived apologetically in response to Europe's standards and judgements. If, for instance, they were told that Hindus were 'polytheistic idolaters', rather than show the fallacy of such a label, they would bend over backward to build their new creeds on monotheism of a Judeo-Christian type. Not long ago we had a revealing echo of such an attitude when a President of India, K.R. Narayanan, on a visit to Kerala, felt obliged to speculate that Adi Shankarāchārya's Monism had been influenced by Islam's monotheism. That is the last stage of intellectual bankruptcy.

As Aleksandr Solzhenitsyn once put it,

> The mistake of the West is that it measures other civilizations by the degree to which they approximate to Western civilization. If they do not approximate it, they are hopeless, dumb, reactionary.[14]

Educated Indians virtually admitted they were 'hopeless, dumb, reactionary', and could only stop being so by receiving salvation from Europe. At the political level, they pinned their hopes on its democracy and secularism, ignoring warnings that those European concepts would wreak havoc once mechanically transposed in India. At the cultural level, they internalized the forced equation between Hinduism and 'caste', *sati* and other perceived 'social evils', without ever developing a critical understanding of the aberrations of Western society. A hundred years ago already, Sri Aurobindo observed:

> They will not allow things or ideas contrary to European notions to be anything but superstitious, barbarous, harmful and benighted, they will not suffer what is praised and practised in Europe to be anything but rational and enlightened.[15]

As a result, it is common to find 'modern' Indians (I have had occasion to hear quite a few of them), and even a number of Swamis, especially those with Western followers, who proudly assert that they are 'not Hindus'. What they usually mean by that is that they are 'tolerant' of everything and anything, and therefore far too broad-minded to be Hindus. They forget that Hinduism in its true form, *sanātana dharma*, is no narrow dogmatic creed and can accommodate any path—provided that path is, like itself, and unlike the three great monotheistic religions,* respectful of other paths, because it knows it is only one small parcel of the whole Truth beyond all paths.

Ram Swarup,** a profound Indian thinker, was not afraid of swimming against this self-deprecating tide nurtured by our intelligentsia and media:

> A permanent stigma seems to have stuck to the terms *Hindu* and *Hinduism*. These have now become terms of abuse in the mouth of the very elite which the Hindu millions have raised to the pinnacle of power and prestige with their blood, sweat and tears.[16]

Such is the painful but logical outcome of two centuries of colonization of the Indian mind.

Mother Hate?

The point is not to glorify India of ancient times or construct an idealized image of Indian society: there can be no dispute that, like any other, it has had its faults alongside its brighter spots.

---

* For simplicity's sake, to designate Judaism, Christianity and Islam collectively I use the common term 'monotheistic religions' rather than 'Semitic religion' or 'Abrahamic religion', as the first is dated as well as incorrect, and the second poorly understood in India. I may add, however, that these religions are not always as 'monotheistic' as they claim to be, while Hinduism is not as polytheistic as they like to portray it, or not in the way they portray it (it is, to be precise, omnitheistic and polymorphic, but we should refrain from stretching Greco-Latin beyond a point).
** The late Ram Swarup's penetrating *Hindu View of Christianity and Islam* is recommended reading for the serious student of religious thought and practice.

But for a critique to be useful, it should be based on an understanding *from within*. Unfortunately, most of the critiques we hear come from a small but vocal class of 'modern' Indians who know very little about India and are in many ways the intellectual inheritors of the colonial era. With his usual keenness, Ananda K. Coomaraswamy put it in a nutshell almost a hundred years ago:

> We, who think we are educated and progressive, ... we ourselves have despised and hated everything Indian. ... I do not think we fully realise the depth of our present intellectual poverty. ... The creative force in us has died, because we had no faith in ourselves—we could only learn to be intellectual parasites.[17]

More recently, the Sanskrit scholar and thinker Kapil Kapoor put the phenomenon into perspective:

> All this [traditional Indian] knowledge has been marginalized by and excluded from the mainstream education system. Efforts to incorporate it or teach it have been politically opposed and condemned as 'revivalism'. Europe's thirteenth-century onwards successful venture of relocating the European mind in its classical Greek roots is lauded and expounded in the Indian universities as 'revival of learning' and as 'Renaissance'. But when it comes to India, the political intellectuals dismiss exactly the same venture as 'revivalism' or 'obscurantism'. ... The educated Indian, particularly the Hindu, suffers from such a deep loss of self-respect that he is unwilling to be recognised as such. He feels, in fact, deeply threatened by any surfacing or manifestation of the identity that he has worked so hard to, and has been trained to reject. But it lies somewhere in his psyche as 'an unhappy tale', as something that is best forgotten. It is these people wearing various garbs—liberal, left, secular, modern—who oppose, more often than not from sheer ignorance, any attempt to introduce Indian traditions of thought in the mainstream education system—a classic case of self-hate taking the form of mother-hate![18]

India's cultural heritage might still have been integrated in mainstream education if, like ancient Egypt or Greece, Indian civilization had reached its glorious death some centuries ago; 'vanished civilizations' make fine objects of study, not those that are stubborn enough to linger on.

It is little wonder that the same educational system has all but succeeded in crippling the Indian child's native talent, which finds it hard to flower anywhere but abroad. Where are the J.C. Boses, P.C. Roys, C.V. Ramans or S. Ramanujans that free India should have produced? Where, the original thinkers, artists and creators all the better able to grapple with the world as they have their feet firmly planted on a millennial soil?

Looking Ahead

But everything has a deeper meaning, we are told, and that of our present confused phase was luminously expressed by Sri Aurobindo in 1909:

> The spirit and ideals of India had come to be confined in a mould which, however beautiful, was too narrow and slender to bear the mighty burden of our future. When that happens, the mould has to be broken and even the ideal lost for a while, in order to be recovered free of constraint and limitation. . . . We must not cabin the expanding and aggressive spirit of India in temporary forms which are the creation of the last few hundred years. That would be a vain and disastrous endeavour. The mould is broken; we must remould in larger outlines and with a richer content.[19]

There is no doubt that the old mould has all but been broken; the question is whether we are moving towards a 'richer content'. There are hopeful signs of an aspiration to a reawakening and a liberation from this intellectual and cultural degeneration. But for this aspiration to be fulfilled, I am convinced that we shall have to rediscover a subtle and supple but profound intellect, and learn to tap anew the inexhaustible source of strength that has sustained India over ages. Take care of India's soul and the rest will take care of itself, as Swami Vivekananda said.[20] Only then will we learn to question West and India alike, past as well as present. Only then will we regain our discernment, our one beacon in the growing gloom.

I will quote Sri Aurobindo once more:

> We must begin by accepting nothing on trust from any source whatsoever, by questioning everything and forming our own conclusions. We need not fear that we shall by that process cease to be Indians or fall into the danger of abandoning Hinduism. India can never cease to be India or Hinduism to be Hinduism, if we really think for ourselves. It is only if we allow Europe to think for us that India is in danger of becoming an ill-executed and foolish copy of Europe.[21]

To recover her true genius in a new body is the seemingly impossible task now facing India. She needs it not only for herself but for the world. 'Europe is destructive, suicidal,'[22] André Malraux told Nehru in 1936.

India's view of the universe, and of ourselves as an integral part of it, this bridge between destruction and renewal, between matter and spirit, is what humanity needs today. India's special contribution should be to show, as she did in her ancient history, how material and spiritual developments can be harmonized—and indeed need each other if human society is to survive. Because the West ultimately believes in death, it ends up destroying the planet; because India ultimately sought the secret of life, it could restore the divinity of the creation, humans included.

This 'Indian genius', as Michelet called it,[23] has been percolating back to the West, where it has inspired new approaches, more 'holistic' thoughts, though not yet a transforming power. Perhaps the tide of colonialism will be reversed, after all. And without bloodshed, this time.

Perhaps Rabindranath Tagore's last testament of April 1941, three months before his death, will be fulfilled:

The spirit of violence which perhaps lay dormant in the psychology of the West, has at last roused itself and desecrates the Spirit of Man. . . .

I had at one time believed that the springs of civilization would issue out of the heart of Europe. But today when I am about to quit the world that faith has gone bankrupt altogether. . . .

Today I live in the hope that the Saviour is coming— that he will be born in our midst in this poverty-shamed hovel which is India. I shall wait to hear the divine message of civilization which he will bring with him. . . . Perhaps that dawn will come from this horizon, from the East where the sun rises.[24]

6

The Age of Confusion

IF we wish to assess the strengths and gifts of Indian culture
and civilization—and some of its weaknesses too—a good deal
of clutter accumulated by decades of intellectual laziness or
effeteness needs to be cleared. One way is to cast a fresh look
at a few important issues which, in India's present intellectual
climate, are usually regarded as 'sensitive' or 'controversial'—in
other words, fit to be discreetly swept under the carpet, or else
cast into wearisome stereotypes. Yet I find that discussing them
critically turns out to be highly profitable, provided we do so
from the standpoint of Indian experience, not from dry philosophy or stereotyped thinking.

Conversely, turning away from them or unthinkingly accepting
conventional ideas about them is, to my mind, the source of the
most serious confusion. Long ago we were warned about this
unmistakable sign of our dark age: in the Mahābhārata, for
example, the sage Mārkandeya tells Yudhishthira that in the
Kaliyuga, 'Men generally become addicted to falsehood in
speech,' and 'intellectual darkness will envelop the whole earth.'[1]
Yet we have done surprisingly little to dispel this darkness from
our own minds to begin with. We have allowed others, unfamiliar
with or contemptuous of the truths discovered by many centuries
of yoga and *sādhanā*, to think for us, speak for us, and ultimately
to dictate to us.

What are these issues, then? Let me choose a few convenient keywords to circumscribe them: 'God', 'religion', 'secularism', and 'tolerance'. Imposing words, no doubt, constantly dinned into our ears. Yet the one thing seldom mentioned about them is that these English words correspond to no clear Indian concepts—hence the confusion they generate when mechanically applied to the Indian context. I will keep returning to this point.

But does not the word 'God', at least, correspond to an Indian concept, you may ask? Apparently it does: we all know how Hindus love to stress that 'God is one' and 'all religions have the same God.' We even find respectable swamis eager to get themselves photographed in front of St. Peter's of Rome or in an audience with the Pope—although they do not seem to realize that the same Pope would not care to visit a Hindu temple and offer worship there. We are also told that 'all religions speak the same truth' or 'are as many paths to the Truth,' and so on. Nice thoughts, full of goodwill, but surprisingly ignorant—in fact slogans rather than thoughts. I agree that synthesis is desirable and essential in the search for truth, but painting the whole world with a single brush will not produce a synthesis, only a jumble. To reach a fruitful synthesis, we must train our minds again to the use of *viveka*, a laser-like spiritual discernment that separates truth and falsehood in each element. It is with good reason that *viveka* is the very first qualification required of a seeker, according to Shankarāchārya.[2]

The Abrahamic God

Our first task, then, is to examine the Abrahamic concept of God at the root of the three monotheistic religions: Yahweh (later Jehovah) or Allah. I do not refer here to more ancient Greek, Norse or Celtic gods since, as we know, they lost the war against God with a capital 'G'. (Some of them are now striving to revive, but even if they partly succeed, they will be little more than pale replicas of their original selves.)

The first thing that strikes the discerning Indian reader of the

Old Testament, especially the Exodus, in which Jehovah first introduces himself to Moses under that name,[3] is his ungodlike character. Jehovah is admittedly jealous: the second of the Ten Commandments reads, 'You shall have no other gods before me,' while the third explicitly forbids the making and worship of any idols, 'for I am a jealous God, punishing the children for the sin of the fathers.' Jehovah does speak as often of punishment as he does of sin, and periodically goes into a state of 'fierce anger', promising the most complete devastation to the Hebrews who reject him. Not content with cursing his reluctant followers, he also curses nation after nation, and finally the earth itself, which, as I pointed out earlier, he holds responsible for man's sins: 'The day of the Lord is coming—a cruel day, with wrath and fierce anger—to make the land desolate and destroy the sinners within it' (Isaiah, 13:9). In fact, he is so obsessed with sin that one looks in vain in his oppressive berating and legislating for any hint of a higher spirituality, such as we find in the Upanishads or the Gītā. Contrast his 'jealousy' with Krishna's insistence on spiritual freedom: 'Whatever form of me any devotee with faith desires to worship, I make that faith of his firm and undeviating' (Gītā, 7.21), or again: 'Others ... worship me in my oneness and in every separate being and in all my million universal faces' (9.15). But the god of the Bible and Koran will have none of this catholicity.

If Jehovah had stopped there, we might have found him to be simply a foul-tempered and libidinous god; after all, some Purānic gods too have such defects, although they usually retain a sense of their limits and a compassion of which Jehovah is spotlessly guiltless. But he has a plan, he means business and knows that coercion alone can establish his rule: when the Hebrews over whom he is so keen to hold sway go back to their former worship of a 'golden calf', he orders through Moses that each of the faithful should 'kill his brother and friend and neighbour' (Exodus 32:27). Instructions which were promptly complied with, for we are informed that 3,000 were killed on that fateful day; to crown his punishment, Jehovah 'struck the people with a plague'.

I find it highly symbolic that Judaism should have been born in blood and fear, not out of love for its founding deity. As Sri Aurobindo put it, 'The Jew invented the God-fearing man; India the God-knower and God-lover.'[4] It probably took centuries for the old cults to disappear altogether, and a stream of prophets who sought to strike terror into the hearts of the Israelites. It was a radical, unprecedented departure from ancient world cultures. Naturally, it did not stop there and went on to find more fertile soils in Christianity and Islam: earlier, Jehovah was content with being the god of the Hebrews alone; now, reborn in the new creeds, his ambition extended to the whole earth.

Increasingly aware of this cruel, irritable, egocentric and exclusivist character of Jehovah, many Western thinkers, especially from the eighteenth century onward, rejected his claim to be the supreme and only god. Voltaire, one of the first to expose the countless inconsistencies in the Bible, could hardly disguise how it filled him with 'horror and indignation at every page'.[5] In particular, he found the plethora of laws dictated by Jehovah 'barbaric and ridiculous'.[6] The U.S. revolutionary leader and thinker Thomas Paine wrote of the Old Testament in his *Age of Reason*:

> Whenever we read the obscene stories, the voluptuous debaucheries, the cruel and torturous executions, the unrelenting vindictiveness with which more than half the Bible is filled, it would be more consistent that we called it the word of a demon than the word of God. It is a history of wickedness, that has served to corrupt and brutalize mankind; and, for my own part, I sincerely detest it, as I detest everything that is cruel.[7]

With the growth of materialistic science, in particular Darwinian evolution, such views, which were revolutionary at the time of a Voltaire, became widespread. Bernard Shaw, for example, described the Biblical god as 'a thundering, earthquaking, famine striking, pestilence launching, blinding, deafening, killing, destructively omnipotent Bogey Man.'[8] Elizabeth Cady Stanton, the courageous U.S. pioneer of the woman rights movement, wrote in 1898, 'Surely the writers [of the Old Testament] had a very low idea of the nature of their God. They make Him not only anthropomorphic, but of the very lowest type, jealous and revengeful, loving violence rather than mercy. I know no other books that so fully teach the subjection and degradation of woman.'[9] Mark Twain put it in his own way: 'Our Bible reveals to us the character of our god with minute and remorseless exactness. The portrait is substantially that of a man—if one can imagine a man charged and overcharged with evil impulses far beyond the human limit. . . . It is perhaps the most damnatory biography that exists in print anywhere. It makes Nero an angel of light and leading by contrast.'[10] On another occasion, he added, 'It ain't the parts of the Bible that I can't understand that bother me, it is the parts that I do understand.'[11] Freud, seeing in Jehovah an all-too-human creation, subjected him to psychoanalysis—a dream of a subject for a psychoanalyst. Aldous Huxley called the Old Testament 'a treasure house of barbarous stupidity [full of] justifications for every crime and folly'.[12] In fact, Huxley traced the 'wholesale massacres' perpetrated by Christianity to Jehovah's 'wrathful, jealous, vindictive' character, just as he attributed 'the wholesale slaughter of Buddhists and Hindus' by invading Muslims to their devotion for a 'despotic person'.[13] Albert Einstein said, 'I cannot imagine a God who rewards and punishes the objects of his creation, whose purposes are modeled after our own—a God, in short, who is but a reflection of human frailty.'[14]

Because a few intellectuals had the courage to state the obvious, the power of Christianity was greatly reduced in the West. Yet I have always marvelled that Indians should learn about Christianity neither from those bold Western thinkers nor from their own inquiry, but from bigots who continue to pretend that the Age of Enlightenment never happened.

But is that all there is to the Abrahamic god? Are we simply faced with a man-made demon or the product of some fevered brain? If you look at Jehovah in the light of Indian experience, it is striking how he has all the characteristics of an *asura*. Recall for a moment a being such as Hiranyakashipu: did he not, too, forbid all other cults? Did he not order that he alone should be worshipped as the supreme god? Did he not use fear and violence to try and coerce Prahlāda? That he was stopped by a divine manifestation, like many other *asura*s eager to possess this world, is another story; the point is that we find here the same seed of pride and cruelty as in a Jehovah.

Now, to pinpoint Jehovah's identity we must remember that he himself explains how 'Yahweh' is a new name to the Hebrews: 'By that name I did not make myself known to them' (Exodus, 3:14–15, 6:3). But in the Old Testament, Jehovah does not reveal his earlier name; it is only the early Christian Gnostic tradition, which was brutally suppressed by the growing orthodox school, that provides us with an answer—or rather two. In the Gnostic Gospels which survived centuries of persecution (see p. 55), Jehovah is named either Samael, which means (appropriately) 'the god of the blind', or Ialdabaoth, 'the son of chaos'. Thus one of those texts contains this revealing passage:

> Ialdabaoth, becoming arrogant in spirit, boasted himself over all those who were below him, and explained, 'I am father, and God, and above me there is no one.' His mother, hearing him speak thus, cried out against him, 'Do not lie, Ialdabaoth; for the father of all, the primal *anthropos*, is above you.'[15]

So not only was Jehovah not the supreme god, but he also had a mother! For the Gnostics, like the Indians, refused to portray God as male only; God had to be equally female—and ultimately everything.

Another text, in the *Secret Book of John*, asks pertinently:

> By announcing [that he is a jealous God] he indicated that another God does exist; for if there were no other one, of whom would he be jealous?[16]

In fact, Jehovah is viewed in the Gnostic Gospels as no more than a demiurge or a subordinate deity—exactly what *devas* and *asuras* are in Indian tradition.

The French novelist Anatole France made use of the apocryphal Gospels (rather the few fragments known in his time, for he wrote a few decades before the Nag-Hammadi finds). In his perceptive novel *The Revolt of the Angels*, one of the rebellious angels depicts Jehovah thus:

> I no longer think he is the one and only God; for a long time he himself did not believe so: he was a polytheist at first. Later on, his pride and the flattery of his worshippers turned him into a monotheist. ... And in fact, rather than a god he is a vain and ignorant demiurge. Those who, like me, know his true nature, call him 'Ialdabaoth'. ... Having seized a minuscule fragment of the universe, he has sown it with pain and death.[17]

Now contrast this notion of God as a tyrannical ruler wholly separate from his creation with the Indian notion of an all-encompassing, all-pervasive, all-loving divine essence. In the language of the Upanishads:

> He is the secret Self in all existences. ... Eternal, pervading, in all things and impalpable, that which is Imperishable ... the Truth of things. ... All this is Brahman alone, all this magnificent universe.[18]

If Jehovah represents a radical departure from ancient worships, it is in that he is 'wholly other', as Huxley puts it. Because of the unbridgeable gulf between him and his creation, no Jew or Christian would dare declare, 'I am Jehovah,' no Muslim would dream of saying, 'I am Allah.' But to the Hindu, *so 'ham asmi*,[19] 'He I am,' or *tat tvam asi*,[20] 'You are That,' is the most natural thing in the world—it is, in truth, the very first fact of the world! Again, can Christian parents christen their son 'Jehovah' or Muslim parents name theirs 'Allah' in the way a Hindu child can be called 'Maheshvarī', 'Purushottama' or 'Parameshvara'?

Clearly, thus, if we use a single word—'God'—for such widely dissimilar concepts, we will land ourselves in total confusion. 'God is one,' perhaps, in the Vedantic sense that all is ultimately one, because all is ultimately divine, and yet Hindu inquiry always discerned a whole hierarchy of beings, not all equally true or luminous: a *rākshasa*, for instance, cannot be equated with a Krishna. Some may object to calling the Biblical or Koranic god an *asura*, but I use the word in the original sense of a mighty god who comes to his fall owing to ambition or pride. Moreover, the Indian approach has always claimed absolute freedom to inquire into every aspect of divinity, from the most personal to the most transcendent: if the Abrahamic god happens to have the attributes of an *asura* rather than those of the supreme Reality, why should we look away from that essential difference?

A more intelligent objection might be that in later Jewish mysticism (especially the Kabala), and in Christian or Muslim mysticism, we do find seekers going far beyond this loud-mouthed self-declared god. That is certainly true, but they did so *despite*, not *thanks to*, their concept of a one and only god; their spiritual thirst led them beyond to a truer experience, as it would have in any other context. In fact, many of them had a brush with 'heresy'; some were ruthlessly suppressed, the Gnostic Christians to begin with, whose writings were condemned as 'madness and blasphemy',[21] for they had little use of dogmas and, instead, insisted on self-knowledge and the inner discovery: 'Look for God by taking yourself as a starting point,' said Monoimus, 'if you carefully investigate . . . you will find him in yourself.'[22] Even a Meister Eckhart, whose teaching has been paralleled with Vedanta, was hounded by the Inquisition. The fact remains, at any rate, that compared to India, those true mystics remained very few, while the masses of Europe and her Christianized colonies were stuck with the cruder notion, their intellectual and spiritual progress slowed down or arrested for centuries.

I am not going here into the more complex question of Jesus as he is portrayed in the New Testament, except for a brief observation or two. A Hindu would probably have no problem with him as a teacher or even a partial *avatāra*, were it not again for his exclusiveness which puts a fatal limit to himself and to God's power to manifest: why should God have an only child (a male one, of course) rather than ten or a thousand? Why should he send us a single saviour for all time to come—and to be saved from what? God creates us, creates sin and ignorance the better to curse us, sends us a single redeemer, writes a single book, and hopes to win our love by warning us that we shall be tortured for ever if we do not accept him! Such incongruous notions are offensive to any discerning mind and to the spiritual perception.

Also, though not quite as foul as Jehovah's, Jesus' language—as reported in the Gospels, for we shall never know what it actually was—makes liberal use of threat and arrogance: 'Fear him who, after killing the body, has power to throw you into hell. . . . Unless you repent, you too will all perish.[23] For judgment I have come into this world. . . . All who came before me were thieves and robbers. . . . No one comes to the Father except through me.'[24] And more in the same vein. How far we are from the Vedic concept of universality: 'The Existent is one, but sages call it by various names' (Rig Veda, 1.164.46).

Thus the first and central object of our inquiry, God, tells us that we have surrendered to facile assimilations. We must reject the use of a single word to describe two wholly different concepts. Sri Aurobindo did not fall into this all-too-common trap, and summarized the whole issue in these words:

> The conception of the Divine as an external omnipotent Power who has 'created' the world and governs it like an absolute and arbitrary monarch—the Christian or Semitic conception—has never been mine; it contradicts too much my seeing and experience during thirty years of *sadhana*. It is against this conception that the atheistic objection is aimed—for atheism in Europe has been a shallow and rather childish reaction against a shallow and childish exoteric religionism and its popular inadequate and crudely dogmatic notions.[25]

Religion vs. Dharma

This takes us to the concept of 'religion'. Here again, we must question the clumping together, under a single term, of a wide array of dissimilar faiths, creeds and practices. Of course, all religions are concerned in some way with a supranatural being or creator; but that is not enough, since there is a fundamental disagreement on who or what the said being is. Moreover, here again, crucial differences between the three monotheistic religions and the older faiths cannot be ignored. The most visible distinctions—the absence in Hinduism of dogmas, of an absolute authority in the form of an only Scripture, of a supreme clergy, or also the belief in reincarnation—have been stressed often enough, and rightly so. But there are differences of a deeper nature.

To begin with, the Indian and the Pagan approaches never made a distinction between the 'faithful' and the 'infidels', the former to be saved in a single lifetime and the latter to be 'eternally barbecued', as Swami Vivekananda once put it; humanity was not divided into two irreconcilable camps, or reconcilable only through mass slaughter or mass conversion. Indeed, in the Hindu view, the only thing one may ever be 'converted' to is one's own concealed divinity, and that can only be done through a long and sincere inner effort, not through unquestioning adherence to rigid and all-too-often cruel dogmas. By contrast, fundamentalist adherents of the three monotheistic religions can see no hope for a Hindu, a Buddhist, a Sikh, a Jain or a Parsi, or, say, an 'animist' Amerindian; today they generally try (with mixed success) to avoid openly condemning such 'idolatry', but a close look at their belief systems shows how this fatal division remains central to their mentality, as I have invariably found in my conversations with Christian missionaries in India.

It is not only humanity that the Bible, and later the Koran, divided into two camps: the creator, too, is separate from his creation, and especially from us humans. In the Indian view, the Divine is you and me, the bird outside and the wide ocean; he *and* she, and also 'it', is boundless, endless, and cannot be limited to any Book or manifestation or dogma. No *rishi* or Buddha or Tīrthankara ever declared salvation to be attainable through him alone; peddling tickets to heaven is something alien to Indian spirituality, as is bribing the gatekeeper with a 'confession of faith'. There is no easy shortcut on the arduous path to self-discovery.

This is an essential, unbridgeable difference: Judaism, Christianity and Islam are founded on specific commandments or utterances—an external agency that takes almost all responsibility away from the faithful; they merely have to obey. Indian 'religions' offer no such lists of 'divine' instructions: whatever outside aids may come your way—books and systems and gurus —an *internal* agency is, in the end, the only tool: you shoulder full responsibility for your actions as well as for your efforts (or lack of them) towards liberation from ignorance.

Moreover, by giving humanity one 'only Son' or one 'last prophet' and a single Scripture—'only one book in all these ages',[26] as Sri Aurobindo remarked—God in effect ended his communication with humans for all time to come: he (not she) left no scope for further revelation, fresh knowledge or new horizons. But Truth, for the Hindu, the Jain or the Buddhist is inexhaustible: there can be no end to the revelation, no only child, no last prophet; no Indian teacher ever said that his message was final and there could be nothing beyond it: anyone is free to start a new teaching, give a new message to the world, found a new school of thought or method of yoga.

It is so because Truth can never be perfectly and wholly expressed in words: it is beyond words, beyond the intellect; it cannot be contained by any brain, although it can be experienced by our innermost or uppermost being: 'The Gita itself thus declares that the Yogin in his progress must pass beyond the written Truth. . . . For he is not the *sādhaka* of a book or of many books; he is a *sādhaka* of the Infinite.'[27] The contrast with the younger monotheistic religions is total: for the Christian or Islamic literalist, Truth has been exhausted once and for all, and all of it is contained in a bunch of printed pages that you can buy with a few coins from your purse; Truth is finite, graspable, on a level with the human mind, and purchasable: you can own it, and, owning it, claim superiority over those who do not.

If one objects that these differences, however radical, are after all only theoretical, or perhaps theological, then we must point out that centuries of crusades, 'holy' wars, *jihad*, Inquisition and persecution of many kinds are ample proof that to the followers of Christianity and Islam, the division between the faithful and the infidels was no abstraction. If they indulged in such behaviour across several continents and for many centuries, it is not because they were intrinsically bad, but because they followed the injunctions of their respective scriptures and religious instructors. If the Hindu and Buddhist cultures did not attempt to destroy other cultures and civilizations or persecute followers of other cults, if they never waged bloody religious wars, it is not because Indians were intrinsically good, but because the fundamentals of their culture were universal enough to make such aberrations nearly impossible, insisting instead on a real spiritual freedom to choose or even create one's own path.

Only the most superficial and hasty view can equate such radically divergent phenomena. I used the word 'culture' to describe Hinduism, Buddhism or Jainism, because I find it confusing to use the word 'religion' in their context; or else, let us call the three monotheistic faiths 'dogmatic and exclusivist credal systems', not 'religions'. Words should have some clear meaning, as long as we have to use them. The Indian concept is neither religion nor any 'ism'—it is dharma, the eternal law of the universe, which cannot be formulated in any rigid and final set of tenets, because it is as infinite and complex and fluid as life. Still, we may say that among its essential values are pluralism, synthesis, universality and oneness, none of which is to be found in the biblical worldview.

I do not mean to denigrate the monotheistic religions in any way. If their followers are happy with their faith and find it helps them, all to the good. But to bring everything down to a single straight line is simplistic. A few years ago, the Vatican proclaimed itself against the idea of 'equality of religions', in conformity with its traditional claim of being the 'sole repository of the truth'. And indeed, the noble goal of equality of religions is a mirage. India's ancient culture is not on the same plane as the religions that flowed from the Bible, neither in its conceptual framework nor in actual practice. There are no doubt a few truths in common here and there, and it is good to note them; there are also in the Bible (especially the New Testament) substantial borrowings from India, as I mentioned in Chapter 2, and it is good to be aware of them. But it is more important, in my view, to note where the two worldviews diverge, and to go to the root of the divergence. The conquering nature of Christianity and Islam found an expression in military conquests and conflicts; no so the quest for a well-ordered human life and society that Hinduism, Jainism and Buddhism promoted, each in its own way.

Secularism and Tolerance

The 'synthesizers', as Ram Swarup called them, or adepts of all-out sameness—'God is the same, all religions are the same and take us to the same goal'—bring in another Western concept, that of 'secularism', and tell us that it means 'equal respect for all religions'. This too we are supposed to accept unquestioningly, like a sort of magic wand that is going to solve all our religious and social problems. But what really is secularism, in theory and practice?

Curiously, as I have observed, the noisiest proponents of secularism in India are careful not to evoke its historical origin; yet that must be our starting point. Secularism was born of a rebellion against the oppression of theocracy in the Christian and Islamic worlds. In medieval Europe, political power was held or at least controlled by one Church or another. It took nearly two centuries, the eighteenth and nineteenth, to curtail that power and establish a complete separation between Church and State—which is what secularism has meant in the West, as any good dictionary will tell us.[28] In France, for instance, the Roman Catholic Church was virtually all-powerful until the French Revolution; only a century later did it finally lose its hold on education. Secularism meant keeping the Church away from political power and from education; it meant a polity free from Christian affiliation. Likewise, when Mustapha Kemal threw out the Sultan in Turkey and established a 'secular republic' in 1923, it was because he had abolished the office of the Caliph of the Islamic world; 'secularism', to the new Turkish republic, simply meant keeping Islam away from political power, as it still does today.

In India, however, theocracy never took root. Hinduism, to begin with, lacking an organized church, clergy or structure, would have been intrinsically incapable of imposing a theocratic rule had it ever wished to. Even so conformist a historian as Vincent Smith noted:

> Hindooism has never produced an exclusive, dominant, orthodox sect, with a formula of faith to be professed or rejected under pain of damnation.[29]

Political rule was the business of the Kshatriya, not of the priestly class, and although kings often took the advice of a sage or a guru in matters of governance, justice or ritual, the very notion of a 'state religion' is alien to Hinduism. We do not hear of a Vaishnavite or a Shaivite rājā imposing his creed on his subjects in the way Catholic or Protestant kings did in medieval Europe, and wars between neighbouring kingdoms were never caused by clashes of belief or cult. On the contrary, Indian kings often prided themselves on protecting all sects without partiality; victors are sometimes on record for adopting the conquered king's god and cult publicly so as to assuage their new subjects' feelings, a practice expressly recommended by the *Arthashāstra*.[30] Other than this injunction, religion appears nowhere in Kautilya's treatise of governance: there is no question of an official faith or of dictating to anyone in religious matters.

The case of Buddhism might have been different, since it did have an organized monastic order, the Sangha, that might have been tempted to acquire political power; however, the absence of an institutionalized supreme head may have kept such ambitions in check. In any case, even when Ashoka converted to Buddhism and actively propagated the *dhamma*, he did nothing to turn it into a state religion; rather, he expressed in his Edicts the wish that 'all religions should reside everywhere, for all of them desire self-control and purity of heart,'[31] and vowed to 'honour ascetics and the householders of all religions'.[32]

This does not mean that religion—rather the complex of tradition, ethics, culture and spirituality that, in India, goes by the name of 'religion'—did not have a place in national life. The Indian temperament endeavoured to spiritualize all aspects of life, including the social and political. If spirituality was of any practical value, why should it be kept out of governance? Sri Aurobindo reflects that spirit when he states,

> There is to me nothing secular, all human activity is for me a thing to be included in a complete spiritual life.[33]

Such is ancient India's attitude to religious and spiritual life: on the one hand, respect, protect and nurture all creeds and sects, without imposing any, and on the other hand, hold in front of everyone, from the humble craftsman to the ruler, the objective of spiritualizing all activities of life. Even if we can point to instances of sect rivalry, intolerance, even cases of fanaticism in India's religious history, they remained isolated. Oft-quoted examples of frictions between Shaivites, Jains and Vaishnavites come from the Tamil land, yet the Tamil epics *Shilappadikāram* and *Manimekhalai* amply testify that what we call today Hinduism, Jainism and Buddhism coexisted harmoniously. 'The sectarian spirit was totally absent,'[34] writes the scholar V.R. Ramachandra Dikshitar. 'Either the people did not look upon religious distinctions seriously, or there were no fundamental differences between one sect and another.'[35] Archaeologist and historian K.V. Raman summarizes the 'religious inheritance of the Pāndyas' in these words:

> Though the majority of the Pandyan kings were Saivites, they extended equal patronage to the other faiths. . . . Their

religion was not one of narrow sectarian nature but broad-based with Vedic roots. They were free from linguistic or regional bias and took pride in saying that they considered Tamil and Sanskritic studies as complementary and equally valuable.[36]

There was thus no need to fight against the oppression of a state religion or a theocratic state. Why, then, should we have to hear of 'secularism' at all in India? And why do its loudest champions—apart from our political class—happen to belong to the very religions against which Europe had to erect the defence of secularism? Why are self-appointed leaders of Christian and Muslim Indians lecturing Hindus about the virtues of secularism, when their own religions were for so long dead against it, and would still be, given a chance? When, in 2004, the European Union decided to keep the word 'God' and any reference to Christianity out of the preamble of its draft constitution, the Vatican and other churches protested that 'Europe cannot deny its Christian heritage.'[37] This attempt to keep a toehold in the new Europe was rightly brushed aside by most of its members.

If classical India was secular without even an awareness of the concept of secularism, modern India, which has made it a nostrum, fails to meet the basic standards of secularism. Separation of religion and state automatically implies equal rights: any distinction on the basis of faith is unacceptable to genuine secularism; Jews, Muslims, Christians or atheists enjoy the same rights in European nations. In today's India, however, the state controls most Hindu temples while keeping off churches and mosques; it is empowered by the Constitution to take over Hindu schools while 'minority' schools are free from government control; it forever seeks to grant special privileges to 'minorities', as it did again in 2008 when it offered special scholarships to children of minority denominations, while denying the same assistance to equally deprived Hindu children. In a word, the Indian state discriminates between its citizens on the basis of religion.

To deflect a debate on this glaring flaw in our Constitution and polity, our leaders and intellectuals tell us that 'secularism' has a different connotation in the Indian context, a positive rather than a negative one: it should be taken to mean equal respect of all religions, or 'tolerance'. Tolerance is a great virtue indeed, one which Christianity and Islam, again, steered clear of through much of their history: how many pre-Christian and pre-Islamic cultures survive in their conquered territories? On the other hand, the concept and practice of tolerance was always so natural in India that there did not even exist a word for it: when Jewish, Parsi or Christian groups sought refuge in Hindu India, no ruler or religious figure thought of asking them to abandon their religion and embrace Hinduism; in Kerala, a few kings readily financed the building of synagogues and churches for them.

The Hindu certainly needs no lesson in tolerance. However, genuine tolerance can only be between mutually respectful faiths or societies or nations. 'How is it possible to live peacefully with a religion whose principle is "I will not tolerate you"?'[38] asked Sri Aurobindo. Whether we like it or not, Hindu society has been growing increasingly restless at practises that target its most vulnerable members with a well-oiled propaganda machine and the lure of monetary or other gain. The tension has been palpably rising from year to year, and Christian leaders often aggravate matters (perhaps consciously so) by raising the bogey of a 'Hindu persecution of Indian Christians' for consumption by the English-language press in India and abroad, making up incidents when possible,[39] or hastening to accuse Hindus even when it is plain that others are involved.[40] It is curious how the two religions that stamped out all Pagans, 'infidels' or 'non-believers' in their path have painted Hindus with the black brush of their very own past.

The net result in the Indian context is that these two world-conquering religions (at this point, we must leave Judaism aside, since it did not develop a proselytizing nature) have managed to project themselves as tolerant, secular, equalitarian, progressive— an image at variance with what they were in their countries of origin at the peak of their strength. On the other hand, Hinduism is portrayed as retrograde, medieval, superstitious, increasingly intolerant. Oxymorons such as 'Hindu fundamentalism' or 'Hindu fanaticism' are bandied about, forgetting that Hinduism has no easily identifiable 'fundamentals', no self-declared conquering mission, no wish to impose itself on anyone, and cannot therefore give rise to a fanaticism of the Christian or Islamist kind. Of course, Hinduism is also equated to the caste system—as though it were nothing else—whose abuses are portrayed wholly through the colonial prism.

At the same time, the persistence of caste discrimination and economic deprivation among converts to Christianity and Islam is well-known[41] but rarely discussed: former (and supposedly 'liberated') Dalits will not be able to marry with former 'upper castes'; in some churches of Kerala and Tamil Nadu, separate benches are kept for them. In Tamil Nadu again, several 'Dalit Christian' groups have started campaigns of protest against such discriminations. The hypocrisy of the main argument for conversion—the liberation from 'caste oppression'—is revealed by the very designation of 'Dalit Christian', but now that it has acquired official status, no one seems to notice the contradiction in terms.

The Task Ahead

While catchwords are hypnotically brandished around, no intelligent debate is permitted on their real meaning and application in the Indian context. When, for instance, a confrontation flares up in some part of the country, the media and the self-appointed guardians of our human rights sit up and express shock and outrage—especially if they think they smell some 'Hindutva' rat—but do not find it necessary to probe the chain of events that led to such a situation and what set them in motion. This, in effect, ensures that wounds will fester instead of healing. Increasingly frequent clashes are sadly predictable, even if we affect a shocked surprise at every occurrence.

Indian scholars and thinkers must develop the courage to

grapple with the real issues behind the cant of the day. Ram Swarup's words of caution need to be heard:

> Hindus are disorganized, self-alienated, morally and ideologically disarmed. They lack leadership; the Hindu elites have become illiterate about their spiritual heritage and history and indifferent and even hostile towards their religion. ... India has been asleep for too long, and it needed all these knocks and probably it would get more.[42]

In 1926, Sri Aurobindo put it in simple terms: 'Aggressive religions tend to overrun the earth. Hinduism on the other hand is passive and therein lies the danger.'[43] The current renewed aggressivity, hiding behind the fig leaf of ersatz secularism, must be resisted by the Indian intelligentsia for two reasons. One, of immediate urgency, to contain the harm done to India's social fabric by artificial conversions, induced ninety-nine times out of a hundred by pecuniary allurements, not by a genuine religious feeling. Unless the tide is stemmed, the web of Indian society may become irretrievably fragmented into thousands of conflicting groups, with the kind of consequences we already see in parts of India where separatism is the inevitable culmination of the process.

The second reason, more essential, is to pursue and renew India's perennial search for the truth, a search compromised by today's institutionalized hypocrisy. 'It is Truth that conquers and not falsehood,'[44] says the Upanishad; to work out that conquest for the world was—and, let us hope, will be—India's sacred calling. This is no ideological question, it is a matter of saving or losing our intellectual independence and ultimately our spiritual freedom—the only one left to the common Indian.

As early as 1910, Sri Aurobindo diagnosed India's intellectual condition as alarming and called for the rebirth of thought in the land of knowledge:

> Our first necessity, if India is to survive and do her appointed work in the world, is that the youth of India should learn to think,—to think on all subjects, to think

independently, fruitfully, going to the heart of things, not stopped by their surface, free of prejudgments, shearing sophism and prejudice asunder as with a sharp sword, smiting down obscurantism of all kinds as with the mace of Bhima.[45]

7

The Gītā
and the Problem of Action

INDIA'S intellectual ailments, which I have tried to outline in the previous two chapters, are, in reality, part of a larger problem—that of action. In a way, India's future course hinges on it: if 'to be or not to be' is the dilemma for the West, 'to act or not to act' has often been India's. And that is a cruel paradox, considering that India gave the world a 'gospel of action'[1]—the Gītā. Let us see if, through it, we can find our way out of the confusion we have made a habit to regard as thought.

Of all Indian scriptures, the Bhagavad-Gītā has likely been the one most commented on. India's sages, yogis, philosophers, thinkers have, as a rule, regarded it a sacred duty to add theirs to the long list of commentaries on these eighteen brief chapters from the Mahābhārata—a mere 700 *shlokas* unrivalled in their sweep and depth.

Sri Aurobindo was no exception to the rule. In his seminal *Essays on the Gita* published from Pondicherry in his monthly *Arya* between 1916 and 1920, he expounded every aspect of the Gītā, ethical and spiritual: its stress on action, its *karmayoga* based on true equanimity, non-attachment and renunciation of the ego, its broad synthesis of Vedanta, Sāmkhya, Jñāna, Bhakti and even Tantra, its insights into the deeper workings of nature, into human nature with its divine as well as diabolical potential, its final call to reach beyond all dharmas to the supreme truth. But here, at the cost of incompleteness, the Gītā's core teaching—the problem of action and the use of force to defend dharma—is what we need to look into.

Sri Aurobindo's acquaintance with the Song of the Lord had begun long before his *Essays on the Gita*. That was no mere intellectual or philosophical inquiry, for, in the true tradition of yoga, he was an experimenter before anything else—he even rejected the label of 'philosopher': '[Modern] philosophy,' he said, 'I consider only intellectual and therefore of secondary value. Experience and formulation of experience I consider as the true aim of philosophy.'[2]

From his return from England to India in 1893, at the age of twenty, and until 1905, Sri Aurobindo worked in the Baroda State Service. That left him enough leisure to immerse himself in Sanskrit scriptures, since, dissatisfied with an exclusively Western education, he was eager to rediscover his roots. Among his favourites were the two Epics, the Upanishads, and Kālidāsa. He translated large portions of the Rāmāyana and Mahābhārata into English, though only a few fragments survived his later tribulations. The well-known scholar Romesh Chandra Dutt, whose own adaptations of the Epics were popular in those days, asked to see the young Aurobindo's translations at Baroda, and remarked that had he seen them earlier, he would never have published his own.[3]

In that very first study of the Gītā before he was even thirty, what struck Sri Aurobindo was its stress on the Kshatriya's 'duty to protect the world from the reign of injustice',[4] a virile and distinctive Indian message as he immediately saw:

> The Christian and Buddhistic doctrine of turning the other cheek to the smiter, is as dangerous as it is impracticable.
> ... [It stems from] a radically false moral distinction and the lip profession of an ideal which mankind has never been able or willing to carry into practice. The disinterested and desireless pursuit of duty is a gospel worthy of the strongest

manhood; that of the cheek turned to the smiter is a gospel for cowards and weaklings. Babes and sucklings may practise it because they must, but with others it is a hypocrisy.[5]

The Gītā and the Nationalists

A few years later, the Gītā's stress on true manhood and 'desireless duty'—*nishkāma karma*—was to be Sri Aurobindo's prime inspiration during his revolutionary days. It is rarely acknowledged that he was, in 1906, the first Indian to openly call for complete independence from the British Empire,[6] at a time when the Congress Moderates were busy praising the 'providential character' of British rule in India and swearing their 'unswerving allegiance to the British crown'. Now in Calcutta, through the pages of the English daily *Bande Mataram* which he edited, Sri Aurobindo exhorted his countrymen to find in themselves the strength to stand up to their colonial masters. He soon became the leader in Bengal of those whom the Moderates contemptuously called the 'Extremists'. In April 1908, a few days before his arrest in the Alipore Bomb Case, he wrote:

> A certain class of minds shrink from aggressiveness as if it were a sin. Their temperament forbids them to feel the delight of battle and they look on what they cannot understand as something monstrous and sinful. 'Heal hate by love, drive out injustice by justice, slay sin by righteousness' is their cry. Love is a sacred name, but it is easier to speak of love than to love. ... The Gita is the best answer to those who shrink from battle as a sin and aggression as a lowering of morality.[7]

The rise of non-violence as a creed is clearly anticipated here (let us recall that Gandhi would only appear on the Indian scene a few years later, in 1915). But Sri Aurobindo took Sri Krishna's admonition of Arjuna as a practical guidance and, like Swami Vivekananda, put his faith in strength, not in ahimsa. Shortly after his release from jail the following year, he developed this point in a speech on the Gītā at Khulna:

The virtue of Brahmins is a great virtue: You shall not kill. This is what *ahinsa* means. If the virtue of *ahinsa* comes to the Kshatriya, if you say 'I will not kill,' there is no one to protect the country. The happiness of the people will be broken down. Injustice and lawlessness will reign. The virtue becomes a source of misery, and you become instrumental in bringing misery and conflict to the people.[8]

Indeed, the revolutionaries in Bengal and Maharashtra drew such inspiration from the Gītā that the colonial authorities came to regard it as a 'gospel of terrorism',[9] and it became one of the most sought-after pieces of evidence in police raids. It is also one of the chief influences cited in the 1918 Rowlatt Sedition Committee Report, side by side with Swami Vivekananda's works.[10] Sri Aurobindo himself gave initiation to aspiring revolutionaries (including his own brother Barinda Kumar[11]) by making them swear on the Gītā that they would do everything to liberate India from the foreign yoke.[12] But in the columns of the *Karmayogin*, he took objection to this summary characterization of the Gītā:

The only doctrine of the Gita the Terrorist can pervert to his use, is the dictum that the Kshatriya must slay as a part of his duty and he can do it without sin if he puts egoism away and acts selflessly without attachment, in and for God, as a sacrifice, as an offering of action to the Lord of action. If this teaching is in itself false, there is no moral basis for the hero, the soldier, the judge, the king, the legislature which recognises capital punishment. ... It is undoubtedly true that selflessness, courage, a free and noble activity have been preached as the kernel of the ethics of the Gita. That teaching has in no country been condemned as ignoble, criminal or subversive of morality. ... We strongly protest against the brand of suspicion that has been sought to be placed in many quarters on the teaching and possession of the Gita—our chief national heritage, our hope for the future, our great force for the purification of the moral weaknesses that stain and hamper our people.[13]

The Yoga of the Gītā

Though he drew strength from the Gītā, Sri Aurobindo knew better than to see in it 'a mere gospel of war and heroic action, a Nietzschean creed of power and high-browed strength, of Hebraic or old Teutonic hardness'.[14] During his year-long solitary imprisonment in the Alipore jail, he intensively practised the yoga spelt out by Sri Krishna. Soon after his unexpected acquittal in May 1909, in his landmark speech at Uttarpara he recounted something of his experience:

> He placed the Gita in my hands. His strength entered into me and I was able to do the *sādhana* of the Gita. I was not only to understand intellectually but to realise what Srikrishna demanded of Arjuna and what He demands of those who aspire to do His work.[15]

To 'realize', let us note again. And what he first realized was the divine Oneness described in the Gītā: 'The man whose self is in Yoga, sees the self in all beings and all beings in the self, he is equal-visioned everywhere. He who sees Me everywhere and sees all in Me, to him I do not get lost, nor does he get lost to Me' (6.29, 30). In Sri Aurobindo's words:

> I looked at the jail that secluded me from men and it was no longer by its high walls that I was imprisoned; no, it was Vasudeva who surrounded me. I walked under the branches of the tree in front of my cell but it was not the tree, I knew it was Vasudeva, it was Srikrishna whom I saw standing there and holding over me His shade. I looked at the bars of my cell, the very grating that did duty for a door and again I saw Vasudeva. It was Narayana who was guarding and standing sentry over me. Or I lay on the coarse blankets that were given me for a couch and felt the arms of Srikrishna around me, the arms of my Friend and Lover. ... I looked at the prisoners in the jail, the thieves, the murderers, the swindlers, and as I looked at them I saw Vasudeva, it was Narayana whom I found in these darkened souls and misused bodies. ...

When the case opened ... I was followed by the same
insight. He said to me, 'When you were cast into jail, did
not your heart fail and did you not cry out to me, where is
Thy protection? Look now at the Magistrate, look now at
the Prosecuting Counsel.' I looked and it was not the Magistrate whom I saw, it was Vasudeva, it was Narayana who
was sitting there on the bench. I looked at the Prosecuting
Counsel and it was not the Counsel for the prosecution that
I saw; it was Srikrishna who sat there, it was my Lover
and Friend who sat there and smiled. 'Now do you fear?'
He said, 'I am in all men and I overrule their actions and
their words.'[16]

Such was the supreme experience Sri Aurobindo received in
jail, which never left him afterwards. And such is the supreme
paradox of the Gītā, that we must act and act boldly and sometimes fiercely, knowing and seeing all the while that all is He,
that there is nothing in this entire universe that is not *essentially*
the Divine. I stress the word 'essentially', because there lies,
according to Sri Aurobindo, the key to the apparent paradox:
all is essentially divine, but until it is manifestly so, this creation
will remain a Kurukshetra in which we will be duty-bound to
fight for the truth. For the Gītā is concerned with our human
duties, not with 'human rights'.

The Gītā, the Gospel of Strength, and Non-Violence

It is customary nowadays to hear that Hinduism is at bottom a
'message of tolerance and non-violence'. I discussed earlier the
question of tolerance, but it is worth recalling these words of Sri
Krishna: 'Even those who sacrifice to other godheads with devotion and faith, they also sacrifice to Me. ... I am equal in all
existences, none is dear to Me, none hated' (9.23, 29)—this,
along with the Vedic affirmation about the many names of
the One Existence, goes far beyond the ordinary meaning of
'tolerance', and, again, marks out Hinduism as distinct from the
monotheistic religions.

But let us rather dwell on the point of non-violence. Our first observation is that, unlike Buddhism or Jainism, Hinduism did not make a universal doctrine of ahimsa, which remained limited to the Brahman's dharma, even then with qualifications. True, we have in the Mahābhārata the maxim *ahimsā paramo dharmah,* 'ahimsa is the highest law,' but it was not intended for the Kshatriya. There is even a very sensible observation made to the Brahman Kaushika:

> When the earth is ploughed, numberless creatures lurking in the ground are destroyed. ... Fish preys upon fish, various animals prey upon other species, and some species even prey upon themselves. ... The earth and the air all swarm with living organisms which are unconsciously destroyed by men from mere ignorance. Ahimsa was ordained of old by men who were ignorant of the true facts. There is not a man on the face of the earth who is free from the sin of doing injury to creatures.[17]

There is also a humorous episode in the *Devī Bhāgavata* (*skanda* 4), in which Brihaspati (in the guise of Shukrāchārya) preaches *ahimsā paramo dharmah* to the *asura*s and enjoins them 'not to injure even those who come to kill you'—but this he preaches to the *asura*s so as to disarm them, not to the *deva*s! Finally, let us note that even Jainism, which made the maxim one of its central teachings, allows monks to attain liberation by fasting to death—an undeniable act of *himsa.* There is clearly nothing absolute about the much-abused saying.

There is also nothing non-violent about the wars in the Rāmāyana and the Mahābhārata, about some of the Veda's fierce gods and violent battles, or Durgā's and Kālī's pitiless and bloody destruction of demons. Sanskrit texts, as also the Sangam literature of Tamil Nadu and folk legends, resound with heroes and heroic deeds. Sri Krishna echoes them when he declares: 'I am the strength of the mighty' (10.36).

As was his wont, Sri Aurobindo analyzed the crux of the problem:

Our very bodily life is a constant dying and being reborn, the body itself a beleaguered city attacked by assailing, protected by defending forces whose business is to devour each other. ... War and destruction are not only a universal principle of our life here in its purely material aspects, but also of our mental and moral existence. ... It is impossible, at least as men and things are, to advance, to grow, to fulfil and still to observe really and utterly that principle of harmlessness which is yet placed before us as the highest and best law of conduct.[18]

Significantly, this passage from his *Essays on the Gita* was published in the December 1916 issue of the *Arya*, in the middle of the First World War, when Mahatma Gandhi had joined the national movement and started propagating his doctrine of 'harmlessness' or ahimsa.

Let us pursue Sri Aurobindo's exploration:

This world of our battle and labour is a fierce dangerous destructive devouring world in which life exists precariously and the soul and body of man move among enormous perils, a world in which by every step forward, whether we will it or no, something is crushed and broken, in which every breath of life is a breath too of death. To put away the responsibility for all that seems to us evil or terrible on the shoulders of a semi-omnipotent Devil, or to put it aside as part of Nature, making an unbridgeable opposition between world-nature and God-Nature, as if Nature were independent of God, or to throw the responsibility on man and his sins, as if he had a preponderant voice in the making of this world or could create anything against the will of God, are clumsily comfortable devices in which the religious thought of India has never taken refuge. We have to look courageously in the face of the reality and see that it is God and none else who has made this world in his being and that so he has made it. We have to see that Nature devouring her children, Time eating up the lives of creatures, Death universal and ineluctable and the violence of

the Rudra forces in man and Nature are also the supreme
Godhead in one of his cosmic figures.[19]

We have here a crucial difference in attitude between the
Hindu and the Judeo-Christian concepts of evil.

> It is only a few religions which have had the courage to
> say without any reserve, like the Indian, that this enigmatic
> World-Power is one Deity, one Trinity, to lift up the image
> of the Force that acts in the world in the figure not only of
> the beneficent Durga, but of the terrible Kali in her blood-
> stained dance of destruction and to say, 'This too is the
> Mother; this also know to be God; this too, if thou hast
> the strength, adore.'[20]

Bracing words, these, but lest one might imagine that Sri
Aurobindo is advocating some bloodthirsty cult, let me add this
conclusion of his:

> A day may come, must surely come, we will say, when
> humanity will be ready spiritually, morally, socially for
> the reign of universal peace; meanwhile the aspect of battle
> and the nature and function of man as a fighter have to be
> accepted and accounted for by any practical philosophy
> and religion.[21]

Gandhi and Ahimsa

It should now be clear that Sri Aurobindo was poles apart from
the Mahatma on the practice of non-violence, and as this difference is usually glossed over, I think we should examine it, since
such differences, far from being awkward, are in fact fecund if
faced honestly.

In April 1907, a year before Gandhi wrote his *Hind Swaraj* in
South Africa, Sri Aurobindo expounded in a series of seven articles
in *Bande Mataram* his 'Doctrine of Passive Resistance' intended
to become a mass movement against British rule. The series was
widely read in the country. In it, Sri Aurobindo advocated non-
cooperation with and passive resistance to the colonial authorities

as the only practicable policy of the day in the face of the rulers' crushing military superiority and the Congress Moderates' lack of support for the ideal of independence. But in his conclusion to the series, he also spelt out the limits of this policy:

> Every great *yajña* has its Rakshasas who strive to baffle the sacrifice. . . . Passive resistance is an attempt to meet such disturbers by peaceful and self-contained *brahmatej*; but even the greatest Rishis of old could not, when the Rakshasas were fierce and determined, keep up the sacrifice without calling in the bow of the Kshatriya. We should have the bow of the Kshatriya ready for use, though in the background. Politics is especially the business of the Kshatriya, and without Kshatriya strength at its back, all political struggle is unavailing.[22]

Decades later, certain similarities in the practical strategies of Sri Aurobindo and the Mahatma prompted some scholars to parallel the two leaders. Sri Aurobindo protested in the following note (written in the third person):

> In some quarters there is the idea that Sri Aurobindo's political standpoint was entirely pacifist, that he was opposed in principle and in practice to all violence and that he denounced terrorism, insurrection, etc., as entirely forbidden by the spirit and letter of the Hindu religion. It is even suggested that he was a forerunner of the gospel of Ahimsa. This is quite incorrect. Sri Aurobindo is neither an impotent moralist nor a weak pacifist.
>
> The rule of confining political action to passive resistance was adopted as the best policy for the National Movement at that stage and not as a part of a gospel of Non-violence or pacifist idealism. Peace is a part of the highest ideal, but it must be spiritual or at the very least psychological in its basis; without a change in human nature it cannot come with any finality. If it is attempted on any other basis (moral principle or gospel of Ahimsa or any other), it will fail and even may leave things worse than before. . . . Sri Aurobindo's position and practice in this matter was the

same as Tilak's and that of other Nationalist leaders who were by no means Pacifists or worshippers of Ahimsa.[23]

It may appear hard to accept that the gospel of ahimsa 'may leave things worse than before'. But can we for a moment picture what would have happened if, in the middle of the Second World War, with much of Europe including France under German occupation, Britain had faced the Nazi wave with non-violence? And yet, that is exactly what the Mahatma exhorted the British to do in his 1940 open letter 'to every Briton', in which he called for them to lay down their arms 'because war is bad in essence,' 'to fight Nazism without arms or ... with non-violent arms,' and to 'invite Herr Hitler and Signor Mussolini to take ... possession of your beautiful island'.[24] No doubt, Hitler would have been delighted had Britain followed this advice, just as Duryodhana would have been highly pleased to see Arjuna lay down his bow.

We note a very different attitude in Sri Aurobindo's approach, also spelt out in 1940:

> Hitler and Nazism and its push towards world domination are ... an assault by a formidable reactionary Force, a purely Asuric force, on the highest values of civilisation and their success would mean the destruction of individual liberty, national freedom, liberty of thought, liberty of life, religious and spiritual freedom in at least three continents.[25]

In September of the same year, in one of his rare public gestures after taking refuge in Pondicherry, Sri Aurobindo sent the Governor of Madras a contribution and a message in support of the Allies during the War. He thus supported the same war that Gandhi abhorred.

Another difference in attitude between them concerns the Nazi persecution of the Jews before and during the Second World War. When, in 1938, a disciple tried to justify this persecution on the ground that 'the Jews betrayed Germany during the [First World] war,' Sri Aurobindo protested:

Nonsense! On the contrary they helped Germany a great deal. It is because they are a clever race that others are jealous of them. Or for anything that is wrong you point to the Jews—it is so much better than finding the real cause. People want something to strike at. So the popular cry, 'The Jews, the Jews'. . . . It is the Jews that have built Germany's commercial fleet and her navy. And the contribution of Jews towards the world's progress in every branch is remarkable.[26]

Persecution of the Jews was a vital constituent of Hitler's grand design of world domination. For Gandhi, however, it had no particular meaning, except that he wanted the Jews to adopt the true spirit of non-violence. Indeed, he blamed them for having 'no thought even of "loving the Enemy".'[27] A few months before the start of the Second World War, while claiming that his sympathies were with Germany's Jews, Gandhi accused them of calling on England and America to wage war against Germany so as to save them. In the face of vehement protests, from Jews and non-Jews alike, he was forced to retract his offending statements.[28] He nevertheless continued to deliver regular sermons to the German Jews, the gist of which can be conveyed by a few of his own statements:

> Sufferings of the non-violent have been known to melt the stoniest hearts. I make bold to say that if the Jews can summon to their aid the soul power that comes only from non-violence, Herr Hitler will bow before the courage which he has never yet experienced in any large measure in his dealings with men, and which, when it is exhibited, he will own is infinitely superior to that shown by his best storm troopers. The exhibition of such courage is only possible for those who have a living faith in the God of Truth and Non-violence, i.e., Love.[29]
>
> A single Jew bravely standing up and refusing to bow to Hitler's decrees will cover himself with glory and lead the way to the deliverance of the fellow Jews.[30]

But what exactly was this 'deliverance'? For all his talk of melting Hitler's heart, Gandhi knew that it was not going to happen. Only one option remained in practice:

> Suffering voluntarily undergone will bring them [German Jews] an inner strength and joy which no number of resolutions of sympathy passed in the world outside Germany can. Indeed, even if Britain, France and America were to declare hostilities against Germany, they can bring no inner joy, no inner strength. The calculated violence of Hitler may even result in a general massacre of the Jews by way of his first answer to the declaration of such hostilities. But if the Jewish mind could be prepared for voluntary suffering, even the massacre I have imagined could be turned into a day of thanksgiving and joy that Jehovah had wrought deliverance of the race even at the hands of the tyrant. For to the godfearing, death has no terror. It is a joyful sleep to be followed by a waking that would be all the more refreshing for the long sleep.[31]

So death, it would appear, was the logical conclusion of a non-violent attitude in this case, along with a promise of thanksgiving and deliverance. A year later, Sri Aurobindo remarked in a conversation with disciples, 'Non-violence cannot defend. One can only die by it.'[32]

The Cripps Mission

Let us now turn to the case of the mission of Sir Stafford Cripps, sent to India in 1942 by a proud and reluctant Winston Churchill. Harried by Germany, increasingly pressured by the U.S.A., eager to secure India's support during the War, Churchill, who had sworn ever to protect the Empire, found himself compelled to present to India on a gold platter an offer of dominion status. (That was the third such offer since the start of the War, but in more explicit terms than ever.)

Sri Aurobindo 'supported the Cripps offer because by its acceptance India and Britain could stand united against the

Asuric forces [of Nazism] and the solution of Cripps could be used as a step towards independence.'[33] As a result, he promptly sent messages to the Congress leaders urging them to accept the proposal which amounted to virtual independence at the end of the War. Although some (including Nehru and Rajagopalachari) favoured it, Gandhi told Sri Aurobindo's messenger that he found it unacceptable, once again 'because of his opposition to war'.[34] (Churchill, I should add, forbade Cripps to show the slightest flexibility.) The result of Gandhi's dogmatic stand on the evil nature of war—a dogma Sri Krishna rebuffs in the Gītā—was to be heavy with consequences for India. It not only meant an unnecessary postponement of Independence, but it made India's bloody vivisection unavoidable, even as the Mahatma promised it would happen only 'over his dead body'; it also meant three wars with our neighbour and the continuing war of attrition and terrorism in Kashmir and elsewhere.

In *The History of the Freedom Movement in India*, R.C. Majumdar referred to Sri Aurobindo's 'advice to the Congress to accept the proposals of Cripps' and noted, 'The Congress rejected it at the time but many of its leaders admitted later that Arabinda was right.' Indeed, Majumdar's verdict was that Sri Aurobindo 'had a much clearer idea as to what should be the future politics of India than most of the leaders who shaped her destiny.'[35]

With due respect to the Mahatma, his rigid insistence on an impracticable non-violence may have cost the country dear, as a detached reassessment of his contribution to the struggle for freedom would, in my opinion, show—a critical appraisal that Gandhi's saintly image has so far kept confined to the scholarly world.

To be fair, we should note that Gandhi did try to understand Sri Aurobindo's viewpoint; in 1924, for instance, he sent his son Devadas to Pondicherry to sound him on non-violence. Sri Aurobindo simply replied, 'Suppose there is an invasion of India by the Afghans, how are you going to meet it with non-violence?'[36] We all know what happened when Kashmir was invaded immediately after Independence, or when Chinese troops poured into north India in 1962, or in 1999 when Pakistani troops occupied peaks in Kargil (and I am afraid there are more Kargils to come). It is a moot point what the Mahatma's advice would be in such cases: to lay down arms and meet the enemy with love and non-violence?

The following words of Sri Aurobindo, written in December 1916 in his *Essays on the Gita*, appear insightful in retrospect:

> We will use only soul-force and never destroy by war or any even defensive employment of physical violence? Good, though until soul-force is effective, the Asuric force in men and nations tramples down, breaks, slaughters, burns, pollutes, as we see it doing today, but then at its ease and unhindered, and you have perhaps caused as much destruction of life by your abstinence as others by resort to violence.[37]

Non-Violence vs. Force

If, therefore, we mean the Gītā's teaching to be a practicable one—which is what Sri Aurobindo and his companions in the fight for freedom did—we are bound to reject non-violence as a collective creed. It may remain an individual's choice, for every individual is free to follow his preferred path, but anyone who has to wage a battle for dharma or for the truth—which comes to the same thing—will find a better ally in the use of force which the Gītā advocates. Arjuna is of course something of all of us, the symbol of 'the struggling human soul', in Sri Aurobindo's words, and Kurukshetra is the 'battle of life', even of our humdrum everyday life if we take the trouble of living for a purpose. Resist a corrupt official and a Kurukshetra opens in front of you; let a women's group take on liquor barons and you can hear the twang of the Gāndīva; if a few villagers or tribals oppose a timber mafia, you will see a hundred Kauravas rise; or simply try to keep your street clean and learn what *ghoram karma* is all about!

Now, a frequent misconception is that if we reject non-violence, we must fall into violence—there is no alternative beyond those two poles. That is a costly confusion, and one which Gandhi hypnotized us into. Yet the Gītā goes to great pains to dispel it: between blind, āsuric violence and noble but impotent non-violence, there is conscious force, free from hatred and ego, which can remain powerfully still or also wage war, as circumstances demand. True, in the world's history, most aggressive expansions followed the āsuric path and washed the earth with blood—there is at least one notable exception, though, and that is India, whose preferred weapon of conquest was the cultural. Yet she was by no means a heaven of ahimsa. Alexander was confronted by Porus's armies; the Gurjara Pratihāras checked the progress of the Arabs into northwest India; we know well enough the great deeds of a Shivaji, a Rani Lakshmibai and countless other heroes of this land, to whom Sri Krishna's injunctions on the Kshatriya's dharma were no dead letter.

As to the present, it is a frequently heard complaint that Mahatma Gandhi's teaching of non-violence is no longer followed in India; but it rather seems to me that it has penetrated the collective Indian consciousness deep enough to make it wince at the very thought of action and put a brake on its use even when and where it is patently needed. Externally, no other country, I am sure, would have 'tolerated' the amount of aggression India has suffered since Independence, and at what terrible cost. Internally, India has been 'non-violent' towards the galloping growth of corruption, the criminalization of politics and the cancer of Naxalism. As a nation, India has lacked the courage to put to effective use the elements of strength in her heritage.

Swami Vivekananda, too, noted the irony behind an ahimsa-preaching Christianity and an action-urging Gītā:

Jesus Christ, the God of the Europeans, has taught: Have no enemy, bless them that curse you; whosoever shall smite thee on thy right cheek, turn to him the other also; stop all your work and be ready for the next world; the end of the world is near at hand. And our Lord in the Gita is saying:

Always work with great enthusiasm, destroy your enemies and enjoy the world. But, after all, it turned out to be exactly the reverse of what Christ or Krishna implied. The Europeans never took the words of Jesus Christ seriously. Always of active habits, being possessed of a tremendous Râjasika nature, they are gathering with great enterprise and youthful ardour the comforts and luxuries of the different countries of the world and enjoying them to their hearts' content. And we are sitting in a corner, with our bag and baggage, pondering on death day and night.[38]

At school, the average Indian pupil will be taught to worship Gandhi as the 'father of the nation', but will learn nothing of the Gītā's spiritual ethics and its call to oppose *adharma*. I wonder how those who drafted India's education policy arrogated the right to deprive young Indians of this pillar of their heritage. Of course, if we decide that education is only intended to prepare children for getting jobs and has nothing to do with making better human beings out of them, then we admit that there is no more meaning to a human's life than to an ant's. The Gītā's message is an effective tool: it offers a purpose in life; it gives strength; it instils self-confidence, elevation in thought, a broader view of life, a deeper understanding of human nature. I believe India would be in a better shape today had the Gītā not been kept out of sight and hearing of young Indians, except for a few *shlokas* at the time of burials.

Because they insisted on building a new, rejuvenated India on the truths of her ancient heritage and not on fleeting and shallow values, neither Sri Aurobindo nor Swami Vivekananda are in favour with current thinking, if it can be called that. In fact, today they would be labelled 'revivalists', and would certainly find themselves swimming against the cheerless tide, at loggerheads with almost every direction the country has taken since Independence, and with the educational system in particular. They could not have pictured education in free India rejecting the positive and enriching elements of Indian culture and preferring to go on with Macaulay's denationalizing methods. Is Indian culture then something so shameful, so ignoble that it has to be concealed from our children, except in the privacy of the home? Well, perhaps it is after all—but if it is, let us have the courage to declare so openly and have done with it instead of peddling it to foreign tourists to attract them to a few temples and ruins.

I cannot resist the temptation of mentioning a case in point: none of our successive education ministers thought it worthwhile to give Swami Vivekananda's or Sri Aurobindo's name to one out of the 274 Central and State universities spread over the country; Mahatma Gandhi has four universities in his name; Dr. Ambedkar has eight, Jawaharlal Nehru five, Rajiv Gandhi three, and a number of much lesser Indians have one. But no 'Swami Vivekananda University', no 'Sri Aurobindo University' —Swami Vivekananda who shook India awake, Sri Aurobindo who in 1906 became the first principal of the newly opened Bengal National College, Sri Aurobindo the nationalist leader, the editor and chief writer of *Bande Mataram* and *Karmayogin*, the creator of an original Indian perspective in yoga, thought, action and life.

This omission may be a small thing in itself, but it is revealing of the establishment's unease towards these awkward personalities. Which Indian student ever learns anything of substance about them?

Sri Aurobindo had and still has a message for his country, and a practical one. Whether working for India's Independence, supporting the Allies, urging acceptance of Cripps' proposal, he practised what he called 'spiritual realism'.[39] Of course, it would be a mistake to equate Sri Aurobindo's entire teaching and yoga with the Gītā. As he said,

> I regard the spiritual history of mankind and especially of India as a constant development of a divine purpose, not a book that is closed and the lines of which have to be constantly repeated. Even the Upanishads and the Gita were not final though everything may be there in seed.[40]

But in his action, Sri Aurobindo faithfully followed the spirit of the Gītā. His life is, in my opinion, the best commentary on the great Scripture. He once wrote to a disciple,

> If one is among the ... seekers of [the] Truth, one has to take sides for the Truth, to stand against the forces that attack it and seek to stifle it. Arjuna wanted not to stand for either side, to refuse any action of hostility even against assailants; Sri Krishna, who insisted so much on *samatā*, strongly rebuked his attitude and insisted equally on his fighting the adversary. 'Have *samatā*,' he said, 'and seeing clearly the Truth, fight.' ... It is a spiritual battle inward and outward; by neutrality and compromise or even passivity one may allow the enemy force to pass and crush down the Truth and its children.[41]

Warmongering in the Gītā?

If the colonial view of a fatalistic, passive and non-violent India was condemnatory, we now hear from the West a diametrically opposite criticism, in a typical damned-if-you-do, damned-if-you-don't situation: the Gītā stands accused of warmongering. Witness this statement made in 2000 by Wendy Doniger, a well-known Indologist and professor of history of religions at the University of Chicago: 'The Bhagavad Gita is not as nice a book as some Americans think,' she informed her audience. 'Throughout the Mahabharata ... Krishna goads human beings into all sorts of murderous and self-destructive behaviors such as war. . . . The Gita is a dishonest book; it justifies war.' And the learned professor added for good measure: 'I'm a pacifist. I don't believe in "good" wars.'[42]

Thankfully, many eminent Western thinkers, from Emerson to Aldous Huxley and André Malraux, showed a far deeper understanding of the Lord's Song. But let us face the professor's statement. Leaving aside its disparaging tone common with some (not all) Western 'Indologists' accustomed to judging Indian civilization by their own standards and personal likes, it does raise a valid problem. Indeed a few Jain texts, for instance, have criticized Krishna on much the same ground and asserted that he would have to be in hell for many ages to atone for his sins.

Is war and killing always bad, then? Well, if it is, it is not India that ought to be condemned but the West with its bloodstained record of Crusades and genocides of Pagan peoples, its 'wars of religion', its smash-and-grab colonial expansion, its two World Wars and recent bombing campaigns across the globe. Indeed, Prof. Doniger's own nation was founded on war and genocide. Where has the West practised 'pacifism' in the last two millennia? On the other hand, we see very few cases of a military conquests of other lands by India, no Indian genocide of other peoples, no stamping out of another culture or religion. Why lay this unjust blame on the innocent rather than on the guilty?

But the problem is deeper, for the Gītā refuses to fall for simplistic oppositions such as war vs. pacifism or violence vs. non-violence. True, there is nothing non-violent about the Gītā, and elsewhere in the Mahābhārata, ahimsa is roundly criticized, as we saw earlier. This does not mean that war should be the preferred solution as a rule: did not Krishna go to the Kauravas on a last-ditch peace mission, even though he knew it was doomed to fail? Only after exhausting all avenues to peace did he advise the Pāndavas to wage war.

However, the crucial point missed by Prof. Doniger is that this was not a selfish war waged out of a desire of conquest or political power: it was a war to end the adhārmic rule of the Kauravas. Krishna's objective was not peace *per se,* but dharma for the universal good.

There lies the radical difference between the Western and the Indian approaches. To the West, and also to Mahatma Gandhi, there is either brute force or pacifism, either violence or non-violence; to the Gītā, the truth is neither one nor the other, but the conscious use of force to protect dharma, the universal order. Rooted in the ancient Indian concept of the Kshatriya, this third way can only be practised by those who have risen above egoism, above āsuric ambition or greed. The Gītā certainly does not advocate war; what it advocates is the active and selfless defence of dharma through all possible means, war being the last of them. Had India, as a nation, sincerely followed it, she might not have lost a large chunk of Kashmir, and might not have today China nibbling at her borders, from Ladakh to Arunachal.

The Gītā is neither a gospel of warmongering nor a feeble advocacy of pacifism. It spells out the only dharmic answer to āsuric aggression, an answer rooted in spiritual discernment. Sri Krishna plunges a dejected Arjuna back into the world, not away from it. No doubt, overcome by egoism, by *tamas* and *rajas*, we live our lives ignorantly. But between blind, unconscious, mechanical living on the one hand, and complete rejection of life on the other, the Gītā offers a practical alternative. And a more satisfying one, especially in today's world which does not appear overeager to renounce action!

The Gītā's answer is 'the greatest gospel of spiritual works',[43] in Sri Aurobindo's phrase. Can works really be spiritual? Yes, we are told, if we sincerely strive to uproot egoism from our actions, 'with [our] consciousness founded in the Self, free from desire and egoism' (3.60), conscious that 'You have a right to action, but only to action, never to its fruits' (2.47). Supremely difficult in practice, yet a most soothing way to recognize that our intellect is incapable of gauging the workings of the universe: we cannot be sure of what is really good or bad, right or wrong, and whether our action is of any use at all, or just some random ripple on the great ocean of life. 'Thick and tangled is the way of works,' admits the Gītā (4.17).

Such is, in a nutshell, the method the Scripture offers us to escape from ignorance without escaping from life. We may not be able to adopt it in a day, but the very attempt of putting it into actual practice changes our whole attitude to life and widens our vision and action. It also relieves us from the unhealthy obsession with 'achievement' and 'success' that pervades today's globalized culture and wants us to 'conquer', to be 'aggressive' and 'assert our personality'. In reality, what conquers is not the human spirit but human greed, what asserts itself is not 'personality' but ego, and its success is often our deeper failure. The older Indian perspective reflected in the Gītā asks us to work not for ourselves but for the world and the divine Intention in it. By doing so, we live a fulfilled life, not a blind race to nowhere.

Spirituality then becomes a constant experience, not just a sublime but elusive moment in meditation. Gradually, inner and outer merge into an integral life: 'Not by abstention from works does a man enjoy actionlessness, nor by mere renunciation does he attain to his perfection' (3.4).

Part Three

INDIA
AND THE WORLD

8

A Wounded Identity

INDIA, it has often been said, is a civilization more than a nation: as a country of unparalleled complexity, with a bewildering social, linguistic and spiritual diversity, and an ancient cultural heritage acting as overall cement, she has generously overstepped the boundaries of what conventionally constitutes a nation, especially in the Western definition of the term. Whichever label we choose, that cement has largely been based on the underlying presence of what may loosely be called a Hindu heritage—'loosely', because the term Hindu is supple enough to accommodate Vedic, Jain, Buddhist, Vedantic, Tantric, Purānic, Sikh, folk and tribal concepts, forms, attitudes, customs and practices. If this appears an objectionable statement, let me quote Rabindranath Tagore on what constitutes India's cultural unity:

> India has all along been trying experiments in evolving a social unity within which all the different peoples could be held together, while fully enjoying the freedom of maintaining their own differences. ... This has produced something like a United States of a social federation, whose common name is Hinduism.[1]

The shocks of time have left this civilization 'wounded', to use V.S. Naipaul's phrase.[2] Over the past centuries and more so after India's Independence, while the Indian identity has been called into question, often reopening the old wounds, there has been no compensatory healing process founded on a frank admission of the past and a collective desire to let it really be 'past'. Instead, 'modern' India appears to have developed the strange doctrine that only by sweeping the past under the carpet can we bring about harmony—until the accumulated debris bursts in our shocked faces.

Part of the problem is that our perspective of India largely remains a colonial one, with the old stereotypes lurking around: her culture was variously condemned as barbaric, stagnant, idolatrous, caste-ridden, at best otherworldly and therefore effete. The echoes of such misportrayal persist in many standard readings of Indian history, from textbooks to more scholarly studies. In effect, the distortions are of two kinds: *factual distortions*, and the more subtle *model distortions*. I will discuss a few examples briefly; each of them would require a full separate treatment (and has often received one from various authors), but even as a superficial survey, the exercise is worthwhile.

1. Factual distortions in Indian History

The Aryan Invasion Theory

According to the Aryan invasion theory, a people called 'Aryans' invaded India around 1500 BCE and subjugated the 'indigenous' inhabitants, possibly the Harappans or their descendants—exactly whom depends on which one of the countless variations of the theory we consider. The conquering Aryans, in horse-drawn chariots, then imposed their Vedic culture, Sanskrit language and caste system on all of India in stages. A weakened version of this theory now puts forth a milder 'migration' into India, followed by a process of acculturation—which amounts to much the same thing: in both cases, the origins of Indian civilization shift to Central Asia or beyond: north Indians (especially higher castes) become 'invaders', while south Indians (especially lower castes) are turned into victims—notions that existed in no Indian text or tradition.

This nineteenth-century theory—the European counterpart of which was to become a pillar of Nazi ideology—helped to legitimize colonial rule and the imperial game of 'divide and rule'. But as archaeological excavations multiplied in the twentieth century, especially in the Indus and Sarasvatī valleys, it became clear that no traces were to be found of such a migration into India around the proposed date: the picture that emerged was one of transition in continuity, with no external disruption. Anthropology, too, through the examination of hundreds of skeletons, rejected the possibility of a new human type entering India around 1500 BCE, or indeed at any time during the third and second millenniums BCE. Several important genetics studies have since confirmed that by and large, Indian populations have been settled in the subcontinent for 40,000 years at least. Finally, many elements of Harappan culture (arbitrarily supposed to be 'pre-Aryan') turned out to be quite compatible with Vedic culture: among them, the worship of fire, of a mother-goddess, of trees and animals, of the *linga*, important sacred symbols such as the swastika or the *trishūla* (trident), ritual purification through water, and, most importantly, a tradition of yoga and meditation. Other symbols, the use of oil lamps, red pigment, conch shells showed that quite a few Harappan customs were transmitted to later Indian civilization. Even in agriculture, town planning, construction techniques and crafts, the rich Harappan legacy is now well-documented. All this evidence has prompted archaeologists to stress that there is no cultural break of the sort implied by the Aryan invasion theory between the Harappan and the later Gangetic civilizations.[3]

The Aryan theory was a potent weapon of division in the colonial arsenal, since it identified Brahmans and other upper castes with 'invaders' and the lower castes as 'aborigines' and reduced Vedic culture to an imported one. Despite accumulating evidence against it, it is still taught in most Indian textbooks and misused by various ideologies and political groups that have recycled and repackaged the divisive strategies of the colonial age.

Dravidian, Dalit and Tribal Separateness

Another consequence of the Aryan invasion theory was the myth of a separate, pre-Aryan, 'Dravidian' identity and culture. While south India and especially the Tamil land do have a stamp of their own, from the beginning we see it imbued with Vedic and Purānic elements. Nowhere in the Sangam literature (the most ancient in Tamil) do we find a hint of a cultural clash with the North or with Vedic culture. Quite the contrary, we find the Vedas and the recitation of Vedic mantras praised from the earliest layers of this literature; Vedic gods such as Indra and Agni and all major gods of the classical Hindu pantheon figure in Tamil poems and epics, along with many concepts and legends drawn from the Mahābhārata and the Rāmāyana, as well as other sacred texts. Archaeological and numismatic evidence also supports an ancient integration of Vedic culture in the South, as can be seen from cultural artefacts found in the earliest cities (third or fourth century BCE).[4] Nowhere can we spot a separate, identifiable 'Dravidian' culture, much less civilization. On the other hand, the South has contributed enormously to Indian culture in terms of music, dance, literature, poetry, and an important devotional movement that spread throughout India in stages, besides generating a huge literature. The South forms an integral part of India's cultural continuum in time and space: distinctiveness is not separateness.

In much the same way, the so-called 'Dalits' (formerly 'Harijans', and still earlier 'Untouchables') are sought to be separated from the mainstream of Indian culture, although they are often more staunchly Hindu than the higher castes; indeed, if Hinduism has survived in India, it is thanks not only to the remarkable transmission of scriptures and other texts by Brahmans, to the resistance put up by many Kshatriya (warrior) clans against Muslim hegemony, but also to the deep attachment to Hindu beliefs, traditions and culture found in the lower strata of Indian society, a fact conspicuous even today through the mushrooming of village temples, rural and tribal pilgrimages and festivals.

Finally, we often hear that India's numerous tribes never had anything to do with Hinduism until it was 'imposed' upon them by Brahman 'missionaries' (I myself heard this from Christian missionaries). Not only is there no trace of any such 'imposition', Hinduism is in reality the result of a long and fruitful interaction between Vedic culture and tribal cults, with many tribal deities enriching the Hindu pantheon and tribal practices, rituals and art forms getting absorbed—a wholly organic process controlled by no authority or clergy. Moreover, tribal chieftains often rose to the Kshatriya class, smoothly fusing into Hindu society.[5] Again, we note an attempt to deny this extraordinary symbiotic feature of the apparently amorphous, decentralized, elusive and almost indefinable phenomenon called 'Hinduism'.

Saint Thomas's Journey to India and Martyrdom

In order to push back Christianity's presence in India and make up for the absence of an 'Indian martyr', the legend of Apostle Thomas's travel to India was promoted a few centuries ago. There is no historical evidence for it, however: the only text on which the legend is based, the apocryphal *Acts of Thomas*, written in Syriac in the third century CE, points to Parthia (near the Caspian Sea) and to Bactria, not to India.[6] This is confirmed by Persian and Bactrian names of kings (e.g., 'Mazdai') and other characters (Iuzanes, Charisius, Mygdonia, Narcia, Siphor . . .), also by physical features such as a 'desert land' or a lion. None of this applies to south India, yet, by dint of repetition, the myth has wormed its way from missionary tracts and tourist guidebooks into respectable reference books. As early as in 1773, Voltaire pointed out that it was another Thomas, a Syrian trader, who led his group of refugees to Kerala's shores in the sixth century CE. Voltaire, in fact, ridiculed the legend of Thomas the Apostle being pursued by spear-brandishing Brahmans, they 'who never speared anyone.'[7]

Let us also point out that St. Thomas is reported in many other parts of the world, so that we can count, in all, twelve graves for this ubiquitous apostle: six between Kerala and Tamil Nadu and six outside India, from Brazil to Tibet to Japan—surely a feat that makes Thomas a greater miracle worker than Jesus himself. Such major problems with the traditional (rather, neo-traditional) account is what made several historians of Christianity, such as Rev. James Hough, depict it as 'most improbable . . . unsupported by the faintest vestige of authentic history'.[8]

While this imagined martyrdom is actively propagated, the documented killing of Hindu priests and devotees and the demolition of temples by Jesuits and others (especially in Goa and Pondicherry) are not considered important enough to be remembered.[9] Worse, the few Hindus who happen to challenge it are promptly accused of promoting 'communal hatred'. This inversion is an integral part of the process of humiliation: the natural right to historical truth is denied, while the victim is made to look like an aggressor.

The Goan Inquisition

Francis Xavier is among the earliest and best known missionaries to operate in India, where he sailed in 1541. Two years later, he described his work among Travancore villagers in a letter to his fellow Jesuits at Rome's Society of Jesus: 'When all are baptized I order all the temples of their false gods to be destroyed and all the idols to be broken in pieces. I can give you no idea of the joy I feel in seeing this done, witnessing the destruction of the idols by the very people who but lately adored them.'[10]

For all his exertions, however, Francis Xavier could not make much headway. His frustration prompted him to write in 1545 to the then king of Portugal, asking to establish the Inquisition in Goa, which was already under Portuguese control. This was done in 1580, and the Goan Inquisition functioned until 1812—making it one of the longest lasting 'Holy Offices' in the world.

It is common for Church officials and Christian historians to claim that the Goa Inquisition only concerned itself with Christian heretics, and that very few were ultimately burnt at the stake.[11]

Such claims play upon the lack of official records left behind by the Inquisition (they were destroyed soon after it was dismantled). However, there is enough evidence left otherwise—including a contemporary account by Charles Dellon, a French physician who was jailed by the Inquisition on false charges—to disprove the claim.[12] In fact, victims included many Hindus and also Indian Jews; we have gruesome descriptions of the tortures they were subjected to, often culminating in their 'confessions' and *auto da fé* executions.

'Goa is sadly famous for its inquisition,' wrote Voltaire as far back as 1773, while it was still in effect. 'The Portuguese monks deluded us into believing that the [Indian] people worshipped the devil, but they are the ones who served him.'[13] Here, too, the humiliation of Indian victims of this 'Holy Office' is compounded by the refusal to acknowledge the horrors it inflicted.

The Portuguese rulers victimized Goa's Hindu population in other ways, too. This is well captured by the Goan (and Christian) historian T.R. de Souza:

> At least from 1540 onwards, and in the island of Goa before that year, all the Hindu idols had been annihilated or had disappeared, all the temples had been destroyed and their sites and building materials were in most cases utilized to erect new Christian Churches and chapels. Various viceregal and Church council decrees banished the Hindu priests from the Portuguese territories; the public practice of Hindu rites including marriage rites, was banned; the state took upon itself the task of bringing up Hindu orphan children; ... the Hindus were obliged to assemble periodically in churches to listen to preaching or to the refutation of their religion. .... The government transferred to the Church and religious orders the properties and other sources of revenue that had belonged to the Hindu temples that had been demolished or to the temple servants who had been converted or banished. Entire villages were taken over at times for being considered rebellious and handed over with all their revenues to the Jesuits.[14]

The destruction in 1747 of Puduchery's Vedapuriswaran temple by Jesuits, recorded in great detail by a witness, is among other cases of violence suffered by Hindus in the name of Jesus.[15]

The Islamic Record in India

In a parallel case, but on a larger scale, the actual record of Muslim rulers in India has been eclipsed. Over several centuries, Islamic sources recorded in gory detail slaughters of Hindus, Buddhists or Jains (all of them regarded as 'Kāfirs' or infidels) and the forcible conversion, massive captures of slaves inflicted on the Indian population,[16] besides great plunder and the demolition of countless Hindu, Buddhist and Jain temples and centres of learning. Historians from Will Durant, Alain Daniélou or Koenraad Elst[17] in the West to R.C. Majumdar,[18] K.S. Lal[19] or Sita Ram Goel[20] in India have documented this blood-soaked period of Indian history. Daniélou, for instance, called it 'a long and monotonous recital of murders, massacres, plunder and destruction',[21] while Durant offered this assessment:

> The Mohammedan Conquest of India is probably the bloodiest story in history. It is a discouraging tale, for its evident moral is that civilization is a precarious thing, whose delicate complex of order and liberty, culture and peace may at any time be overthrown by barbarians invading from without or multiplying within.[22]

But it was not merely a matter of 'slaughtering the idolaters' or 'ending the conceit of the infidels by means of the sword and the spear,'[23] as Fīrūz Shāh Tughluq put it in the fourteenth century; it was also the imposition of a tax (jizya) on the survivors and the practice of very public humiliations: desecrating 'idols', burying them 'in front of the mosques' so that they may be 'trampled by the shoes on the feet of the Muslims'.[24] Islamic chronicles faithfully recorded such practices, too, page after grisly page.[25]

There is a watertight case for the suffering and humiliation inflicted on Hindu, Buddhist and Jain communities by Islamic invaders and rulers, and no more reason to sweep it under the carpet than to conceal the genocides and ravages perpetrated by colonial powers in America and Africa.[26] Timur's account of his conquest of Baghdad in August 1401, when he built 120 pyramids with 90,000 severed heads of its inhabitants, is not the object of any controversy, but all hell breaks loose if mention is made of similar massacres and depredations by him on his way to Delhi, or by Mahmūd of Ghazni, Alā'-ud-Dīn Khaljī, Malik Kāfūr, Muhammad ibn Tughluq, Fīrūz Shāh Tughluq, Sikandar Lodī, Aurangzeb, among many others, in much of India—all deeds, again, proudly recorded by the perpetrators of those atrocities or their chroniclers. Inexplicably, drawing attention to such chapters of Indian history instantly raises colourful labels of 'Hindu communalism', 'chauvinism' or even 'hatred mongering': other nations, it appears, have a right to know facts of their history, pleasant or repellent, but not India.

Conversely, Muslim invasions of India have sometimes been glorified; M.N. Roy, for instance, claimed that Islam brought a welcome 'message of hope and freedom'.[27] If at all a few instances of destruction are acknowledged in passing, we are told that temples were plundered only because they were centres of wealth, or sometimes for 'political motives'[28]—a clumsy excuse amply rejected by the Islamic rulers themselves, for instance Timur who spoke in his autobiography of 'the sword of Islam being washed in the blood of the infidels'.[29] The intention appears to be to dodge an objective discussion of Islamic fanaticism, the driving force behind the above depredations, apparently for fear of offending today's Muslim Indians. Yet the latter are no more responsible for them than today's Germans are responsible for Nazi atrocities. The difference is that Germany has fully acknowledged this dark phase of her history and made reparations for it, while in India we stubbornly remain in denial mode—forgetting that it is only by acknowledging the past, with all its horrors, that it can be effectively healed; clumsily trying to suppress it will only ensure that wounds continue to fester. No self-respecting nation wants its victims to be denied remembrance.

The Case of Ayodhya

A slightly different case is that of Ayodhya, a long-festering controversy which has recently resurfaced with the September 2010
judgment of the Allahabad High Court (some of the adjudged
suits were filed sixty years earlier!). Here is a place spoken of in
the Rāmāyaṇa and many subsequent texts as the birthplace of
Rāma, a place where, in any case, worship of Rāma has been
attested for centuries (by numerous Muslim documents, an
eighteenth-century Austrian traveller to India, the Jesuit and
geographer Joseph Tieffenthaler, and revenue records of British
times), finally a place where, according to Hindu tradition, a
temple dedicated to Rāma had existed before it was demolished
by Muslim invaders, who built a mosque in its place. Numerous
Muslim records show that the Hindus never gave up their claim
to worship there and often fought for it; for some periods they
were even allowed to worship in the mosque's courtyard, a con-
cession without parallel in the Islamic world. In 1936, the mosque
was locked and forgotten by the Muslim community; thirteen
years later, Hindus got images of Rāma and Sītā installed in it.
Tensions rose, especially as both the courts and the government
tried to dodge the issue and postpone a decision, until in 1992
the mosque was demolished by a group of Hindu activists, who
promptly erected a makeshift shrine in its place.

Besides the above traditions, hard evidence existed from other
sources, textual as well as archaeological. The Hindu tradition
of associating the Babri mosque with Rāma's birthplace was
recorded by many Muslim writers, such as Abul Fazl, Akbar's
chronicler. The demolition of the Rāma temple followed by the
construction of the Babri mosque in 1528 by Mir Baqi is also
mentioned, and proudly so, in several Muslim documents, beginning with one by a granddaughter of Aurangzeb. Turning to
physical evidence, fourteen black-stone pillars bearing Hindu
motifs and deities could be seen inside the mosque, which would
not have been the case if it had been built on a virgin location.
Then, in 1975, the archaeologist B.B. Lal conducted limited

excavations close to the mosque; they brought to light rows of pillar bases below the mosque's level, which suggested a pre-existing large structure. Crucially, a large stone inscription emerged from the demolition; written in a Devanāgarī script of the eleventh century and deciphered by leading Indian epigraphists (including Ajay Mitra Shastri and K.V. Ramesh), it spoke of a magnificent temple to 'Vishnu-Hari' and to the 'killer of the ten-headed demon' (i.e., Rāma, killer of Rāvana). Lastly, in 2003, the High Court ordered fresh excavations by the Archaeological Survey of India, which found in early layers numerous Hindu designs and artefacts as well as some fifty pillar bases indicating a 'huge structure'; it concluded that the evidence showed 'distinctive features found associated with the temples of north India'.

Taken together, this massive evidence convinced the Allahabad High Court, which allotted to two Hindus organizations two-thirds of the disputed land, including the crucial site where the mosque had stood, acknowledging that for centuries it had indeed been regarded by Hindus as Rāma's birthplace; the last third was allotted to the Muslim litigants. Expectedly, a group of 'secular' historians of the Marxist school, who had stubbornly opposed all Hindu claims during the failed negotiations that preceded the mosque's demolition, started a fresh campaign against the court's verdict, recycling their old arguments: for instance, since Rāma was not a historical character, the question of his birthplace did not arise; or the large building beneath the mosque could have been an older mosque; or even if it was indeed a Hindu temple, it would have been abandoned and ruined long before the mosque was built. There was no end to such convoluted and mutually contradictory denials, all of them of a negative nature. They have been rebutted at length,[30] but I must stress here that the question of Rāma's historicity is essentially irrelevant to the whole Ayodhya issue: the proven long-standing tradition of Rāma worship at the spot is sufficient to establish that this has long been a sacred site for Hindus, a sentiment that ought to have been respected, just as the Christian belief that Jesus was born at Bethlehem is respected worldwide even though there is no historical proof for it. Instead, the intransigence we have seen in this controversy can legitimately be viewed as a conscious will to humiliate Hindus.

As always, it would be wrong to identify all Muslim Indians with the small political groups claiming to represent them. In the 1980s, a few Muslim voices had already expressed a wish that their community should hand over the site to Hindus, since it had no major religious significance for Muslims (it was not, for instance, a pilgrimage site). Sadly, those voices were drowned in the din of the controversy, and rarely highlighted by the media. They were heard again in 2010 after the Allahabad High Court's judgement, this time more clearly. For instance, one of the original Muslim litigants, now ninety years old, wanted the verdict accepted; a group of young Muslims from Uttar Pradesh also declared their opposition to an appeal in the Supreme Court and additionally announced a donation of 15 lakhs of rupees for the construction of a Rāma temple at the site.[31]

On the other hand, in October 2010, the All India Muslim Personal Law Board decided to challenge the Allahabad High Court's verdict in the Supreme Court, on the ground that 'This issue can only be sorted out when the claim of Muslims is upheld. We cannot surrender our claim.'[32] This predictable stand, which brushes aside the far more genuine Hindu claim to the site, is bound to harden positions once again. The only way out seems to be for moderate Muslim Indians to exert a pressure on such groups so they agree to the Hindus' claim to the site, which can have no significance for Muslims unless they wrongly choose to identify themselves with a conquering and iconoclastic Babar.

When prompted to condemn the Babri Masjid's demolition, writer and Nobel laureate V.S. Naipaul said, 'I would call it an act of historical balancing. The mosque built by Babar in Ayodhya was meant as an act of contempt. Babar was no lover of India. I think it is universally accepted that Babar despised India, the Indian people and their faith.'[33]

There can be no logic—except that of conquest and humiliation—in identifying with such a character. On the other hand, the positive gesture that a growing section of Muslim Indians are asking for would generate powerful currents of goodwill in today's India and would enable her to bring this chapter to a close after almost five centuries.

British Rule: Denigration of Indian Civilization

To legitimize its 'civilizing mission' in India, Britain needed to portray her as barbaric and uncivilized—a standard colonial practice from America to Africa and Asia. Hinduism, in particular, was denigrated as 'barbaric', 'superstitious', 'idolatrous', and generally responsible for India's depressed social condition. This legitimized the spread of a 'superior' civilization and religion through the colonial rule. In colonial histories, India's ancient accomplishments were generally obscured or, as in the case of science, portrayed as deriving from Greece's influence. More recent, precolonial advances, such as India's indigenous and remarkably efficient system of schooling,[34] extensive medical traditions or democratic village administration were systematically eclipsed.

Despite the accumulation of valuable material on precolonial India, this framework endures with varying degrees of subtlety. India's socioeconomic stability, her contributions to world civilization in science, technology, art, architecture, philosophy, religion, spirituality, literature, scripts, continue to be underrated: the average Indian student, for instance, learns almost nothing of them, and is unable to form a proper idea of Indian civilization and its role in the history of humanity.

British Rule: Concealment of Colonial Barbarity

From the late eighteenth century, the chief policy of the East India Company, and later of the Empire, was that 'India must be bled', in the words of R.A. Salisbury, Secretary of State for India. Starting from Bengal, a massive drain of wealth largely fuelled Europe's Industrial Revolution—the 'Bengal plunder', as the British historian Brooks Adams called it.[35] But taxes were imposed so cruelly that, according to figures compiled from British sources, 30 to 50 million deaths were caused by famines between the late eighteenth century and the 1940s, mostly in the peasantry. Respected Indian personalities such as Dadabhai Naoroji,[36] Romesh Dutt[37] or S.G. Deuskar[38] added their voices to those of British historians like William Digby in recording this large-scale tragedy. The last scholar, author of a monumental and impassioned study, wrote in 1901:

> Modern England has been made great by Indian wealth, wealth never proffered by its possessor, but always taken by the might and skill of the stronger. The difference between the eighteenth and the twentieth centuries is simply that the amount received now is immensely larger, is obtained 'according to law'. .... England struck down the ancient industries of India and, during a whole century, has done naught that is worthy to constitute India a land of varied industries.[39]

The full extent of this plunder, however, finds no place in Indian textbooks, nor does the systematic destruction of India's crafts and her indigenous systems of education, administration and medicine. If the sheer brutality of the colonial rule must be documented, it is not in order to nurture any hatred for today's Britain, but because it played a part in orienting the later evolution of Indian society, from the peasant class to the so-called elite.

The Struggle for Freedom

Official histories of the freedom movement lay an almost exclusive emphasis on Mahatma Gandhi and the Indian National Congress, at the expense of those who really prepared the ground: Bal Gangadhar Tilak, the Marāthā leader who ignited the Independence movement late in the nineteenth century; Lala Lajpat Rai, the powerful Punjabi leader; Bipin Chandra Pal, the inspired Bengali orator; Sri Aurobindo, the leader whose incisive pen and high vision of India's destiny wielded so much influence in the first decade of the twentieth century that India's Viceroy, Lord Minto, regarded him as 'the most dangerous man we have to deal with at present'.[40] Such leaders are usually glossed over in two or three lines in history textbooks; many more, who left few or no writings, are completely forgotten.

Or they are demonized: a recent textbook on *Modern India* used the words 'terrorists' and 'terrorism' seven times in just two pages to describe revolutionaries in India's freedom struggle, no doubt aware of how the word's connotation has shifted in recent decades and of the resulting impact on the minds of schoolchildren.[41] The term 'terrorist' was, of course, used by the British to characterize freedom fighters who had recourse to weapons; there is no excuse for using it in a modern textbook without a suitable explanation: India's freedom fighters did not explode bombs in public places with a view to causing as many deaths as possible, nor did they take hostages or use suicide bombers—the current implications of the word 'terrorist'.

While Gandhi is credited with vanquishing the mighty British Empire almost single-handedly, we find hardly any discussion of other factors that contributed to its fall: the irreversible world trend towards decolonization, the debilitating impact of the Second World War on Britain, or U.S. pressure on Britain—factors that helped other nations achieve independence, including Burma (Myanmar, in 1948) or Ceylon (Sri Lanka, also in 1948), without their having had the leadership of a Gandhi. Naturally, there is even less discussion of Gandhi's blunders, such as the Khilafat movement which in effect strengthened the demands of radical Muslim politics, ultimately paving the way for India's partition.

On the other hand, the few historians who discussed the shortcomings of Gandhi and the Congress and gave due place to other freedom fighters suffered discrimination and were labelled 'communal'. Such was the case of one of India's most distinguished twentieth-century historians, R.C. Majumdar, who, after Independence, was entrusted with the writing of an official history of the freedom movement; when the first government of 'free India' realized that he would not indulge in the expected adulation of

Gandhi and the Congress, it unceremoniously withdrew him from the direction of the project.[42] Majumdar went on to publish on his own a three-volume *History of the Freedom Movement in India*, which acquired the status of a classic. In it, he felt compelled to reject 'the generally accepted view which gave Mahatma Gandhi the "sole credit for the freedom of India" '.[43] He explained:

> It has been my painful duty to show that ... the popular image of Gandhi cannot be reconciled with what he actually was. ... Gandhi was lacking in both political wisdom and political strategy ... and far from being infallible, committed serious blunders, one after another, in pursuit of some Utopian ideals and methods which had no basis in reality. It will also be seen that the current estimate of the degree or extent of his success bears no relation to actual facts.[44]

In official histories, on the other hand, the Congress, which had scotched the calls for independence made by Tilak, Sri Aurobindo and their associates (the so-called 'Extremists') from 1905 onward, now credited Nehru with being the first to have voiced this demand in 1929, at the Congress session of Lahore. India's Communists followed suit: while they had actually collaborated with the colonial powers, they now claimed that they had been at the forefront of the struggle for Independence. This is nothing to be surprised at when one remembers Communism's liberties with historical truth in Soviet and Maoist regimes.

Beyond such controversies, the whole spirit of the Independence movement, which was to build a nation on the foundation of a revivified and spiritualized Indian culture, is now frowned at, and the fight for freedom 'secularized'. The same textbook that referred to freedom fighters as 'terrorists' held Sri Aurobindo's 'concept of India as mother and nationalism as religion' to be a 'step back' because it had 'a strong religious and Hindu tinge'.[45] Viewing India as the Mother, which was regarded as a supreme virtue by most freedom fighters, is portrayed as unacceptably communal—of course, by ideologies that opposed the very idea of Independence in the first place.

As a corollary, the concept of 'nationalism', for which many heroically offered their lives, is now the instrument of a second demonization: the undiscerning reader will be subtly led to assimilate India's nationalist movement with European ones bearing the same label; through this simple device, with the latter culminating in the dark developments we know (fascism and so forth), their shadow will now automatically extend to the former.

2. Model Distortions in Indian History

Factual distortions of the above kind do not follow a random pattern; they stem from a flawed approach to Indian history. There is probably no better summary of the issue than this anguished statement penned by Rabindranath Tagore in 1903:

> Our real ties are with the Bharatavarsha that lies outside our textbooks. If the history of this tie for a substantially long period gets lost, our soul loses its anchorage. After all, we are no weeds or parasitical plants in India. Over many hundreds of years, it is our roots, hundreds and thousands of them, that have occupied the very heart of Bharatavarsha. But, unfortunately, we are obliged to learn a brand of history that makes our children forget this very fact. It appears as if we are nobody in India; as if those who came from outside alone matter.[46]

This 'brand of history' divided Indian history into Vedic / Buddhist / Hindu / Muslim / British periods, but those neat labels concealed as many misconceptions. As little is known today about a 'Vedic period' as two centuries ago. Buddhism and Hinduism were much less compartmentalized than we are told, and their interplay was much more than a crude power game. There was never a time when Muslims ruled over the whole of India without a few Hindu kingdoms putting up some resistance. And if we name the first four 'periods' after religions, should we call the last a 'Christian period'?

In time, the phrase 'Muslim period' got replaced by 'medieval period', but that is hardly better: the term carries a baggage, suggesting the pre-rational, pre-scientific mind of medieval Europe's 'Dark Ages'. But there were no such ages in India, which used reason and logic (*nyāya*) before the Greeks and had a long tradition of encouraging debate (*samvāda*), free inquiry and criticism, as a cursory look at the two Epics alone shows. The creation of new schools of thought or even new cults was never discouraged: it was understood that truth could not be limited to one or a few modes of expression. That is also why Hinduism, Buddhism or Jainism never had a problem with modern science, be it its cosmological time scales, its concept of an infinite universe, or the evolution of species. The multiplicity of India's intellectual traditions promoted scientific inquiry instead of shackling it as happened in 'medieval' Europe.

Periodization apart, the current prevailing models of Indian history, which are broadly Marxist,* tend to look upon India's history as nothing but a history of invasions, in conformity with Karl Marx's diktat:

India could not escape the fate of being conquered [by England], and the whole of her past history, if it be anything, is the history of the successive conquests she has undergone. Indian society has no history at all, at least no known history. What we call its history, is but the history of the successive intruders who founded their empires on the passive basis of that unresisting and unchanging society.[47]

In such a perspective, not only do the invaders receive more attention than the invaded, as Tagore complained, but Marxist historiography, based on a purely materialistic, socioeconomic

* More correctly, the prevailing school of historiography in India may be said to be a fusion of post-Marxist and postmodernist models. Let me add that I use the word 'Marxist' here not in any derogatory sense, but in the manner those historians and scholars use it to describe their own school of thought. D.D. Kosambi's *Introduction to the Study of Indian History* (1956) set the tone, declaring its intent to use 'dialectical materialism, also called Marxism' to read the evolution of Indian society, complete with a 'proletariat' and class war. My use of the term 'Marxist' is the same as Romila Thapar's in her *Penguin History of Early India: From the Origins to AD 1300*, Penguin Books, New Delhi, 2003, pp. 22 ff.

definition of the human being, belittles what it cannot compre-
hend: the Vedic religion becomes 'primitive animism' (Romila
Thapar[48]); the Bhagavad-Gītā promotes 'feudalism'[49] and is
stained by the 'fundamental defect' of attempting 'to reconcile
the irreconcilable' (D.D. Kosambi[50]); and so on.

Omitting all unifying cultural and spiritual elements, Marxist
dialectics lays a disproportionate emphasis on caste: Indian
history, in R.S. Sharma's view, is worth studying only to understand the 'gross social injustice' of the caste system and to thwart
those who 'clamour for the restoration of ancient culture and
civilization' because they want 'to prevent [India's] progress,' a
progress based of course on 'the achievements of modern science
and technology'.[51] It did not occur to Sharma that without
wanting to restore India's 'ancient culture and civilization', we
may yet turn to it to understand the Indian mind, study its
explorations of human life, and draw useful lessons from the
past. Turning science and technology into new gods will lead us
nowhere, except perhaps to a 'scientific' destruction of the planet.

Here are, in a nutshell, some of the problems Marxist
historiography comes up against when it is mechanically applied
to India:

♦ Since it is founded on a purely socioeconomic definition of
the human being, no spiritual dimension is acknowledged.
India's religious and spiritual currents and movements are
interpreted purely from a materialistic standpoint. When,
for example, the Bhakti movement is discussed, it is turned
into a rebellion against higher castes, when, in actual fact,
it cut across caste barriers; the unifying sociocultural impact
of this unique movement spreading through the whole
subcontinent is quite simply ignored.

♦ As a corollary, Indian philosophy and spirituality are of no
value, nor are India's spiritual figures. In this perspective,
Swami Vivekananda's or Sri Aurobindo's or Tagore's understanding of Indian history and civilization can be of no relevance. In other terms, a prerequisite to an understanding

of India is a rejection of the fundamentals of her civilization and culture. An outsider alone can make sense of them; an insider stands automatically disqualified.

♦ A second corollary is the denial of India's cultural continuity and identity. Artificial breaks are introduced in time (for instance, the imaginary Aryan invasion of India) or in society (the Brahmans vs. the rest of India). We do hear of India's 'diversity' but not of what constitutes its 'unity'. India's cultural cement is not thought to be a worthwhile object of study; its existence, in fact, is denied, since Hinduism is merely 'a mosaic of distinct cults, deities, sects and ideas' and communities in ancient India were only 'segmented identities'.[52]

♦ India's civilizational achievements and contributions to world culture are underemphasized, or omitted altogether, as they were in the colonial era.

♦ The defects of Indian society, ancient, medieval or modern, are magnified and invariably put down to Hinduism, but the same procedure is not applied to defects of Christian and Islamic societies.

♦ Even those defects, undeniable as they are, are not studied objectively. The caste system, for instance, is invariably seen as a source of conflict, even if it provided a measure of stability and economic prosperity to Indian society and promoted cultural pluralism. Also, the impact of Islam and the British rule on Hindu society and the consequent hindering of caste mobility is glossed over.

♦ Finally, India's history is forcibly squeezed into a Eurocentric framework seen through Marxist categories: 'barbarism', 'feudalism', 'class war', etc., become omnipresent labels as a matter of course, as though their relevance to the Indian context required no critical discussion.

D.P. Singhal offered this insight in 1978:

Where the Marxist, imperialist and communalist historians converge is in their attitude towards Hindu culture which forms the bulk of India's heritage. Marxists, as did Marx himself, regard culture as bourgeois and anti-revolutionary. ... Culture, therefore, had to be denounced, including religion, God and morals, as an obstacle to proletarian change. Culture in the Indian context meant mainly Hindu religion and heritage. ... Marxist attacks on culture also aim at hitting at the roots and source of inspiration of nationalism, which in fact is the movement they dread most. ...[53]

In this de-Indianized academic teaching of Indian history, the fundamentals of Indian civilization are non-existent. The logical outcome can only be the atomization of India. As the Communist leader Ashok Mitra cheerfully told a Dutch newspaper a few years ago: 'India was never the solution.'[54]

Marxist historiography is in many ways the inheritor and continuer of the colonial, Eurocentric view of India, although in a new garb. Some of its contributions to India's social conditions have been valuable, but like its predecessor, it finds no intrinsic or enduring value in Indian civilization or in its contributions to humanity. It wants to study a skeleton, or at best a corpse, and is upset to find it alive.

Looking Forward

India presents us with a unique situation: an ancient culture shies away from the task of healing its past and present wounds for fear of offending conquering ideologies that are, in many respects, the apologists of its aggressors. In India's present intellectual climate, a Hindu identity is either denied or projected as regressive, obscurantist and divisive, while in historical fact, it proved to be assimilative, non-aggressive and open to new knowledge. Subtly or not so subtly, the Hindu is made to feel guilty for being one; the 'majority' becomes marginalized in its own land. The very word 'Hindu'—the same which evoked in a Schopenhauer, an Emerson or a Carl Sagan some of the human mind's boldest explorations—is made to acquire a dubious odour.

As a result, India's educational system blanks out any teaching of Indian culture, or else clumsily promotes the undefined and indefinable concept of a 'composite culture'—a slogan more than a concept.

A recent case in point illustrates the phenomenon of Hindu humiliation. In 2005, California's Department of Education (through its Education Curriculum Commission) invited suggestions from Christian, Jewish, Islamic and Hindu scholars on sections of the California textbooks dealing with their respective faiths and civilizations. Suggestions did pour in, and were largely accepted—until a petition by U.S., European and Indian academics impressed upon the Commission members that the proposed changes should be rejected as they reflected a dangerous Hindu fundamentalism. Hindu groups rose in protest, with one Hindu scholar writing an open letter entitled, 'Why do 50-odd "international academics" humiliate the Hindu?'[55]

In 2007, U.S. courts accepted the pro-Hindu lobby's charge of illegality in the review procedure followed by the Department of Education, but later refused to reverse the contentious edits themselves; finally the Department of Education paid a large sum to the plaintiffs' representative organization, and the matter came to rest. However, what matters more than legalities is the very fact that a few academics with no direct experience of India succeeded in imposing their views on a textbook portrayal of Hinduism; certainly, no such interference would have been tolerated from outsiders in the case of Christian, Jewish, or Islamic faiths. Once more, the Hindu was expected to accept being viewed through another's eyes.

'History,' writes the columnist Swapan Dasgupta in the context of the Ayodhya controversy, 'is essentially a conversation between the past and the present.'[56] And the past will keep knocking at our doors—sometimes barging in uninvited—until an honest and meaningful dialogue is permitted.

9

The Conqueror
and the Conquered

THE story of humanity is not a happy tale. No animal species has been so cruel and destructive to itself as *Homo sapiens*. The age-old maxim goes, *Homo homini lupus*—'Man is a wolf to man.' With rare exceptions or brief lulls, war, conquest, plunder and bloodshed, ruthless exploitation have been crimson constants in the shifting equations of 'human' history.

Of course, this behaviour has its roots in animal nature: territorial conquest and expansion, defending one's kin, preying upon other species. Still, there are species and species: the tiger's nature is not that of the deer. But even the tiger—or the wolf, for that matter—does not destroy its fellow creatures. Only man does. The difference is our mind, this instrument that has multiplied our possibilities animal or human, sordid or sublime, divine or devilish.

Conquering Creeds

But if the human mind could be purified or controlled, perhaps things would change? Such has always been the idealist's hope. And what better means than religion? Religion which claims to make humanity better, nobler, purer. Yet looking at history from a Western standpoint, it appears that the opposite happened: man's rapacity reached its height when it put on the cloak of religion. The torments of Europe's Pagans that began with Constantine the Great ended with their extinction a few centuries later. Even afterwards, the common people had to live in the shadows of the Crusades, the witch hunts, the Inquisition and the wars of religion. The Renaissance sowed seeds that were going to free minds, but also an expansionist fervour that spelt doom for people across the seas. Wherever they went, Columbus and his successors killed, enslaved and plundered in the name of Jesus —a century ago, the French writer Anatole France called it 'the crimes of the whole military and commercial Christianity'.[1] Europe's advance was more recently described by Chinweizu, an African commentator, in these words:

> White hordes ... fortified in an aggressive spirit by an arrogant, messianic Christianity ... motivated by the lure of enriching plunder, ... sallied forth from their western European homelands to explore, assault, loot, occupy, rule and exploit the rest of the world.[2]

Assault and plunder were also, to some extent at least, a part of the history of Islam's lightning-fast expansion. So long as conquests were in the name of their god, those two creeds legitimized and titanized unregenerate human nature instead of seeking to transform it. Such is religion of the aggressive and conquering type, claiming the earth and humanity as its God-given fiefdom. It sets out to make people better but ends up encouraging their worse propensities, if in so doing it can grow in power and influence. As the U.S. physicist Steven Weinberg said in a speech in 1999, 'Religion is an insult to human dignity. With or without it you would have good people doing good things and evil people doing evil things. But for good people to do evil things, that takes religion.'

Monotheistic religions doubtlessly had higher elements, too, a rudimentary ethical guide and a few lines of mystical experience and teaching. But much of these can be traced to earlier traditions, from Gnosticism and Mithraism to Buddhism and older Indian influences. And in practice, the Pagan, the heathen, the infidel saw very little of Jesus' love or Allah's mercy; what they experienced across Europe, the Americas, Africa, Asia (and in Asia, particularly India), was the ruin of countless lives, uprooted ethnic groups and the brutal disappearance of hundreds of cultures, scriptures and art forms. 'With all your brags and boastings, where has Christianity succeeded without the sword?'[3] asked Swami Vivekananda of missionaries. As unpleasant as the reality may be, we must face it. If we are told, for instance, that Christianity and Islam preach peace, love and brotherhood, we must ask why their histories are full of the very opposite values. We must ask why in their obsessional quest for heaven, they strove so hard to turn this earth into a living hell. And we must keep asking until we get an honest answer.

It took Europe centuries to emerge from the Dark Ages that followed the rise of Christianity, and many thinkers of the fibre of a Voltaire, who in 1765 addressed the Church thus:

> You are right, gentlemen, do overrun the earth; it belongs to the strong or the clever who grabs hold of it. You have made the most of the times of ignorance, superstition, insanity, you have divested us from our heritages, trampled on us, you have grown fat on the substance of the wretched—dread the coming of the day of reason.[4]

And indeed, with the advent of enlightenment and reason, many announced the demise of religion—by which they meant the irrational belief in a god enthroned in heaven who keeps himself busy sending the greater part of humanity to eternal torture. Christianity, and to a lesser extent Islam, did lose much of their grip on the more advanced minds, and therefore much of their political power, and by the end of the nineteenth century were in a state of semi-slumber. Science, industry, commerce were the new gods. The good Lord was no longer needed, nor were his son and prophets. Order, prosperity and progress were at last going to reign in the world. That they never made it is another story, and with the increasing seething and boiling the earth has seen since the Second World War, the two slumbering titans have woken up again, like Kumbhakarna, as eager as ever to swallow the world.

Islam has expanded its horizons, thanks to colossal profits from the oil trade, a policy of rapid demographic growth, and a steady penetration into disadvantaged sections of Western societies. Christianity could not recover much of the lost ground in a largely materialistic West: 'Christianity has now almost been vanquished,'[5] one of its spokesmen recently pronounced. Missionaries, finding Westerners too tough to preach to, prefer to sell salvation to benighted Africans or Hindus. Hence Pope John Paul II's call for 'a great harvest of faith from Asia', made during his November 1999 visit to India. Hence the deployment of armies of missionaries, operating now with sophisticated strategies and a more canny language, and supported by colossal funds from the West. (According to figures released by India's Ministry of Home Affairs, foreign contributions amounting to tens of billions of rupees reach Christian organizations every year.[6])

More than ninety years ago, commenting on the methods of Christian missionaries in India, A.K. Coomaraswamy showed considerable foresight in this word of warning:

> All that money, social influence, educational bribery and misrepresentation can effect, is treated as legitimate. ... But even Hindu tolerance may some day be overstrained. If it be intolerance to force one's way into the house of another, it by no means necessarily follows that it would be intolerance on the owner's part to drive out the intruder.[7]

A State within the State

During my two-decade-long stay in the small district of the Nilgiris, which boasts some 350 churches, I saw Bible colleges sprouting, some of them offering fat cash rewards to students who committed themselves to proselytism. Government-aided (and therefore supposedly secular) Christian schools would start the day with prayers to our 'Father in Heaven', offer 'free tuitions' in the evening with heavy biblical content, and warmly encourage students to attend mass; Hindu girls were often prohibited from wearing a *bindī*. I was told of Christian activists visiting hospitals and threatening patients on their sickbeds with damnation if they did not convert, or barging into peaceful Hindu *satsang*s with shouts of 'Halleluiah!', confident that local authorities would be reluctant to intervene for fear of being called 'unsecular' or 'anti-minority'. Groups of young Christians would sometimes invade the place where I stayed, under the pretext of offering prayers—we would decline with thanks and show them out, but my middle- and lower-class Hindu friends were too polite to do so when they experienced the harassment of frequent visits to their homes by representatives of Seventh-Day Adventists, Jehovah's Witnesses, Unitarians, Open Bible Church, and dozens of other Christian denominations, with unsolicited preaching and glowing promises of material benefits upon conversion: cash rewards, promises of new houses, easy admissions to Christian-controlled schools, free treatment at Christian-controlled hospitals, etc. Reports of some poor Hindu yielding to the temptation came in with increasing frequency.

The disruption inflicted on India's social fabric in the name of 'religious freedom' by the 'soldiers of Christ', as they often call themselves, is the least concern of our leaders. Most of India's tribes have already suffered deep inroads, and are fast on the way to alienation, rootlessness and division—the bitter fruits of conversion. Tribal groups and other communities which had lived in relative peace and harmony for centuries suddenly find themselves divided into two opposite camps (we have seen in recent years the tensions among the Santhal and Dangs tribes of Orissa and Gujarat, and I could give examples of cultural alienation among tribes of the Nilgiris). Taught the virtues of separateness and unrest, they move on to the next logical step—separatism. This is painfully clear in India's Northeastern States, where the map of secessionist movements coincides with the regions of intense missionary activity. The same pattern is now reproduced in many parts of central India.

In 1956, the Niyogi Committee, appointed by the Madhya Pradesh government two years earlier, submitted its *Report of the Christian Missionary Activities Enquiry Committee*.[8] Its two volumes provided a massive documented study of proselytizing practices in the region; it should be prescribed reading for all those interested in the subject of religious freedom. A sample of its conclusions:

> Missionary organisations are so widespread in this country that they seem to constitute 'a State within the State'.[9]
> Enormous sums of foreign money flow into the country for Missionary work.... Conversions are mostly brought about by undue influence, misrepresentation, etc., or in other words not by conviction but by various inducements offered for proselytization in various forms....
> As conversion muddles the convert's sense of unity and solidarity with his society, there is a danger of his loyalty to his country and State being undermined....
> A vile propaganda against the religion of the majority community [i.e., Hinduism] is being systematically and deliberately carried on so as to create an apprehension of breach of public peace.
> Evangelization in India appears to be a part of the uniform world policy to revive Christendom for re-establishing Western supremacy and is not prompted by spiritual motives. The objective is apparently to create Christian minority pockets with a view to disrupt the solidarity of the non-Christian societies, and the mass conversions of a considerable section of Adivasis with this ulterior motive is fraught with danger to the security of the State.[10]

Over half a century later, we can see in India the results of this 'world policy', from Jharkhand to the Northeast. I could also cite an example from my own experience, in the Nilgiris again: in 2002, I came to know a Tamilian father in the Don Bosco organization, one of the richest and most active missions in India.

A self-styled environmental activist (which is how I met him), he was a nonconformist, wore jeans and a leather jerkin, and claimed to be an admirer of Swami Vivekananda and Sri Aurobindo. One evening, he confided in me that he was leaving the next day on one of his regular visits to Maharashtra tribals, telling them that tribes had 'no future within the Indian Union', and their only hope was therefore to 'take up guns' (his exact words). Ostensibly, of course, Don Bosco is an 'educational' organization. How much more such 'education' is India going to need before she breaks up into a hundred warring fragments?

Christian pamphlets and websites publish in great detail the regions they concentrate on, the reasons why they think conversions are easier to obtain there, district-wise statistics of non-Christians and Christians, how many of the latter are prepared to work for conversion, and so forth. One such website proclaimed a decade ago, 'Unreached peoples are being identified, researched, profiled, and adopted as targets of focused, fervent prayer and outreach with an urgency that is unprecedented.'[11] It then dilated on north India, because

> This part of the world is of enormous importance. The needs and the opportunities are staggering. ... The time is right. North India is poised to receive an outpouring of His grace and His glory. ...[12] North India is strategically important in completing the unfinished task of world evangelization.[13]

And coming to Varanasi, we got a sudden whiff of the nineteenth century: 'Many consider this city the very seat of Satan.'[14] Impressive statistics followed on the number of churches, baptisms, 'intercessors', etc., concluding that 'Research information on this part of India is available as never before.'[15] Similar campaigns targeting Hindu and Buddhist populations are visible in other Asian countries such as Sri Lanka, Nepal, Myanmar or Korea.

Islam adds a military dimension to the missionary one, with militants from Kashmir to Chechnya fighting for Islamic rule and asking for re-establishment of a Khalifat, in Central Asia to begin with, and London ultimately, where they dream of seeing 'the green flag atop Downing Street'.[16]

Alarm is palpably growing across Europe, where most leaders persist in the hope that multiculturalism will somehow take care of the problem. A fast dwindling hope, if we go by the German Chancellor Angela Merkel's admission, in October 2010, that Germany's multicultural approach has 'failed, utterly failed', leaving her country with 'integration' as the only option—but what if some sections do not wish to be integrated?

A Triple Task

The rich non-aggressive indigenous cultures of Amerindians, Africans, Polynesians, Australians or Indians represent the saner and deeper side of humanity. It behoves them to show the way to a third option—the way of the thousand-branched tree. Their immediate task is triple.

First, they must reject collective amnesia and study the history of religions—the conquering ones and the conquered. As the Belgian thinker François Perin wrote a few years ago,

> Europe's ancient civilization, chiefly developed on the shores of the Mediterranean, was not submerged by a religion of love, but indeed forcibly destroyed by a fanatical Church. ... It is easy to understand why the history of Christianity is so uncommon at school; the spread of such knowledge would have a disastrous effect on what is left of faith today.[17]

Forgetting the past only serves the aggressor, not the victim. The latter's motto should be not 'Forgive and Forget' but 'Lest We Forget'. And since we hear so much of apologies for past wrongs—most of them vague and without reparations—we may wonder why, for instance, independent India failed to ask for an apology from the Vatican and Portugal for the horrors inflicted during the Goan Inquisition. This would have been the natural way to show respect to those victims, and it is the way wounded generations in Canada, Ireland, Australia and elsewhere have followed.[18]

Secondly, non-aggressive cultures must avoid the snare of 'unity of religions'—an impossible proposition as long as any of them claims exclusive property of the truth and a divinely ordained mission to overrun the earth. Unity of religions and cultures is only possible between fraternal and mutually respectful faiths. If some belief systems explicitly reject such a unity, why waste time and mental clarity in trying to force it upon them? They are, at least, honest in claiming the exclusive (and mutually exclusive!) possession of the truth. Also, how can any interreligious dialogue be of any use if one side's declared objective is to have the whole world adopt its creed? Those are awkward facts that followers of non-proselytizing religions have been reluctant to face, often out of ignorance of the fundamental difference between a non-aggressive belief system and a world-conquering creed. Sometimes, indeed, we even find a lamb eager to defend the wolf's gospel.

As Sri Aurobindo said a century ago,

> The inner principle of Hinduism ... has been synthetic, acquisitive, inclusive. ... It is in the first place a non-dogmatic inclusive religion and would have taken even Islam and Christianity into itself, if they had tolerated the process.[19]

'If' ... Until proselytizing religions renounce all desire to conquer followers from other faiths, the latter will find a better use of their energies in nurturing their own withering tree.

They must also work to share, rediscover and revivify their common worldview and heritage—a considerable one—and formulate it anew, in the language of our age, not in that of bygone times. In so doing, they need not shrink from shedding externals that, however picturesque, have lost all usefulness. Any tradition that refuses to adapt itself to changing world conditions is doomed to extinction. Abandoning forms that have outlived their relevance can only help to keep the central spirit alive and evolving. A century ago, Sri Aurobindo, again, made this highly unorthodox statement: 'The soul of Hinduism languishes in an unfit body. Break the mould that the soul may live.'[20]

Lastly, the surviving ancient cultures of the world must strengthen their naturally fraternal bonds and join forces, realizing that in union there is strength. Strength not to conquer or convert, but simply to survive and enrich one another.

As always in human history, aggressive elements are winning short-term victories. And as always, what the conquered represent in the evolutionary experiment will outlive their conquerors.

Sri Aurobindo concluded a poem entitled 'The Tiger and the Deer' with these two lines:

> The mighty perish in their might;
> The slain survive the slayer.[21]

10

Dialogue among Civilizations: An Indic Perspective

WE are told that the world has shrunk to a 'global village'. Indeed, if that is so, there is hardly any room left for East or West, much less for distinct civilizations; perhaps the brave new world was only meant to be a noisy and crowded market-place, after all. In that case, all our questioning, discoursing and dialoguing will soon die down in a well-regulated monoculture and one-track life, in which cultures will be no more than an academic curiosity of the past.

But that is unlikely to happen. Our very nature rebels against uniformity and drives to multiplicity. Not just human nature: all of nature does, from viruses and bacteria to galaxies. If one fact is certain, it is that humanity will continue to experiment with many lines, village or no village, globalization or not. That is what postmodern exponents of pluralism and multiculturalism have realized. But how do we ensure that the various lines and cultures still produce a harmony and not a cacophonous bloodbath?

In dealing with such questions, the now dominant academic approach is to steamroller various lines of human experience onto a two-dimensional map from which all reliefs have disappeared; it then tries to read the map as best it can, with the verdict naturally reflecting the personal cultural preferences or persuasions of the particular map-reader. At best, we get a flattened vision in which a motley crowd of cultures abut one another, and this 'diversity' seems to become an end it itself. Just after 9/11, Ibn Warraq, a well-known critic of Islam, protested against such levelling:

> Multiculturalism is based on some fundamental misconceptions. First, there is the erroneous and sentimental belief that all cultures, deep down, have the same values; or if these values are different, they are all equally worthy of respect. Multiculturalism, being the child of relativism, is incapable of criticising cultures, of making cross-cultural judgments. The truth is that not all cultures have the same values, and not all values are worthy of respect.[1]

A forthright and, of course, politically incorrect statement, which we need to explore, as it is intimately related to the terms under which any fruitful 'dialogue of civilizations' can be conducted.

The Titans and the Sage?

Before we do so, I may propose an alternative approach, which is to look upon humanity as nothing more than an experiment— by what Experimenter, with what primary ingredients, catalysts and reacting conditions, are questions I will leave aside. We are concerned here with the few dominant lines that stand out in this wide-ranging, long-lasting, manifold process.

In its expansion and brilliant achievements, the West has been driven by an aggressive conquering impulse; it has been *rajas* in action and is ever impelled to seek and overrun the earth. It was founded on military and political expansionism, as we can see with ancient Egypt, Akkad, Greece, Persia or Rome, the Hittites or the Vikings. The advent of Christianity turned this into a politico-religious expansionism, which, refurbished, was later the engine of colonial conquests, too. The postcolonial age has focused more on the manipulation of markets and economic expansionism, but the two earlier forms have hardly disappeared—they have only become more discreet, more adept at garbing the old impelling force in modern terminology: today's political language is one of 'constructive engagement', 'defence of national interests', 'spread of democracy', the building of a 'new world order', etc.; the religious drive still speaks openly of evangelization, conquest of continents for the faith, but generally prefers the more artful nomenclature of 'education', 'social service', 'social liberation', 'empowerment', and of course 'human rights'—the same human rights it denied in the name of God when it held the reins of power.

Politics, religion and economy are thus the three branches of the West's *trishūla*, one and the same phenomenon at bottom— a prodigious generator of strife and instability, upheaval and brutality, but also a tireless explorer, shaper and creator, a first-rate catalyst for change and evolution. Islam, with its Judeo-Christian foundations, has behaved in much the same way: though its cultural background and outer forms are more Oriental than Western, it has been a politico-religious power machine conquering minds and nations, again sowing destruction as well as change in its wake.

Religions, cultures, societies, nations, empires disappeared under the onslaught of those two Titans. The experiment may seem cruel, but in reality, it is neither moral nor judgemental.

Another line of human experiment has been that of Asia and more particularly India. It would be tempting to say that if the West is rājasic, Asia is both tāmasic and sāttvic. But that is not likely to account for the complexity of reality. Nor is it true that the West is predominantly materialistic and intellectual while the East is primarily spiritualistic: until recent centuries, Eastern civilizations were more developed materially than the West, and produced many more and deeper intellectuals. Nor also is it correct that the East yearns for peace in contrast to the West's love of strife: warring in India and the rest of Asia has been an almost permanent feature. So where exactly does the difference, if there is one, lie?

Looking at India, we saw an attempt to place a comprehensive spiritual culture at the centre of all life, while monotheistic religions dug an abyss between the divine and the mundane, the heavenly and the earthly, the creator and the created. India's expansionism was rarely as a military phenomenon; it was, as Sri Aurobindo put it almost a century ago, 'an invasion of peace and not of war, for to spread a spiritual civilisation by force and physical conquest, the vaunt or the excuse of modern imperialism, would have been uncongenial to the ancient cast of her mind and temperament and the idea underlying her Dharma.'[2]

Dialogue Yesterday and Today

An 'invasion of peace' sums up the whole issue and the difference in civilizational behaviour. For it is not as if civilizations have not dialogued in the past; they have never stopped doing so. The Egyptian with the Mesopotamian, the Mesopotamian with the Dilmunian and the Elamite, the Greek with the Egyptian, the Roman with the Greek, the Chinese with the Central Asian, Korean or Japanese, the Arab with the Asian and the European, and the Indian with all of them and a few more.

If, today, we hear so much about the need for a 'dialogue of civilizations', it is out of necessity—and fear. Perhaps for the first time in recent history, the West feels profoundly threatened. Columbus or Vespucci did not exactly invite America's 'savages' to a civilizational powwow around a cup of cocoa, nor did the Portuguese, the Dutch, the French or the British feel the need for an intellectual exchange with African slaves or with India's natives. Today's call for a dialogue is mostly in the context of a perceived threat: with Islam—clearly a physical threat—and to a lesser extent with China, a rising economic rival. India is beginning to receive attention only insofar as she might become another economic 'superpower'. Surely, we have heard no loud call for a dialogue with African cultures, Amazonian tribes or Australia's aborigines. Power thus remains the first rule of engagement, which means that we have an interface of barbarisms rather than of civilized entities. A century ago, the sociologist Benjamin Kidd opined that civilization had not yet arrived, and that Western civilization 'is as yet scarcely more than glorified savagery.'[3] Have things much improved?

To state the obvious is not to be anti-Western—we can ill afford any 'anti-ism' when we are all teetering on the edge of extinction—and if late in the day and for the wrong reasons, the process of dialogue must be welcomed, not with a naïve hope that it will produce quick results, overnight wisdom and all-round peace, but because it is valuable in itself, an exploration that, at the least, offers a challenge worthy of a humanity in search of new definitions, a new language and ultimately a new nature.

For such a process to offer any hope, two conditions will have to be met. They are so self-evident as to be banal, yet offer a supreme difficulty when we look at them from the point of view of the 'dialoguee'—for it soon becomes apparent that current notions of dialogue hinge around a dialoguer-dialoguee interface, not an exchange between equal partners.

Such, in fact, is the first condition: a true respect of difference, an absence of any sense of superiority, racial or cultural, an openness that enables one to appreciate and attune to an alien culture. (That, again, has little to do with the much-vaunted 'tolerance', which rather suggests an effort to veneer one's contempt for the Other.) True, we hear a lot more today about native cultures of America, Africa or Australia, restoration of tribal lands or apologies for past genocides. And we find more and more individuals and groups working towards lasting cross-cultural understanding and interaction.[4] Yet, seeing the persistence of the old prejudices and sometimes their resurgence, as in the fresh rise of racism and anti-Semitism in parts of Europe, it is clear that we have a long way to go.

The second condition is far more difficult: an end to all forms of political, economic, religious or cultural aggression. If the will for dialogue were sincere, real non-aggression, not only in deed but in intent, would automatically follow. Instead, the picture the West gives us—India and the rest of the Third World—has the following components:

- politically, the proliferation of shrill 'strategic doctrines' affirming the right to strike at any perceived enemy, but denying the same right to less powerful nations;
- economically, the luring of weaker economies into a debt trap and the consequent manipulation of their markets and depletion of their natural resources, with the result that, by way of debt servicing, Third World countries today contribute more to the World Bank than do Western countries, in effect paying for the West's wasteful lifestyles;
- on the religious level, myriads of missionary campaigns ever ready to raise an outcry in the name of 'religious freedom' if their efforts are resisted—religious freedom being in effect taken to mean not the respect of other religions, but the freedom to stamp them out; and
- culturally, an aggressive spread of 'American culture', riding piggyback on media power and economic conquest, and forcing generally ill-prepared traditional cultures to clash with 'modernity', often at the cost of their disappearance.

Should this overview appear sweeping or lopsided, it would help to narrow it down to the case that is of immediate concern to us, that of India's interface with the West in recent decades.

The West and India

Politically, India has for decades been a victim not only of terrorism but of the most biased treatment by the U.S.A., the U.K. and a few other Western countries. In the last three decades, hundreds of murderous attacks on Kashmiri pandits and the 'ethnic cleansing' that drove them out of their home state hardly drew a few whispers. Massive and incontrovertible evidence of Pakistani support to numerous acts of terrorism in India from Coimbatore to Mumbai and Hyderabad to the Lok Sabha, produced only a few homilies on the need for restraint, the more trigger-happy Western nations being the loudest, while supplies of weapons to Pakistan continued in order 'to combat terrorism'. Naturally, India has only herself to blame ultimately for putting up with such constant bloodletting, but the fact is that the West remains the referee of the political game with two sets of rules: one for the self-appointed 'leading nations', another for the rest. The very structure of the United Nations with its fundamentally flawed and undemocratic Security Council is evidence enough that might is right.

Economically, colossal diversion of resources to corruption and a wasteful bureaucracy and public sector forced India to beg at the door of the World Bank; while she was yearning for liberalization after decades of the most regressive Socialist regime, the sudden arrival of the steamroller of globalization has spelt doom for native small industries and thrust upon thrifty Indians the most wasteful consumerist habits. Now that Western economy has shown its feet of clay and deep-rooted ill-health, one wonders whether there is still time for India to find her own path to sustainable development.

The religious field is equally problematic; I have sufficiently described dominant strategies in previous chapters. The very existence—or rather survival—of a predominantly Hindu society appears to be unacceptable to the two conquering religions. To establish their 'tolerance', some Christian leaders have of late been calling for 'interfaith dialogues'. If they were based on a genuine desire to understand other cultures and religions, to achieve mutual enrichment or at least harmonious coexistence, such dialogues would be a natural part of a fruitful interface. But with the Roman Catholic Church, for instance, calling for a 'harvest of faith' from Asia in the third millennium, it is hard to see the usefulness of such initiatives: laudable as they may appear on the surface, they are bound to lead nowhere. They are not 'dialogues', except in the sense of a dialogue of the wolf with the lamb.

In India's case, the problem is compounded by misportrayals in the cultural field by Western (and sometimes Indian) academia and the media. All too often, it is considered acceptable and desirable to ridicule some aspect of Indian culture, to submit some Hindu god or saint to psychoanalysis so as to reach the most grotesque conclusions, and in a general way to trace India's social evils to her religion. There are still in India and abroad many genuine students of Indian civilization, content to do their work silently, while the more visible and sometimes vociferous 'experts' spend a lifetime denigrating the object of their studies. Indian scholars generally maintain an attitude of indifference, having seen 'a long list of misunderstanding works abusive of our country and its culture', but as John Woodroffe wrote in 1918, in a masterly rejoinder to one such work, 'This indifferent attitude is a mistake. India cannot at the present moment allow any charges against her to go unanswered.'[5] Today, a few scholars, thinkers and writers, from inside and outside the academia, have taken up the gauntlet.[6] This is all the more urgent since, as colonial history showed eloquently, the denigration of a culture is only the first form of aggression against the nation that holds it—with other forms waiting to follow. As Woodroffe again put it very lucidly:

> The question of the value of Indian culture is not merely an academic one. It has present practical bearing on the future of India and the World. ... Is Indian civilization about to be renewed or to be broken up—another instance of that disintegration which has followed the introduction of Western civilization amongst Eastern peoples? ... In every way, the coming assault on Hindu civilization will be the greatest which it has ever had to endure in the whole course of its long history.[7]

This 'assault' is no longer 'coming'. Expectedly, it targets India's weak points to start with. The result of many strands and conflicting pulls, ancient, traditional and modern, with endless vertical and horizontal variety, Indian society is an infinitely complex evolving process, with numerous black spots but also dynamic undercurrents of change. Assume we painted a portrait

of Western society by concentrating on its mafias, its large desti-
tute classes, drifting communities, dysfunctional families, rootless
youths, on drug abuse, all-pervading violence and high levels of
criminality, on resurgent racism and anti-Semitism. Assume we
added a long list of sickening facts, from the feeding of cattle
with meat from infected cattle, or of calves with blood from
slaughtered cattle,[8] to the Church's endless sex scandals and the
destroyed generations of native children in Christian schools in
Canada, the U.S.A. and Australia. Would the resulting picture
be a truthful one, let alone legitimate? Yet that is exactly the
method we have seen used in recent years not only in the field of
Indology ('South Asian studies', as the discipline now calls itself),
but in English-language Indian media and its Western counterparts.

One saving grace in the interface between the West and India
is found at the popular level: people-to-people contact, as the
phrase goes. Here, we have an organic process which, thankfully,
escapes all control, as it has done since Harappan times and
perhaps earlier. In a way, that is a truer interface than the
academic, and if it is allowed to pursue its present expanding
trend, it will offer not only a corrective to the limitations of the
academic debate, but a healthy example of civilizational dialogue.
One only wishes that, in the process, India were exposed to a
few beneficial traits of the West, such as civic discipline and ecological awareness, rather than the sort of degenerate non-culture
flooding the country.

The Indic Model

In the twentieth century, leading Western nations thought they
could offer a viable model of integration of non-White, non-
Western communities: the U.S.A.'s 'melting pot' model, which
has worked up to a point, also the 'assimilation' that former
colonial masters like France or Britain boasted of. Today, with
the growing assertiveness of multiculturalism—the 'mosaic' or
'salad bowl' model—the emphasis has shifted to preserving the

distinct identities of those communities.[9] There should be nothing wrong with either approach, except that they often appear to clash in practice. Recent controversies in France about the wearing of religious symbols, the veil and the *burqa*, in Italy about the display of crucifixes in public schools, in Switzerland about banning the construction of new minarets, the demand by some Muslim groups in Europe and in the U.S.A. for separate laws in tune with the Shariat, are pointers to the West's growing inability to deal with the problem of 'minorities' and to harmonize multiculturalism with its concept of secularism. Indeed, nothing was more ironic than an Italian cardinal recently fuming against the 'tyranny of minorities'[10] (Muslim ones, in that case), when in the Indian context we hear the same voices loudly calling for special rights and privileges for minorities!

If these trends are any indication, rather than dialogues we are on the way back to the Tower of Babel. Indeed, delicate ears opine that we are already there. And it is not hard to grasp the cause of the whole confusion: diversity and pluralism are all very well, but they cannot reach a harmony without finding some underlying unity, and hopes that some loose humanism could provide it have repeatedly been belied.

For long periods of time and on a large geographical scale, India has shown a unique ability to harmonize her regional cultures; different rituals, customs, languages, ethnic origins were no bar, as long as the central spirit of the land—a ready acceptance of otherness and a worldview that can merge with any non-dogmatic culture—was respected.

India's model, if she has one, is neither the melting pot nor the mosaic, but the thousand-branched tree of the Rig Veda: an endless diversity growing out of a common trunk. I am tempted to evoke the proverbial banyan tree, constantly replanting itself, but unlike the banyan, Indian culture allows a lot of undergrowth to thrive.

The New World Disorder

The world is not going to adopt the Indic model overnight. It must first reach the end of its line of experiment. It could veer towards a less destructive line only if conquering creeds learned the secret of lasting peaceful coexistence, which they are unwilling or unable to do within their current power structures. We do find many Muslim moderates, and more Christian ones, who would happily live with more liberal versions of their religion, free from their institutionalized straitjackets, but their voices, though important, have not reached critical mass.

How the present turmoil will end remains the secret of the gods—although, clearly, the answers will come from circumstances rather than from intellectual debates. Here is how, almost a century ago, Sri Aurobindo analysed the problem:

> That stupendous effort [of the West] is over; it has not yet frankly declared its bankruptcy, but it is bankrupt. It is sinking in a cataclysm as gigantic and as unnatural as the attempt which gave it birth. On the other hand, the exaggerated spirituality of the Indian effort has also registered a bankruptcy; we have seen how high individuals can rise by it, but we have seen also how low a race can fall which in its eagerness to seek after God ignores His intention in humanity. Both the European and the Indian attempt were admirable, the Indian by its absolute spiritual sincerity, the European by its severe intellectual honesty and ardour for the truth; both have accomplished miracles; but in the end God and Nature have been too strong for the Titanism of the human spirit and for the Titanism of the human intellect. The salvation of the human race lies in a more sane and integral development of the possibilities of mankind in the individual and in the community. The safety of Europe has to be sought in the recognition of the spiritual aim of human existence, otherwise she will be crushed by the weight of her own unillumined knowledge and soulless organisation. The safety of Asia lies in the recognition of

the material mould and mental conditions in which that
aim has to be worked out, otherwise she will sink deeper
into the slough of despond of a mental and physical incom-
petence to deal with the facts of life and the shocks of a
rapidly changing movement.[11]

So far, the West has been half deaf to its own saner voices; the
dialogue of civilizations remains a non-starter, because it has been
neither a dialogue nor between truly civilized entities. Whether
it does take off or not depends on the collective will behind the
human experiment and the course of circumstances; for only if
those are compelling enough will the destructive course we have
adopted be altered. As Mother, Sri Aurobindo's companion and
co-worker, once put it,

> The only hope for the future is in a change of man's con-
> sciousness and the change is bound to come. But it is left
> to men to decide if they will collaborate in this change or
> if it will have to be enforced upon them by the power of
> crushing circumstances.[12]

Almost half a century after she made this statement, we can
better understand the shape of the 'crushing circumstances' to
come: an undeclared Third World War among a hundred rather
than two or three blocks. Oil wars, market wars, currency wars,
food wars, water wars appear likelier with every passing year. On
the philosophical side, the collapse of our last ideals, humani-
tarian and Gandhian included, is as unavoidable as the collapse
of the ideals of Europe's intellectuals before the Second World
War. In reality, from an evolutionary perspective, their failure is
desirable, for they are half luminous but half dark, half enlightened but half blind, and relentless evolution always sweeps such
palliatives aside to confront us with the real problem.

Can anything deflect this apparently unstoppable race to ugly
self-destruction? Perhaps only a greater cataclysm. A chain reaction of ecological disasters, the collapse of health systems and a
global economic burnout are a few distinct possibilities—we
have had enough recent hints of all three. However unpleasant,

'alarmist' such prospects may appear to weak minds, this 'great implosion', as Pierre Thuillier called it in 1995,[13] would be merely logical. Whether it is a sudden implosion or a gradual grinding to a halt, whether it takes place in five, ten or twenty years, whether we should desire it or not are not the issues. 'The whole of the Western world is on a volcano which may burst tomorrow,'[14] said Swami Vivekananda upon his return to India.

What can India do in this scenario? It is not inept governmental policies or catchwords such as 'democracy', 'secularism' or 'non-violence' that will help. Swami Vivekananda called for strength and energy above all else, and spoke of using 'aggression, aggression in a religious sense only . . . [to] find the common bases of Hinduism and awaken the national consciousness to them.'[15] Sri Aurobindo wrote in 1918, 'I believe in an aggressive and expanding, not in a narrowly defensive and self-contracting Hinduism.'[16]

What these two politically incorrect seers meant by 'Hinduism' was not what most of us have in mind. They meant, simply, the exploration and growth of our human potential, the tools developed over millennia to lead us to the one discovery that really matters: ourselves. Our true self, our true fulfilment. We can all be part of this great adventure, for as Vivekananda put it,

> One atom in this universe cannot move without dragging the whole world along with it.[17]

Or Sri Aurobindo:

> [India] can, if she will, give a new and decisive turn to the problems over which all mankind is labouring and stumbling, for the clue to their solutions is there in her ancient knowledge. Whether she will rise or not to the height of her opportunity in the renaissance which is coming upon her, is the question of her destiny.[18]

Epilogue

IN the last two decades—perhaps coinciding with India's phase of 'liberalization'—I have seen and talked to many Indians, young ones especially, in the throes of what is commonly called an identity crisis: beneath apparently successful studies or careers, they rarely know who or what they are, what they can or should expect from life (beyond a fat salary), who their role models should be, or how they should orient their lives.

Also—or perhaps above all—they do not know what it means to be Indian. They are 'patriotic', in the sense that they are ready to go into a frenzy if the country's cricket team is in a tight spot, but this patriotism, good or bad, is not India's privilege. Is there something more to Indianness?

Through this book's meanderings, I have tried to touch on what constitutes Indian identity. Without attempting a strict definition, it may be summarized as a sense of civilizational belonging. Let me propose twelve manifestations of Indian civilization that any Indian, regardless of religion, ethnic group, language and customs, can relate to and legitimately feel proud of. I do not claim that India is wholly defined through these achievements, but they do provide pointers to what she has sought to achieve and express as a civilization.

1. **The Indus–Sarasvatī civilization** (third millennium BCE): largely peaceful, with a remarkable civic discipline despite the invisibility of rulers; high technical achievements in metallurgy, crafts, town planning, water harvesting, agriculture; an interface with at least five other bronze-age civilizations; effective cultural integration of the subcontinent's Northwest.

2. **Experiments with democracy** (from the first millennium BCE at least): early republicanism, community-based and dharma-based governance resulting in stability and relative prosperity; functional systems of assemblies with a degree of representation and participation.

3. **Peaceful cultural integration of India**: early cultural concept of India; spread and ready acceptance of the Epics across the subcontinent; networks of sacred sites adding up to a sacred geography; a two-way organic process controlled by no authority or political power, which stamped out no local culture.

4. **India's interface with other civilizations**: generous contributions to other civilizations in religion, philosophy, art, literature, science, technologies, from Far East and Southeast Asia to Central Asia, China, the Near East, Greece, etc.; a peaceful interaction that suppressed no pre-existing culture.

5. **India's perspectives on nature**: sacredness of the creation; no chasm between nature and the divine; milking, not 'conquering' nature; respect for all life forms; simplicity of living; excellence in water structures.

6. **Spiritual freedom and pluralism**: acceptance of otherness: *svabhāva* (individual nature) and *svadharma* (individual law or truth); freedom to strike out a new path; a celebration of diversity.

7. **Scientific and technological advances**: advanced concepts and pioneering developments in mathematics, astronomy, medicine, chemistry, architecture, technologies.

8. **Spiritualization of all life**: literature, music, dance, painting, architecture as expressions of the divinity.

9. **Integral development and fulfilment**: systems of yoga, elaborate methods of self-exploration and self-realization; transformation of the human person.

10. **The nineteenth-century renaissance**: in spirituality, literature, thought, art and science.

11. **India's impact on the West**: nineteenth-century outflow from India reflected in European and American literature,

thought and humanism; a spirituality compatible with
modern science; impact on the New Age movement; the
spread of yoga, meditation, concepts of rebirth and karma.
12. **Survival of Indian civilization**: difficult to account for, but
in the end perhaps the most shining accomplishment of all.

These twelve achievements denote a culture with enviable
dynamics, an indefatigable creativity and a discreet generosity,
which any civilization would be legitimately proud of. How this
culture could at the same time appear so frail as to allow the
degree of degradation we see in India's national life remains a
troubling question. Not merely all-pervasive corruption, the
hypocritical deference to decaying institutions, the cowardly
turning away from real issues, but, perhaps more irretrievably,
the loss of original thinking and aesthetic sense — two of classical
India's crown jewels. An objective assessment of our average
politician's and bureaucrat's intellectual level and a glance at our
hideous cities ought to convince a sensitive observer of the extent
of the damage.

To be sure, there is no point in being nostalgic about the
past—golden ages exist only in our imagination—but an ignorance of the past is even less justified if that past can help us to
understand ourselves. The first function of cultural history, I
would suggest, is to give us a sense of belonging: from separate
individuals lost in time and space, we become part of a stream
of civilization.

At a collective level, if we lose sight of this core of India, her
political unity can only be seen as an artifice. The country's
integrity becomes questionable—and is being questioned in this
twenty-first century, with increasing brutality. Cultural concepts
have a knack of spilling out of sedate academic circles, their true
worth tested by the bullet. A deep red scar runs across the map,
from Kerala to the Northeast, while a section of our intelligentsia
rejoices at the prospect of India's further dismemberment and our
rulers sleep and betray the trust of the common Indian.

But if India does falls apart, the loss will not merely be that of a land where genuine and profound seekers walked and toiled. It may mean the end of one line of experiment for humanity. For in the world of the ideal—a world more real than our compartmentalized minds imagine—India is more than a piece of land; she is a continent in humanity's inner geography: a quest for the true, the beautiful, the lovable.

The quest must continue.

More than forty years ago, on 3 February 1968, Mother gave this message:

> India has become the symbolic representation of all the difficulties of modern mankind.
> India will be the land of its resurrection—the resurrection to a higher and truer life.

Today, the first part of this message is conspicuous enough; we must hope that we will live to see its second part realized.

Notes*

Introduction: Is Indian Culture Obsolete?

1. *Letters of Swami Vivekananda*°, p. 164.
2. Sri Aurobindo, *The Renaissance in India*°, p. 56.
3. James Vicini, 'U.S. has most prisoners in world due to tough laws', *Yahoo News*, 9 December 2006, rss.crossmap.com/article/u-s-has-most...in.../ story140082.htm (retrieved 20.01.2010).
4. See two reports: 'Gun Violence in the United States', http://ojjdp.ncjrs.gov/pubs/gun_violence/sect01.html, and 'Gun Statistics', www.wagv.org/gun-violence.php (both retrieved 20.08.2010).
5. Swami Vivekananda, *Lectures from Colombo to Almora*°, pp. 64–65.
6. Pierre Thuillier, *La Grande Implosion: Rapport sur l'effondrement de l'Occident 1999–2002*, Fayard, Paris, 1995, pp. 17–19. (My apologies to the author for taking the liberty to use the present tense in this extract, while his whole book is written in the past tense, being humorously presented as a 'report' written in 2081 by a commission of inquiry on the West's collapse.)
7. André Malraux, quoted by Pierre Thuillier, op. cit., p. 55.
8. Will Durant, *Story of Our Civilization*, vol. I, *Our Oriental Heritage*, Simon & Schuster, New York, 1954, p. 633.
9. Sri Aurobindo, 'A Preface on National Education', *Early Cultural Writings*, vol. 1 in *The Complete Works of Sri Aurobindo*, Sri Aurobindo Ashram, Pondicherry, 2003, p. 422.
10. See Michel Danino, *The Lost River: On the Trail of the Sarasvati*°, ch. 10.
11. Figures are provided by Angus Maddison and Paul Kennedy, quoted by P. Kanagasabapathi, *Indian Models of Economy, Business and Management*, Prentice–Hall of India, New Delhi, 2nd edn, 2009, pp. 35–40.
12. Will Durant, *The Case for India*, Simon & Schuster, New York, 1930, p. 2. An excellent summary of the British plunder of India, with facts and figures, can be found in P. Kanagasabapathi, *Indian Models of Economy, Business and Management*, op. cit.

---

* To quickly locate the desired reference, follow the page range in the header at the top of the page. Works mentioned in the following Suggested Further Readings figure here under their titles alone, without subtitles or bibliographical details; to make this clear, their titles are followed here by the symbol ° (thus, *India's Rebirth*°).

13. Will Durant, *The Case for India*, op. cit., p. 1.
14. Ibid., p. 7.
15. Ibid., p. 2.
16. Ibid., p. 55.
17. Sri Aurobindo, *The Renaissance in India*°, p. 58.
18. Sri Aurobindo, *India's Rebirth*°, p. 202.
19. Rabindranath Tagore, *The Centre of Indian Culture*°, pp. 31–34.
20. Sri Aurobindo, *India's Rebirth*°, p. 110.
21. Swami Vivekananda, *Lectures from Colombo to Almora*°, p. 214.

1. India's Scientific Mind

1. *Āryabhatīya of Āryabhata*, K.S. Shukla and K.V. Sarma, (eds), Indian National Science Academy, New Delhi, 1976, II.10.
2. Ibid., II.4–5.
3. Ibid., I.12.
4. Ibid., I.7. Āryabhata defines the *yojana* as 8,000 human heights or about 13.6 km, which gives a circumference of the earth equal to 1050 x 13.5 x π ≈ 44,860 km; this is 12 per cent greater than the correct value of 40,075 km. His value for the moon's diameter (315 *yojanas*) is too large: 4,252 km instead of 3,476 km (22 per cent in excess). However his values for the Sun and the planets are far too small.
5. Ibid., IV.6–10. Contrary to some interpretations, however, Āryabhata's system remained basically geocentric; heliocentrism appears first with Parameshvara (c. 1360–1455) and more clearly with his disciple Nīlakantha Somayāji (1444–1545), two celebrated Kerala astronomers who predate Copernicus. See M.S. Sriram, K. Ramasubramanian and M.D. Srinivas, *500 years of Tantrasangraha: A Landmark in the History of Astronomy,* Inter-University Center & Indian Institute of Advanced Study, Shimla, 2002.
6. Roger Billard, *L'Astronomie indienne*, École Française d'Extrême-Orient, Paris, 1971, p. 83.
7. *Āryabhatīya of Āryabhata*, op. cit., IV.37: 'The Moon eclipses the Sun and the great Shadow of the Earth eclipses the Moon.'
8. Ibid., I.3, from which Āryabhata's value for the sidereal day works out to 23 h 56 m 4.1 s, almost identical to the real value of 23 h 56 m 4.091 s.
9. Ibid., IV.5, although Āryabhata wrongly attributes the same property to stars.
10. Ibid., III.11.
11. Carl Sagan, *Cosmos*, Ballantine Books, New York, 1980, pp. 213–14.
12. *Āryabhatīya of Āryabhata*, op. cit., I.13.
13. Georges Ifrah, *The Universal History of Numbers*°, vol. 2, p. 209 (as I find the published English version inadequate here, this is my translation from the original French, *Histoire universelle des chiffres*, Robert Laffont, Paris, 1994). Most of the following information on large numbers is drawn from this book.
14. E.g. 4.4.11. Let us note that all larger numbers (and many of the smaller ones too) mentioned in the Vedic texts are multiples of ten, a clear indication that

from the earliest stages, India had a decimal view of numbers. Interestingly, the Indus–Sarasvatī civilization also shows evidence of partial use of the decimal system in town planning, street and house proportions, also in its weight system. Centuries later, this evolved into the decimal place-value system of numeral notation, one of India's greatest contributions in the scientific field.

15. Georges Ifrah, *The Universal History of Numbers°*, vol. 2. I could not locate this passage in the English edition; it is my translation from the original French, *Histoire universelle des chiffres*, op. cit., vol. 1, p. 953.

16. Georges Ifrah, *The Universal History of Numbers°*, vol. 2, p. 147 (but in my translation).

17. According to Ifrah, ibid, p. 139. (My calculation of the *paramāṇu's* length would be slightly different, but that would hardly change the order of magnitude of the result.)

18. S. Balachandra Rao, *Indian Astronomy: an Introduction°*, p. 55.

19. I have adapted here the version given by Georges Ifrah, *The Universal History of Numbers°*, vol. 1, pp. 633 ff.

20. This quotation as well as the gist of the account are taken from http://klein.math.okstate.edu/IndrasPearls/cover-art/ (retrieved on 12.2.2010)

21. David Mumford, Caroline Series and David Wright, *Indra's Pearls: The Vision of Felix Klein,* Cambridge University Press, 2002.

22. F. David Peat, *Infinite Potential: The Life and Times of David Bohm,* Basic Books, 1997, p. 186.

23. Georges Ifrah, *The Universal History of Numbers°*, vol. 2, p. 134.

24. This number is obtained by multiplying the number of revolutions of the Moon in a yuga of 4,320,000 years, which Āryabhata tells us is 57,753,336, by 12 and again by 30, 60 and 10 (*Āryabhaṭīya of Āryabhata,* op. cit., I.6).

25. Āryabhata's *yojana* is about 13.6 km (see note 4 above); 12,474,720,576,000 *yojana*s is therefore 17 10^{13} km, which yields a diameter of roughly 5.4 10^{13} km. The diameter of Pluto's orbit (if we take the solar system to mean up to Pluto) is 1.18 10^{10} km.

26. Quoted by K.S. Shukla and K.V. Sarma, *Āryabhaṭīya of Āryabhata,* op. cit., p. 12.

27. These figures are taken from the *Encyclopaedia Britannica,* electronic edn, 1997, under the article 'Stars and Star Clusters: Light from the Stars'.

28. See T.R.N. Rao and Subhash Kak, (eds), 'The Speed of Light and Puranic Cosmology' in *Computing Science in Ancient India,* Center for Advanced Computer Studies, University of Southwestern Louisiana, 1998, Indian repr. Munshiram Manoharlal, New Delhi, 2000.

29. Rig Veda, 1.50.4. 'Swift and all beautiful are you, O Surya, maker of the light, illumining all the radiant realm'.

30. A.K. Bag, *History of Technology in India,* Indian National Science Academy, New Delhi, 1997, vol. 1, pp. 665–68.

31. S. Balachandra Rao, *Indian Astronomy: an Introduction,* op. cit., p. 55.

32. Subhash Kak, *The Astronomical Code of the Rgveda,* Munshiram Manoharlal, New Delhi, 2000, ch. 6.

33. Ibid, ch. 9.
34. Holger Wanzke, 'Axis systems and orientation at Mohenjo-daro' in M. Jansen and G. Urban, (eds), *Interim Reports on Fieldwork Carried out at Mohenjo-daro, Pakistan 1982–83,* German Research Project Mohenjo-daro & Roma, Istituto Italiano Per Il Medio Ed Estremo Oriente, Aachen, 1984, vol. II, pp. 33–44.
35. Erkka Maula, 'The Calendar Stones from Mohenjo-daro' in ibid., vol. I, pp. 159–70.
36. J. McKim Malville and Lalit M. Gujral, *Ancient Cities, Sacred Skies: Cosmic Geometries and City Planning in Ancient India,* Indira Gandhi National Centre for the Arts and Aryan Books International, New Delhi, 2000.
37. *Ashtāngahridayasamhita,* 14.51, information and translation by courtesy of Dr. P. Ram Manohar.
38. *The Mahabharata of Krishna-Dwaipayana Vyasa,* tr. Kisari Mohan Ganguli, Vana Parva, ch. 207, first edn in the 1890s; republ. Munshiram Manoharlal, New Delhi, 2000, vol. I, p. 432.
39. *Shāndilya Upanishad,* 2.2.
40. *Āryabhatīya of Āryabhata,* op. cit., IV.49.

2. India's Gifts to the World

1. Sri Aurobindo, *The Renaissance in India°,* p. 8.
2. Will Durant, *The Case for India,* Simon &Schuster, New York, 1930, p. 4.
3. Sylvain Lévi, quoted by Jawaharlal Nehru, *Discovery of India,* Jawaharlal Nehru Memorial Fund and OUP, New Delhi, 1981, p. 210.
4. Peter Francis, 'Early Historic South India and the International Maritime Trade', in *Man and Environment,* vol. XXVII, no. 1, Pune, January–June 2002, p. 159. This issue of *Man and Environment* is a special issue titled 'Indian Ocean in Antiquity', with many valuable articles on ancient contacts across the Indian Ocean.
5. Pliny the Elder, *Natural History,* quoted in Rosa Maria Cimino, (ed.), *Ancient Rome and India,* Istituto Italiano Per Il Medio Ed Estremo Oriente and Italian Embassy Cultural Centre, New Delhi, p. 141.
6. Among the scholars who have argued for ancient contacts between America and the 'Old World', let us mention Robert Heine-Geldern, Gordon F. Ekholm, David H. Kelley, Kornelia B. Giesing and Karl Dieter Gartelmann. Graeme R. Kearsley's recent work *Mayan Genesis: South Asian Myths, Migrations and Iconography in Mesoamerica,* Yelsraek, 2001, provides an overview of the issue. An interesting paper is Neil Steede and David J. Eccott, 'Comalcalco: A Case for Pre-Columbian Transoceanic Contact', *Migration and Diffusion,* vol. 1, issue no. 5, 2001, pp. 76–111.
7. H.G. Rawlinson, 'Early Contacts between India and Europe', in A.L. Basham, (ed.), *A Cultural History of India°,* p. 426.
8. Quoted by W.H. Siddiqi, 'India's Contribution to Arab Civilization', in *India's Contribution to World Thought and Culture°,* p. 583.

9. Most points in this section are from: (a) R.C. Majumdar's ch. XXIV in *The Age of Imperial Unity*, vol. 2 in *The History and Culture of the Indian People°*; (b) *India's Contribution to World Thought and Culture°*; (c) *Imprints of Indian Thought and Culture Abroad*, Vivekananda Kendra Patrika, vol. 9, no. 1, Madras, February 1980; (d) H.G. Rawlinson, 'Early Contacts between India and Europe' in A.L. Basham, (ed.), *A Cultural History of India°*.

10. See Subhash Kak, 'Akhenaten, Surya, and the Rgveda', *The Golden Chain*, G.C. Pande, (ed.), Centre for the Study of Civilizations, New Delhi, 2005.

11. Ibid.

12. Nicholas Kazanas, *Indo-Aryan Origins and Other Vedic Issues*, Aditya Prakashan, New Delhi, 2009, ch. 7, 'Vedic and Mesopotamian cross influences'.

13. S.H. Levitt, 'The Dating of the Indian Tradition', *Anthropos*, 2003, vol. 98, 2nd part, pp. 341–60, quoted by N. Kazanas, 'The Rigveda and Harappa', in Ashvini Agrawal, (ed.), *In Search of Vedic–Harappan Relationship*, Aryan Books International, New Delhi, 2005, p. 92.

14. E.g., Myles Dillon, Nora Chadwick, Anne Rodd or J.A. MacCulloh. Also Peter Ellis (see following note).

15. Peter Berresford Ellis, *The Druids*, Constable, London, 1995, p. 24.

16. See (in alphabetical order) Edwin Bryant, *The Quest for the Origins of Vedic Culture: The Indo-Aryan Migration Debate*, Oxford University Press, New York, 2001; Michel Danino, *The Dawn of Indian Civilization and the Elusive Aryans* (forthcoming); Koenraad Elst, *Update on the Aryan Invasion Debate*, Aditya Prakashan, New Delhi, 1999; Georg Feuerstein, Subhash Kak and David Frawley, *In Search of the Cradle of Civilization*, Quest Books, Wheaton, U.S.A., 1995, reprint Motilal Banarsidass, Delhi, 1999; Nicholas Kazanas, *Indo-Aryan Origins and Other Vedic Issues*, Aditya Prakashan, New Delhi, 2009; B.B. Lal, *The Homeland of the Aryans: Evidence of Rigvedic Flora and Fauna*, Aryan Books International, New Delhi, 2005; Shrikant G. Talageri, *The Rigveda: A Historical Analysis*, Aditya Prakashan, New Delhi, 2000, and *The Rigveda and the Avesta: The Final Evidence*, Aditya Prakashan, New Delhi, 2008.

17. See in particular the works of Koenraad Elst, Nicholas Kazanas and Shrikant Talageri above.

18. H.G. Rawlinson, 'Early Contacts between India and Europe', op. cit., p. 429.

19. Some of these shared beliefs have been highlighted by Bharat Gupt, 'Indo-European Beliefs in Classical Greek and Indian Drama' published in *Studies in Jaina Art and Iconography and Allied Subjects in Honour of Dr. U.P. Shah*, Oriental Institute, Vadodara, and Abhinav Publications, Delhi, pp. 311 ff. The essay is also available online at: www.ifih.org/Indo-EuropeanBeliefsinClassical GreekIndianDrama.htm (retrieved 21.1.2010)

20. See Nicholas Kazanas, 'Plato and the Upanishads', The Adyar Library and Research Centre, Wheaton and Chennai, 2005.

21. Voltaire, *Fragments historiques sur l'Inde*, first publ. 1773, in *Œuvres Complètes*, Hachette, Paris, 1893, vol. 29, p. 408.

22. H.G. Rawlinson, 'Early Contacts between India and Europe', op. cit., p. 429.

23. Ibid., p. 427.
24. T. Lomperis, *Hindu Influence on Greek Philosophy*, Minerva Associates, Calcutta, 1984, p. 76.
25. Strabo's *Geography*, quoted by John W. McCrindle, *Ancient India as Described in Classical Literature*, 1901, republished by Oriental Books Reprint Corporation, New Delhi, 1979, pp. 66–67.
26. *Expressions of Christianity, with a Focus on India°*, pp. 63–64.
27. Voltaire, *Fragments historiques sur l'Inde*, op. cit., pp. 417, 459.
28. Roy Amore, *Two Masters, One Message*, Abingdon, Nashville, 1978, p. 177.
29. Ibid., pp. 178–86.
30. Ibid., p. 186.
31. See more details in Subhash Kak's online article, 'The Church and the Temple' (http://subhash-kak.sulekha.com/blog/post/2002/10/the-church-and-the-temple.htm, retrieved 21.1.2010).
32. See Elaine Pagels, *The Gnostic Gospels*, Penguin Books, London, 1990.
33. Ibid., p. 18.
34. Koenraad Elst, *Update on the Aryan Invasion Debate*, Aditya Prakashan, New Delhi, 1999.
35. See 'Indian Influences in South-East Asia as Reflected in the Personal Names' and 'Indian Influences on the Place-Names of South-East Asia', ch. 33 & 34 in K.V. Raman, *Temple Art, Icons and Culture of India and South-East Asia*, Sharada Publishing House, Delhi, 2006.
36. Sachchidanand Sahai, *Rāmāyana in Laos: A Study in the Gvy Dvorahbī*, B.R. Publishing Corporation, Delhi, 1976.
37. Malini Saran and Vinod C. Khanna, *The Ramayana in Indonesia*, Ravi Dayal Publisher, Delhi, 2004.
38. For instance V. Raghavan, (ed.), *The Ramayana Tradition in Asia*, Sahitya Akademi, New Delhi, 1980.
39. Schopenhauer, quoted in Jawaharlal Nehru's *Discovery of India*, Jawaharlal Nehru Memorial Fund and OUP, New Delhi, 1981, pp. 92-93.
40. Ralph Waldo Emerson, quoted by Sushama Londhe, *A Tribute to Hinduism°*, pp. 17–18.
41. Henry David Thoreau, ibid., pp. 24–25.
42. Mark Twain, *Following the Equator*, 1897, ch. 57.
43. George Cœdès, *Les états hindouisés d'Indochine et d'Indonésie*, Editions de Boccard, Paris, 1948. In its English translation, the title was altered to *The Indianized States of Southeast Asia*, George Cœdès and Walter F. Vella, (eds), East-West Center Press, Honolulu, 1964.
44. Steve Muhlberger, 'Democracy in Ancient India', www.infinityfoundation.com/ECITdemocracyindiaframeset.htm (retrieved 13.2.2010).
45. A. Seidenberg, 'The Origin of Mathematics', in *Archive for History of Exact Sciences*, vol. 18, no. 4, 1978, p 329.
46. S. Balachandra Rao, *Indian Mathematics and Astronomy: Some Landmarks*, Bhavan's Gandhi Centre of Science and Human Values, Bangalore, 3rd edn, 2004, p. 14.

47. S.N. Sen and A.K. Bag, (eds), *The Sulbasutras*, Indian National Science Academy, New Delhi, 1983, p. 4.
48. Arvind Kumar Singh, 'Zero in Early Indian Inscriptions', *Puratattva*, no. 38, 2008, pp. 121–26.
49. Georges Ifrah, *The Universal History of Numbers°*, vol. 2, pp. 87–131.
50. Georges Ifrah, *Histoire universelle des chiffres*, Robert Laffont, Paris, 1994, vol. 2, p. 3. (Inexplicably, the first part of this quotation is missing or unrecognizable in the English translation, which is why this translation is mine.)
51. Georges Ifrah, *The Universal History of Numbers°*, vol. 2, ch. 24.
52. S.N. Sen, 'Astronomy', in *A Concise History of Science in India°*, p. 153.
53. W.H. Siddiqi, 'India's Contribution to Arab Civilization', in *India's Contribution to World Thought and Culture°*, p. 584.
54. Ibid., pp. 584 ff.
55. See B.V. Subbarayappa, 'India's Contributions to the History of Science', in *India's Contribution to World Thought and Culture°*, p. 47.
56. Georges Ifrah, *The Universal History of Numbers°*, vol. 2, pp. 144, 182.
57. K.V. Sarma, 'A Survey of Source Materials', in S.N. Sen and K.S. Shukla, (eds), *History of Astronomy in India,* Indian National Science Academy, New Delhi, 1985, p. 17.
58. *Albêrûnî's India*, tr. Edward C. Sachau, 1888, republ. Rupa, New Delhi, 2002, pp. 5–6.
59. K.V. Sarma, *A History of the Kerala School of Hindu Astronomy (in Perspective),* Vishveshvaranand Institute, Hoshiapur, 1972.
60. Ian G. Pearce, *Indian Mathematics: Redressing the Balance,* website of St. Andrews University, Scotland, 2002, ch. 9 & Conclusions, available online at: www-history.mcs.st-andrews.ac.uk/history/Projects/Pearce/index.html (retrieved 21.1.2010).
61. E.g., George Gheverghese Joseph, *The Crest of the Peacock*, Penguin Books, London, 2000, and C.K. Raju, 'The Indian Origins of the Calculus and its Transmission to Europe Prior to Newton and Leibniz: www.svabhinava. org/ Dia-Gnosis/RajuCK/CalculusAbstractAuckland2.pdf (retrieved 13.2.2010).
62. K.V. Sarma, (ed.), *Science Texts in Sanskrit in the Manuscripts Repositories of Kerala and Tamil Nadu*, Rashtriya Sanskrit Sansthan, New Delhi, 2002, p. 16.
63. Jean Filliozat, 'The Expansion of Indian Medicine Abroad', in *India's Contribution to World Thought and Culture°*, pp. 67 ff.
64. B.V. Subbarayappa, 'India's Contributions to the History of Science', in ibid., p. 58.
65. R.C. Majumdar, 'Medicine', in *A Concise History of Science in India°*, p. 323.
66. B.V. Subbarayappa, 'India's Contributions to the History of Science', op. cit., p. 58.
67. Personal communication from Claude Brun, a French acupuncturist trained in Korea, who translated into French the *Canons of Acupuncture (Huangti Nei Ching Ling Shu)*, Sciences et Tradition, Editions de l'Aire, Lausanne,1988.
68. Sharada Srinivasan and Srinivasa Ranganathan, *India's Legendary 'Wootz' Steel: An Advanced Material of the Ancient World,* National Institute of

Advanced Studies, Bangalore, and Indian Institute of Science, Bangalore, 2004, pp. 50–51.

69. Quoted by Sushama Londhe in www.hinduwisdom.info/Hindu_Culture1.htm.
70. Swami Vivekananda, letter of 13 February 1896, *The Complete Works of Swami Vivekananda*, vol. 5, Advaita Ashrama, Almora, 1947, p. 77.
71. See Subhash Kak, *The Wishing Tree°*, pp. 5 ff.
72. Walter Moore, quoted by Subhash Kak, *The Wishing Tree°*, p. 6.
73. Fritjof Capra, *Uncommon Wisdom°*, p. 43.
74. Fritjof Capra, *The Tao of Physics°*, p. 272.
75. F. David Peat, *Infinite Potential: The Life and Times of David Bohm*, Basic Books, 1997, p. 322.
76. E.F. Schumacher, *Small is Beautiful: Economics as If People Mattered*, Hartley & Marks Publishers, 2000, p. 41.
77. See Harold G. Coward, *Jung and Eastern Thought*, State University of New York Press, 1985.
78. Carl Gustav Jung, *Modern Man in Search of a Soul*, Routledge, 2005, p. 224.
79. Ibid., p. 220.
80. Census figures published in 1996 by the Australian Bureau of Statistics mentioned 199,812 Buddhists in Australia; this was an increase of nearly 60,000 from the 139,847 Buddhists recorded in the 1991 census. As regards Buddhism in France, see for instance www.religionnewsblog.com/1079-_Buddhism_in_France_is_booming.html (retrieved 26.1.2010)
81. Sri Aurobindo, *India's Rebirth°*, p. 42.
82. Hu Shih, 'East and West: The Indianization of China: A Case Study in Cultural Borrowing', in Harvard Tercenary Conference of Arts and Science, *Independence, Convergence, Borrowing*, p. 225, quoted by D.P. Singhal, *India and World Civilization°*, vol. 1, p. 338.
83. D.P. Singhal in *India and World Civilization°*, vol. 1, p. 337.
84. Philip S. Rawson, *The Art of South East Asia*, 1967, repr. Thames & Hudson, 1990.

3. India in France

1. Roger-Pol Droit, *L'oubli de l'Inde: Une amnésie philosophique*, Presses Universitaires de France, Paris, 1989.
2. For this chapter, I have consulted a number of works, but two stand out in the field: (1) Raymond Schwab, *La Renaissance orientale*, Payot, Paris, 1950 (I have not seen its English translation, *The Oriental Renaissance: Europe's Rediscovery of India and the East 1680–1880*, Columbia University Press, New York, 1984); (2) Jean Biès, *Littérature française et pensée hindoue des origines à 1950*, Librairie C. Klincksieck, 1974, unfortunately not available in English.
3. Voltaire, *Lettres sur l'origine des sciences et sur celle des peuples de l'Asie*, first published Paris, 1777, letter of 15 December 1775.
4. Voltaire, *Essai sur les mœurs et l'esprit des nations*, Bordas, Classiques Garnier,

Paris, 1990, p. 228.

5. Voltaire, *Fragments historiques sur l'Inde,* first publ. 1773, in *Œuvres Complètes,* Hachette, Paris, 1893, vol. 29.

6. Voltaire, *Essai sur les mœurs et l'esprit des nations,* op. cit., p. 237.

7. Voltaire, *Fragments historiques sur l'Inde,* op. cit., p. 386.

8. An excellent collection of such testimonies can be found in Guy Deleury, (ed.), *Les Indes Florissantes: anthologie des voyageurs français* (1750–1820), Robert Laffont, Paris, 1991.

9. Louis Renou and Jean Filliozat authored a masterly study of classical India, which remains a much consulted reference: *L'Inde classique: Manuel des études indiennes,* vol. I: Payot, Paris, 1947, republ. Librairie d'Amérique et d'Orient, 1985; vol. II: École Française d'Extrême-Orient, Paris, 1953, repr. 2001.

10. Louis Renou gives a brief account of French Indology in 'The Influence of Indian Thought on French Literature', *Adyar Library Bulletin,* Madras, vols XII & XIII, reprinted in the Adyar Library Pamphlet Series no. 15 in 1948. Another can be found in Michel Danino, 'Indian Texts, French Translations: France's Contribution to Indology', unpublished, 2003.

11. Quoted by Jean Biès, *Littérature française et pensée hindoue des origines à 1950,* op. cit., p. 108.

12. Ibid, p. 100.

13. Michelet, *La Bible de l'humanité,* Éditions Complexes, Bruxelles, 1998, p. 23.

14. Michelet, *Le Peuple,* GF Flammarion, Paris, 1974, p. 176.

15. Michelet, *La Bible de l'humanité,* op. cit., p. 25.

16. Ibid, pp. 19–20.

17. Lamartine, *Opinions sur Dieu, le bonheur et l'éternité d'après les livres sacrés de l'Inde,* Sand, Paris, 1984, p. ix.

18. Victor Cousin, *Cours d'histoire de la philosophie,* Pichon & Didier, 1829, p. 155 (translation adapted from John Woodroffe, *Is India Civilized?°,* p. 132).

19. See two essays by François Chenet and Roger-Pol Droit on these philosophers in *L'Inde inspiratrice: Réception de l'Inde en France et en Allemagne (XIXᵉ & XXᵉ siècles),* Michel Hulin and Christine Maillard, (eds), Presses Universitaires de Strasbourg, 1996.

20. René Daumal's essays, as well as a few translations from the Veda and other texts, were collected in *Bharata: L'origine du théâtre, la poésie et la musique en Inde,* Gallimard, Paris, 1970.

21. André Malraux, *Antimémoires,* Gallimard, Paris, 1957, p. 339.

22. See, in addition to *Antimémoires,* the well-documented bilingual *Malraux and India: A Passage to Wonderment,* Ambassade de France en Inde, New Delhi, 1996.

23. See note 1 above.

24. See *Séance commémorative de Sri Aurobindo à la Sorbonne le 5 décembre 1955* (presided over by Jean Filliozat), Sri Aurobindo Ashram, Pondicherry. Several collections of articles paid tributes to Sri Aurobindo, e.g. 'Hommage à Shri Aurobindo' in *France–Asie,* Saigon, nos. 58 & 59, March and April 1951, and 'Hommage à Sri Aurobindo', *Synthèses,* Bruxelles, December 1965.

25. Satprem's *Sri Aurobindo or the Adventure of Consciousness*, 4th edn, The Mother's Institute of Research, Delhi, and Mira Aditi, Mysore, 2000, provides an excellent introduction to Sri Aurobindo's life and yoga.

4. For the Love of Nature

1. See for instance Shakti M. Gupta, *Plant Myths and Traditions in India*, 3rd edn, Munshiram Manoharlal, New Delhi, 2001; Bansi Lal Malla, *Trees in Indian Art, Mythology and Folklore*, Aryan Books International, New Delhi, 2000; *Brahma's Hair: The Mythology of Indian Plants*, Maneka Gandhi, Rupa, New Delhi, 1989.

2. B.B. Lal, *Excavations at Sringaverapura (1977-86)*, vol. 1, Archaeological Survey of India, New Delhi, 1993.

3. See Anil Agarwal and Sunita Narain, (eds), *Dying Wisdom: Rise, Fall and Potential of India's Traditional Water-Harvesting Systems*, Centre for Science and Environment, New Delhi, 1997; Kalyan Kumar Chakravarty, Gyani Lal Badam and Vijay Paranpye, (eds), *Traditional Water Management Systems of India*, Indira Gandhi Rashtriya Manav Sangrahalaya, Bhopal, and Aryan Books International, New Delhi, 2006; T.M. Mukundan, *The Eris Systems of South India: Traditional Water Harvesting*, Akash Ganga Trust, Chennai, 2005.

4. Quoted by Jitendra Bajaj and Mandayam Doddamane Srinivas, *Annam Bahu Kurvīta*, Centre for Policy Studies, Madras, 1996, p. 2.

5. 'Tropical species decline by 60 per cent', *The Telegraph*, 13 October 2010.

6. Genesis, 1: 26 & 1: 28.

7. Ibid., 29: 10, 12.

8. Isaiah, 24: 1, 3.

9. Genesis, 3: 17.

10. Rig Veda, 1.164.33.

11. *Shiva Purāna*, II.1.24, *The Shiva Purana*, Motilal Banarsidass, Delhi, 1970-86, vol. 1, p. 37.

12. Rig Veda, 10.85.1.

13. Pierre Thuillier, *La Grande Implosion: Rapport sur l'effondrement de l'Occident 1999–2002*, Fayard, Paris, 1995, p. 251.

14. Edward Goldsmith in *Krisis*, Paris, no. 20–21, November 1997, p. 29.

15. Chief Seattle's 1855 speech, available in many publications and websites. (Note that while there is disagreement on the authenticity of some of the statements, there is no dispute that Chief Seattle's message had a profound ecological importance.)

5. The Colonized Indian Mind

1. Rev. John Wilson in 1858.

2. Sidgwick, quoted by Sri Aurobindo on 19 June 1907 in *Bande Mataram*°, pp. 512–13.

3. Quoted in *British Paramountcy and Indian Renaissance*, vol. 10 in *The History*

and Culture of the Indian People°, pp. 83–84.

4. Lord Canning quoted by P. Hardy, *The Muslims of British India*, Cambridge University Press, 1972, p. 72.

5. Quoted in *British Paramountcy and Indian Renaissance*, op. cit., p. 321.

6. George Otto Trevelyan, *Life and Letters of Lord Macaulay*, vol. 1, 2nd edn, 1876, republ. ICON Group International, 2008, p. 406.

7. Kuldip Singh and B.L. Hansaria, judgement of 4 October 1994 in Writ petition (C) no. 299 of 1989, online at www.ifih.org/resourcessupremecourtonsanskrit.htm (retrieved 05.11.2010).

8. Etymology of 'vernacular' as given in *Webster's New World Dictionary*, *verna* meaning 'native slave' in Latin.

9. Klaus Klostermaier, 'Questioning the Aryan Invasion Theory and Revising Ancient Indian History', in *ISKCON Communications Journal*, 1999.

10. Sri Aurobindo, 'The National Value of Art', *Early Cultural Writings*, vol. 1 in *The Complete Works of Sri Aurobindo*, Sri Aurobindo Ashram, Pondicherry, 2003, p. 433.

11. *Swami Vivekananda on India and her Problems*, Advaita Ashram, Calcutta, 1985, pp. 38–39.

12. Ananda Coomaraswamy, *The Dance of Shiva°*, p. 170.

13. See Nicholas B. Dirks, *Castes of Mind: Colonialism and the Making of Modern India*, Permanent Black, Delhi, 2003; Meenakshi Jain, 'The Plight of Brahmins' and 'The Myth of Caste Tyranny', *Indian Express*, 18 & 26 September 1990; Ram Swarup, 'Logic behind perversion of caste', *Indian Express*, 13 September 1996; Kevin Hobson, 'The Indian Caste System and The British: Ethnographic Mapping and the Construction of the British Census in India' available online at www.infinityfoundation.com/mandala/h_es/h_es_hobso_caste_frameset.htm (retrieved 15.09.10).

14. Aleksandr Solzhenitsyn, interviewed in *Time* of 24 July 1989.

15. Sri Aurobindo, 'Social Reform', *Essays Divine and Human,* vol. 12 in *The Complete Works of Sri Aurobindo,* Sri Aurobindo Ashram, Pondicherry, 1997, p. 52.

16. Ram Swarup, quoted in *Hinduism Today*, October 1998, p. 16.

17. Ananda K. Coomaraswamy (in 1910), *Art and Swadeshi,* Munshiram Manoharlal, New Delhi, 1994, p. 9.

18. Kapil Kapoor, 'Sanskrit Literary Theory: A Rejoinder to Eleven Objections', in *Critical Practice*, vol. VIII, no. 2, June 2001.

19. Sri Aurobindo, 'The Past and the Future', 25 September 1909, *Karmayogin°*, p. 247.

20. Adapted from Swami Vivekananda, in Ram Swarup, 'His Vision and Mission', *The Observer*, 28 August 1993.

21. Sri Aurobindo, 'On Original Thinking', *Essays Divine and Human,* op. cit., p. 41.

22. In *Malraux and India*, Embassy of France in India, New Delhi, 1996, p. 46.

23. Michelet, *La Bible de l'Humanité, Œuvres,* Larousse, Paris, 1930, vol. 5, p. 119.

24. Tagore, *Crisis in Civilization*, Visva-Bharati, Calcutta, 1988, pp. 22–23.

6. The Age of Confusion

1. *Mahabharata*, Vana Parva, from K.M. Ganguli's translation, Munshiram Manoharlal, Delhi, 2000, vol. I, sections 187 & 189.
2. *Vivekachūdamāni*, 17.
3. Exodus, 3:14. (The god of Hebrews does not exactly name himself 'Yahweh' but utters four Hebrew consonants, YHWH, generally rendered as 'I am who I am'; later, specific vowels were added to YHWH to produce 'Jehovah'.)
4. Sri Aurobindo, *Thoughts and Aphorisms*, no. ^14, in *Essays Divine and Human*, vol. 12 in *The Complete Works of Sri Aurobindo*, Sri Aurobindo Ashram, Pondicherry, 1997, p. 482.
5. Voltaire, 'Homily on the Interpretation of the Old Testament', in *A Treatise on Toleration and Other Essays*, Prometheus Books, New York, p. 137.
6. Voltaire, 'The Questions of Zapata', in *A Treatise on Toleration*, p. 54.
7. Thomas Paine, *The Age of Reason*, 1796, etext at www.gutenberg.org/ebooks/3743, part 1, ch. 7 (retrieved 14.2.2010).
8. Bernard Shaw, *The Black Girl in Search of God and some lesser tales*, Penguin Books, London, 1946, p. 17.
9. Elizabeth Cady Stanton, *Eighty Years and More*, ch. 24, etext at www.gutenberg.org/etext/11982 (retrieved 14.09.2010).
10. Mark Twain, 'Reflections on Religion', in Charles Neider, (ed.), *The outrageous Mark Twain: some lesser-known but extraordinary works*, Doubleday, 1987, p. 30.
11. Mark Twain, quoted by Dave Lane, *Isn't Religion Weird? Quotations for Atheists*, Lulu.com, 2008, p. 93.
12. Quoted by Ram Swarup, *On Hinduism*, Voice of India, New Delhi, 2000, p. 152.
13. Ibid., p. 151.
14. Albert Einstein, *New York Times*, 9 November 1930, quoted in Charles Bufe, *The Heretic's Handbook of Quotations: Cutting Comments on Burning Issues*, See Sharp Press, 1992 p. 186.
15. Elaine Pagels, *The Gnostic Gospels*, Penguin Books, London, 1990, p. 132.
16. Ibid., p. 56
17. Anatole France, *La Révolte des Anges*, Calmann–Lévy, Paris, 1980, pp. 80 & 193.
18. *Katha Upanishad*, I.III.12, *Mundaka Upanishad*, I.I.6, II.I.1, II.II.12 (all translations by Sri Aurobindo).
19. *Īsha Upanishad*, 16.
20. *Chāndogya Upanishad*, 6 etc.
21. Elaine Pagels, *The Gnostic Gospels*, op. cit., p. 17.
22. Ibid., p. 18.
23. Luke 12: 5, 13: 3. See also Luke 10: 8–15 for Jesus' threats of destruction to cities that might refuse his teaching.
24. John 9: 39, 10: 8, 14: 6.
25. Sri Aurobindo, *India's Rebirth°*, p. 189.
26. Ibid., p. 69.

27. Sri Aurobindo, *The Synthesis of Yoga, The Complete Works of Sri Aurobindo*, Sri Aurobindo Ashram, Pondicherry vol. 23–24, 1999, pp. 55–56.

28. E.g., *Webster's New World Dictionary*, 1997: 'The belief that religion and ecclesiastical affairs should not enter into the functions of the state, esp. into public education.'

29. Vincent Smith, *Asoka*, quoted by Ananda K. Coomaraswamy, *Essays in National Idealism*, Munshiram Manoharlal, New Delhi, 1981, p. 131.

30. *Arthashāstra* 13.5.8 & 11. See R.P. Kangle, *The Kautiliya Arthasastra*, Motilal Banarsidass, New Delhi, 1986, part II, pp. 491–92.

31. King Ashoka, Edict 7. See *The Edicts of King Ashoka*, an English rendering by Ven. S. Dhammika, Buddhist Publication Society, Kandy, 1993 (online at www.cs.colostate.edu/~malaiya/ashoka.html, retrieved 23.1.2010).

32. King Ashoka, Edict 12. Ibid.

33. Sri Aurobindo, *India's Rebirth*°, p. 149.

34. V.R. Ramachandra Dikshitar, *Cilappatikaram*, Madras, 1939, repr. International Institute of Tamil Studies, Chennai, 1997, p. 53.

35. Ibid., p. 58.

36. K.V. Raman, 'Religious Inheritance of the Pandyas', in *Sree Meenakshi Koil Souvenir* (Madurai, n.d.), pp. 168–70.

37. E.g., www.freerepublic.com/focus/f-news/937602/posts or www.hindu.com/fline/fl2102/stories/20040130000206100.htm (retrieved 23.01.2010).

38. Sri Aurobindo, *India's Rebirth*°, p. 165.

39. For example the case of the imaginary rape of a nun in Orissa in February 1999. After the usual outcry against 'fundamentalist Hindus', the complaint turned out to be false and the case was quietly dropped.

40. As, for instance, at Jhabua in Madhya Pradesh where several nuns were indeed raped in September 1998; it turned out that half of the tribals responsible for the crime were Christians. Or the case of the serial bomb blasts at churches in Andhra Pradesh, Karnataka and Goa in 2000, promptly blamed on Hindu organizations, until the culprit was found to be an extremist Muslim organization, the Deendar Anjuman (outlawed in May 2001). Of course none of the Christian leaders and 'secular' journalists who had promptly accused Hindus even thought of apologizing for their false statements.
  Even in the case of the January 1999 murder of the Australian missionary Graham Staines in Orissa, the Wadhwa Commission of inquiry ruled out in its report the involvement of any Hindu organization, and in fact complained that with such incidents, 'the press indulged in speculation and did not exercise restraint in their reporting'. Similarly, in February 2001, the National Commission for Minorities exonerated any 'organization or religious [i.e., Hindu] body' in recent attacks on Christians and blamed the media for overplaying such incidents.

41. See for instance Zariuna Bhatty, 'Social Stratification Among Muslims in India' and J. Tharamangalam, 'Caste Among Christians in India', both in M.N. Srinivas, (ed.), *Caste: Its Twentieth Century Avatar*, Penguin Books, New Delhi, 1996.

42. Ram Swarup, *Hindu View of Christianity and Islam°*, p. 113.
43. Sri Aurobindo, *India's Rebirth°*, 2000, p. 181.
44. *Mundaka Upanishad*, III.I.6.
45. Sri Aurobindo, *India's Rebirth°*, pp. 87–88.

7. The Gītā and the Problem of Action

1. Sri Aurobindo, 'On the Mahabharata', *Early Cultural Writings,* vol. 1 in *The Complete Works of Sri Aurobindo,* Sri Aurobindo Ashram, Pondicherry, 2003, p. 327.
2. A.B. Purani, *Evening Talks,* Sri Aurobindo Society, Pondicherry, 1982, p. 105.
3. Sujata Nahar, *Mother's Chronicles—Book Five: Mirra Meets the Revolutionary,* Mira Aditi, Mysore, 1997, p. 97.
4. Sri Aurobindo, 'On the Mahabharata', *Early Cultural Writings,* vol. 1 in *The Complete Works of Sri Aurobindo,* Sri Aurobindo Ashram, Pondicherry, 2003, op. cit., p. 336.
5. Ibid.
6. Sri Aurobindo, *India's Rebirth°*, p. 19.
7. Ibid., p. 46.
8. Sri Aurobindo, 25 June 1909, *Karmayogin°*, p. 50.
9. Sri Aurobindo, 'The Gita and Terrorism', 12 February 1910, *Karmayogin°*, pp. 452–53.
10. *Sedition Committee 1918 Report under Hon'ble Mr. Justice Rowlatt,* repr. New Age Publishers, Calcutta, 1973, pp. 17, 23.
11. Barindra Kumar Ghose, quoted in M.P. Pandit, (ed.), *Champaklal's Treasures,* Sri Aurobindo Ashram, Pondicherry, 2nd edn, 2008, p. 167.
12. R.C. Majumdar, *History of the Freedom Movement in India°*, vol. 1, p. 408.
13. Sri Aurobindo, 'The Gita and Terrorism', 12 January 1910, *Karmayogin°*, pp. 452–53.
14. Sri Aurobindo, *Essays on the Gita°*, pp. 57–58.
15. Sri Aurobindo, 'Uttarpara Speech', 30 May 1909, *Karmayogin°*, p. 5.
16. Ibid., pp. 6-7.
17. *Mahābhārata*, Vana Parva, ch. 207, adapted from K.M. Ganguli's translation, Munshiram Manoharlal, Delhi, 2000, vol. I, pp. 431–32.
18. Sri Aurobindo, *Essays on the Gita°*, pp. 40–42.
19. Ibid., pp. 381–82.
20. Ibid., p. 45.
21. Ibid., p. 49.
22. Sri Aurobindo, *Bande Mataram°*, 23 April 1907, p. 302.
23. Sri Aurobindo, *On Himself,* Sri Aurobindo Ashram, Pondicherry, 1972, p. 22.
24. *Amrita Bazar Patrika,* 'Method of Non-violence—Mahatma Gandhi's appeal to every Briton', 4 July 1940. See a longer extract and Sri Aurobindo's reaction to the open letter in *India's Rebirth°*, p. 227.
25. Sri Aurobindo, *Autobiographical Notes and Other Writings of Historical Interest,* vol. 36 in *The Complete Works of Sri Aurobindo,* Sri Aurobindo

Ashram, Pondicherry, 2006, pp. 453–54.

26. Nirodbaran, *Talks with Sri Aurobindo,* vol. 1, Sri Aurobindo Society, Calcutta, 2nd edn, 1986, p. 79.

27. M.K. Gandhi, *Harijan,* 18 February 1939, in *Complete Works,* vol. 75, p. 39.

28. M.K. Gandhi, *Harijan,* 27 May 1939, in *Complete Works,* vol. 75, pp. 417–18.

29. M.K. Gandhi, *Harijan,* 17 December 1938.

30. M.K. Gandhi, *Harijan,* 7 January 1939.

31. M.K. Gandhi, *Harijan,* 26 November 1938.

32. Sri Aurobindo, *India's Rebirth°,* p. 224.

33. Sri Aurobindo, *Autobiographical Notes and Other Writings of Historical Interest,* op. cit., 2006, p. 66.

34. Sri Aurobindo, *India's Rebirth°,* pp. 235–36.

35. R.C. Majumdar, *History of the Freedom Movement in India°,* vol. 2, p. 186.

36. A.B. Purani, *Evening Talks,* Sri Aurobindo Society, Pondicherry, 1982, p. 53.

37. Sri Aurobindo, *Essays on the Gita°,* p. 42.

38. Swami Vivekananda, 'The East and the West', *The Complete Works of Swami Vivekananda,* electronic edition, vol. V.

39. Sri Aurobindo, *The Human Cycle, The Ideal of Human Unity, War and Self-Determination,* vol. 25 in *The Complete Works of Sri Aurobindo,* Sri Aurobindo Ashram, Pondicherry, 1997, p. 242.

40. Sri Aurobindo, *On Himself,* op. cit., p. 125.

41. Sri Aurobindo, *Letters on Yoga,* Sri Aurobindo Ashram, Pondicherry, 1972, pp. 665–66.

42. Sri Aurobindo, *The Synthesis of Yoga,* vol. 23–24 in *The Complete Works of Sri Aurobindo,* Sri Aurobindo Ashram, Pondicherry, 1999, p. 94.

43. Wendy Doniger, as reported in *Philadelphia Inquirer* of 19 November 2000.

8. A Wounded Identity

1. Rabindranath Tagore, *Nationalism in India,* republ. Macmillan, New Delhi 1999, p. 69.

2. V.S. Naipaul, *India: A Wounded Civilization,* Penguin Books, New Delhi, 1977.

3. On the Aryan invasion issue, see p. 221, note 16.

4. I developed this literary and archaeological evidence in my paper 'Vedic Roots of Early Tamil Culture', in P. Chenna Reddy, (ed.), *Saundaryashri: Studies of Indian History, Archaeology, Literature and Philosophy* (Festschrift to Professor Anantha Adiga Sundara), Sharada Publishing House, New Delhi, 2009, pp. 19–30 (also online at: www.omilosmeleton.gr/pdf/en/indology/Vedic_Roots_of_Early_Tamil_Culture.pdf, retrieved 01.10.2010).

5. See Sandhya Jain, *Adi Deo Arya Devata: A Panoramic View of Tribal–Hindu Cultural Interface,* Rupa, New Delhi, 2004.

6. *The Acts of Thomas,* extracted from *The Apocryphal New Testament,* tr. M.R. James, Clarendon Press, Oxford, 1924, online at www.gnosis.org/library/actthom.htm (retrieved 19.11.2009).

7. Voltaire, *Fragments historiques sur l'Inde*, first publ. 1773, in *Œuvres Complètes*, Hachette, Paris, 1893, vol. 29, p. 410.
8. Rev. James Hough, *History of Christianity*, 1839, vol. 1, p. 40, quoted in K.V. Raman, *The Early History of the Madras Region*, 1959, 2nd edn, C.P. Ramaswami Aiyar Foundation, Chennai, 2008, p. 29.
9. See Ishwar Sharan, *The Myth of Saint Thomas and the Mylapore Shiva Temple*, Voice of India, New Delhi, 2nd edn, 1995; and A.K. Priolkar, *The Goa Inquisition*, Bombay, 1961, republ. Voice of India, New Delhi, 1991.
10. Henry James Coleridge, *The life and letters of St. Francis Xavier*, vol. 1, republ. Asian Educational Services, 1997, p. 281.
11. E.g., Leonard Fernando and G. Gispert-Sauch, *Christianity in India: Two Thousand Years of Faith*, Penguin–Viking, New Delhi, 2004, p. 124.
12. For material on the Goan Inquisition, see A.K. Priolkar, *The Goa Inquisition*, op. cit., and *Expressions of Christianity, with a Focus on India°*, Part 3.
13. Voltaire, *Fragments historiques sur l'Inde*, op. cit., p. 407.
14. Teotonio R. de Souza, 'The Portuguese in Asia and their Church Patronage', in *Western Colonialism in Asia and Christianity*, M.D. David, (ed.), Bombay, 1988, quoted in *Expressions of Christianity With a Focus on India°*, p. 289.
15. See Sita Ram Goel, *History of Hindu–Christian Encounters°*, ch. 7.
16. E.g., Scott C. Levi, 'Hindus Beyond the Hindu Kush: Indians in the Central Asian Slave Trade', *Journal of the Royal Asiatic Society*, Series 3, 12, 3 (2002), pp. 277–288.
17. See Koenraad Elst, *Negationism in India: Concealing the Record of Islam*, Voice of India, New Delhi, 1993.
18. See *The History and Culture of the Indian People°*, vol. 6: *The Delhi Sultanate* and vol. 7: *The Moghul Empire*.
19. K.S. Lal, *Legacy of Muslim Rule in India*, 1992; *Growth of Scheduled Tribes and Castes in Medieval India*, 1995; *Theory and Practice of Muslim State in India*, 1999 (all published by Aditya Prakashan, New Delhi).
20. See Sita Ram Goel, (ed.), *Hindu Temples: What Happened to Them°*.
21. Alain Daniélou, *A Brief History of India*, Inner Traditions India, Vermont, 2003, p. 195.
22. Will Durant, *The Story of Civilization*, part I, *Our Oriental Heritage*, Simon & Schuster, New York, 1954, p. 459.
23. Firuz Shah Tughlaq, *Tarikh-i-Firuz Shahi*, quoted by Arun Shourie, *Eminent Historians*, ASA, New Delhi, 1998, p. 109.
24. R.C. Majumdar, 'Firuz Shah', *The Delhi Sultanate*, vol. 6 in *The History and Culture of the Indian People°*, pp. 105–6.
25. See numerous examples in Sita Ram Goel, (ed.), *Hindu Temples: What Happened to Them°*, vol. II, section III, 'From the Horse's Mouth'.
26. E.g., Mike Davies, *Late Victorian Holocausts*, Verso, UK, 2001, and David E. Stannard, *The American Holocaust*, Oxford University Press, 1992.
27. Quoted by Ram Swarup in 'Historians Versus History', in Sita Ram Goel, (ed.), *Hindu Temples: What Happened to Them°*, vol. 1, p. 286.
28. Satish Chandra, *Medieval India*, textbook for Class XI, NCERT, New Delhi,

1990, 9 reprints till 2001, p. 231. See also Romila Thapar, *Medieval India*, textbook for Class VII, NCERT, 1989, 13 reprints till 2001, p. 108.

29. From Timur's autobiography, quoted in Meenakshi Jain's *Medieval India*, textbook for Class XI, NCERT, New Delhi, 2002, p. 100.

30. There is a vast literature on the Ayodhya controversy. The following selected titles represent what may be called the Hindu case: *Ram Janmabhumi Vs. Babri Masjid: A Case Study in Hindu-Muslim Conflict*, 1990; *Ayodhya and After: Issues Before Hindu Society*, 1991; *Ayodhya: The Case Against the Temple*, 2002; *Ayodhya: the Finale*, 2003—all authored by Koenraad Elst. A collective work, *History Vs. Casuistry*, 1991. Arun Shourie et al., *The Ayodhya Reference: Supreme Court Judgement and Commentaries*, 1995. (All preceding titles published by Voice of India, New Delhi.) J.C. Aggarwal and N.K. Chowdhry, *Ram Janmabhoomi through the Ages*, S. Chand, New Delhi, 1991. Harsh Narain, *The Ayodhya Temple Mosque Dispute: Focus on the Muslim Sources*, Penman Publishers, New Delhi, 1993. B.B. Lal, *RAMA: His Historicity, Mandir and Setu, Evidence of Literature, Archaeology and other Sciences*, Aryan Books International, New Delhi, 2008.

31. 'Muslim youth group against moving SC', *The New Indian Express*, 1st October 2010.

32. 'Muslim Law Board to appeal in SC against Ayodhya verdict', *The Times of India*, 16 October 2010.

33. ' "Hindu Revivalists Are Mimicking Islamic Fundamentalists": V.S. Naipaul and Khushwant Singh in Conversation', *Outlook*, 8 May 2000, www.outlookindia.com/article.aspx?209362 (retrieved 18.10.2010).

34. See Dharampal, *The Beautiful Tree*, 2nd edn, Keerthi Publishing House with AVP Printers & Publishers, Coimbatore, 1995, also Other India Press, Mapusa, 2000; and Joseph Dibona, *One Teacher One School: The Adam Reports on Indigenous Education in 19th Century India*, Biblia Impex, New Delhi, 1983.

35. Brooks Adams, *The Law of Civilisation and Decay: An Essay on History*, Sonnenschein, London, 1895, p. 259.

36. Dadabhai Naoroji, *Poverty and Un-British Rule in India*, London, 1901, republ. Publications Division, Government of India, New Delhi, 1962 & 1996.

37. Romesh Dutt, *The Economic History of India under Early British Rule*, London, 1901, 2nd rev. edn 1906, and *The Economic History of India in the Victorian Age*, London, 1903, 3rd rev. edn 1908.

38. Sakharam Ganesh Deuskar, *Desher Katha*, 1904 (in Bengali).

39. William Digby, *"Prosperous" British India*, T. Fisher Unwin, London, 1901, pp. 33–36.

40. Lord Minto, quoted by Manoj Das, *Sri Aurobindo in the First Decade of the Century*, Sri Aurobindo Ashram, Pondicherry, 1972, p. 137.

41. Bipin Chandra, *Modern India – A History Textbook for Class XII*, NCERT, New Delhi, 1990–2000, pp. 200–01.

42. R.C. Majumdar, *History of the Freedom Movement in India°*, vol. 1, preface and appendix, and vol. 3, preface.

43. Ibid., vol. 3, p. xiii.

44. Ibid., p. xviii.
45. Bipin Chandra, *Modern India – A History Textbook for Class XII*, op. cit., p. 207.
46. Rabindranath Tagore, 'The History of Bharatavarsha', available at www.ifih.org/TheHistoryofBharatavarsha.htm (retrieved 24.1.2010).
47. Karl Marx, 'The Future Results of the British Rule in India', *The New York Daily Tribune*, 8 August 1853, reproduced in *Marx–Engels, The First Indian War of Independence, 1857–1859*, Progress Publishers, Moscow, 1959, p. 29.
48. Romila Thapar, *A History of India*, Penguin Books, London, 1987, vol. 1, p. 43.
49. D.D. Kosambi, quoted by Romila Thapar, *Interpreting Early India*, Oxford University Press, New Delhi, 1992, p. 93.
50. Kunal Chakrabarti, 'Recent Approaches to the History of Religion in Ancient India', in Romila Thapar, (ed.), *Recent Perspectives of Early Indian History*, Popular Prakashan, Mumbai 1998, p. 193.
51. The last few quotes are from R.S. Sharma, *Ancient India– A History Textbook for Class XI*, NCERT, New Delhi, 1999, pp. 3–6.
52. Romila Thapar, *History and Beyond*, Oxford University Press, New Delhi, 2000, pp. 68, 77.
53. D.P. Singhal, 'Battle for the Past', repr. in *History Today*, no.1, 2000, p. 11.
54. Ashok Mitra in an interview in the Rotterdam daily *NRC Handelsblad*, 20 March 1993, quoted by Koenraad Elst, *Update on the Aryan Invasion Debate*, Aditya Prakashan, New Delhi, 1999, p. 36.
55. A summary of the issue is available at: http://en.wikipedia.org/wiki/California_textbook_controversy_over_Hindu_history and www.hafsite.org/index.php?q=campaigns_education_california_intro.htm (retrieved 20.10.2010). Corrections recommended by Hindu scholars are listed in: www.cde.ca.gov/be/ag/ag/yr05/documents/bluenov05item05.doc (retrieved 26.1.2010).
56. Swapan Dasgupta, 'Remembering Right: India is a country with a rich history and poor historians', *The Telegraph*, 29 October 2010, online at www.telegraph india.com/1101029/jsp/opinion/story_13114321.jsp (retrieved 29.10.2010).

9. The Conqueror and the Conquered

1. Anatole France, *Sur la pierre blanche* (written in 1905), Calmann–Lévy, Paris, 1928, p. 163.
2. Chinweizu, *The West and the Rest of Us: White Predators, Black Slavers and the African Elite* (Vintage, 1975), p. 3, quoted in Noam Chomsky, *The Culture of Terrorism*, South End Press, Boston 1988, p. 3.
3. Swami Vivekananda, 'Hindus and Christians', reported in *The Detroit Free Press* of 21 February 1894, *The Complete Works of Swami Vivekananda*, 1951, vol. 8, p. 212.
4. Voltaire, *Dictionnaire philosophique*, GF–Flammarion, Paris, 1964, p. 22.
5. Cardinal Cormac Murphy-O'Connor, Archbishop of Westminster, quoted in

The Times and reproduced in *The New Indian Express* of 7 September 2001. He refers to England, but his statement could be extended to much of Europe, where church attendance has been dwindling and priests are increasingly harder to recruit.

6. Reports can be downloaded from http://mha.nic.in/fcra.htm, the last being for the year 2007–08 report (retrieved 27.09.10).
7. Ananda K. Coomaraswamy, *Essays in National Idealism*, p. 131.
8. Originally published in 1956 and republished as *Vindicated by Time: The Niyogi Committee Report on Christian Missionary Activities*, Voice of India, New Delhi, 1998, with an introduction by Sita Ram Goel (online at www.bharatvani.org/books/ncr/, retrieved on 23.1.2010). See also Arun Shourie, *Missionaries in India: Continuities, Changes, Dilemmas*, and *Harvesting Our Souls: Missionaries, Their Designs, Their Claims*, ASA, New Delhi, 1994 & 2000.
9. *Vindicated by Time: The Niyogi Committee Report on Christian Missionary Activities*, op. cit., vol. I, part II, p. 31.
10. Ibid., vol. I, part IV, pp. 131–32.
11. See www.ad2000.org/utercall.htm. (Though the website remains, with detailed statistics, targets, etc., this page is no longer available; I have an original printout, complete with colour photographs and tables, dating late 1999.)
12. Ibid.
13. www.ad2000.org/utermost.htm (same remark as above).
14. www.ad2000.org/uters4.htm (same remark as above).
15. www.ad2000.org/utermost.htm (same remark as above).
16. The phrase is by Sheikh Omar Bakri Mohammed, well-known London-based head of the Al-Muhajirun network (also called Maddad, Hezbet-Tahrir ...), which openly advocates the re-establishment of Khilafat and helps train militants fighting from Chechnya to Kashmir.
17. François Perin, *Franc-Parler* ('Frankly Speaking'), Quorum, Ottignies, 1996, p. 64.
18. See several official reports in *Expressions of Christianity, with a Focus on India°*, Part 5.
19. Sri Aurobindo, *The Renaissance in India°*, pp. 133, 147.
20. Sri Aurobindo, 'Epistles from Abroad', *Early Cultural Writings*, vol. 1 in *The Complete Works of Sri Aurobindo*, Sri Aurobindo Ashram, Pondicherry, 2003, pp. 552–53.
21. Sri Aurobindo, 'The Tiger and the Deer', *The Future Poetry*, vol. 26 in *The Complete Works of Sri Aurobindo*, Sri Aurobindo Ashram, Pondicherry, 1997, p. 385.

10. Dialogue among Civilizations: An Indic Perspective

1. Statement by Ibn Warraq on The World Trade Center atrocity, available on www.secularislam.org/ (retrieved 26.1.2010).
2. Sri Aurobindo, *The Renaissance in India°*, pp. 426–27.

3. John Woodroffe, *Is India Civilized?*°, pp. viii–ix.
4. As an example among many, the COMPAS programme is inspiring. See *Food for Thought: Ancient Visions and New Experiments of Rural People*, Bertus Haverkort and Wim Hiemstra, (eds), COMPAS, Leusden, Books for Change, Bangalore & Zed Books, London, 1999, and for instance pp. 30–31.
5. John Woodroffe, *Is India Civilized?*°, p. i.
6. E.g., Krishnan Ramaswamy, Antonio de Nicolas and Aditi Banerjee in *Invading the Sacred*°, also a number of online essays by Rajiv Malhotra.
7. John Woodroffe, *Is India Civilized?*°, pp. v–vii.
8. E.g., 'FDA toughens safeguards to protect against mad cow disease', by Shankar Vedantam in *Washington Post*, 27 January 2004.
9. See for instance Matthew Parris, 'Multiculturalism. A dangerous word ... just like apartheid', *The Times*, 24 January 2004 (www.hvk.org/articles/0104/main.html, retrieved 27.1.2010).
10. See 'Cardinal Tucci Warns Against "Dictatorship of Minorities" In Wake of Judge's Decision to Bar Crucifix From School', Rome, 2 November 2003 (www.zenit.org/english/visualizza.phtml?sid=43843, retrieved 27.1.2010).
11. Sri Aurobindo, 'Our Ideal', *Essays in Philosophy and Yoga*, vol. 13 in *The Complete Works of Sri Aurobindo*, Sri Aurobindo Ashram, Pondicherry, 1998, pp. 143–44.
12. Mother, excerpt from a message of January 1964, in *Mother's Agenda – 1964*, vol. 5, Institute for Evolutionary Research, New York, 1988, p. 46.
13. Pierre Thuillier, *La Grande Implosion: Rapport sur l'effondrement de l'Occident 1999–2002*, Fayard, Paris, 1995.
14. Swami Vivekananda, *Lectures from Colombo to Almora*°, p. 204.
15. Swami Vivekananda, *The Complete Works of Swami Vivekananda*, vol. 5, Advaita Ashrama, Almora, 1947, p. 155.
16. Sri Aurobindo, *India's Rebirth*°, p. 131.
17. Swami Vivekananda, *Lectures from Colombo to Almora*°, p. 194.
18. Sri Aurobindo, *The Renaissance in India*°, p. 40.

Suggested Further Readings

I am often asked to suggest books on Indian culture. To be fair, a suitable list of recommended reading should itself be the size of a book; the list below is necessarily very limited and based on my own preferences. I have included a few classics, but also a few recent books accessible to the lay reader. (Many scholarly studies are mentioned in the preceding Notes.)

1. Introduction to Indian culture

Aurobindo, Sri, *The Renaissance in India and Other Essays on Indian Culture*, vol. 20 in *The Complete Works of Sri Aurobindo*, Sri Aurobindo Ashram, Pondicherry, 1997

Aurobindo, Sri, *Essays on the Gita*, vol. 19 in *The Complete Works of Sri Aurobindo*, Sri Aurobindo Ashram, Pondicherry, 1997

Aurobindo, Sri, *India's Rebirth*, Mira Aditi, Mysore, 3rd edition, 2000

Paranjape, Makarand, *The Penguin Swami Vivekananda Reader*, Penguin Books, New Delhi, 2005

Raghavan, V., *The Indian Heritage*, Dr. V. Raghavan Centre for Performing Arts, Chennai, 5th edn, 1998

Sharma, Arvind, *Classical Hindu Thought*, Oxford University Press, New Delhi, 2000

Tagore, Rabindranath, *The Centre of Indian Culture*, Visva-Bharati, Calcutta, 1988

Tagore, Rabindranath, *Selected Essays*, Rupa, New Delhi, 2004

Vivekananda, Swami, *Letters of Swami Vivekananda*, Advaita Ashrama, Calcutta, 1991

Vivekananda, Swami, *Lectures from Colombo to Almora*, Advaita Ashram, Calcutta, 1992

2. India's cultural heritage

Bajaj, Jitendra, and M.D. Srinivas, *Timeless India, Resurgent India*, Centre for Policy Studies, Chennai, 2001

Basham, A.L., (ed.), *A Cultural History of India*, Oxford University Press, New Delhi, 1975–1983

Bose, D.M., S.N. Sen & B.V. Subbarayappa, (eds), *A Concise History of Science in India*, Universities Press, Hyderabad, 2nd edn, 2009

Coomaraswamy, Ananda K., *Essays in National Idealism*, Munshiram Manoharlal, New Delhi, 1981

Coomaraswamy, Ananda K., *The Dance of Shiva*, Munshiram Manoharlal, New Delhi, 1997

Datta, Bibhutibhushan, & Avadesh Narayan Singh, *History of Hindu Mathematics*, 1935, repr. Bharatiya Kala Prakashan, Delhi, 2004

Gupta, S.P., and Shashi Prabha Asthana, *Elements of Indian Art: Including Temple Architecture, Iconography & Iconometry*, D.K. Printworld, New Delhi, 2nd edn, 2007

Ifrah, Georges, *The Universal History of Numbers*, Penguin Books, New Delhi, 2005, 3 vols.

Joseph, George Gheverghese, *The Crest of the Peacock*, Penguin Books, London & New Delhi, 2000

Kramrish, Stella, *The Hindu Temple*, Motilal Banarsidass, Delhi, 1976, 2 vols.

Krishna, Nanditha, *Sacred Animals of India*, Penguin Books, New Delhi, 2010

Mitchell, George, *Hindu Art and Architecture*, Thames & Hudson, London, 2000

Rao, S. Balachandra, *Indian Mathematics and Astronomy: Some Landmarks*, Bhavan's Gandhi Centre of Science and Human Values, Bangalore, 3rd edn, 2004

Sarasvati Amma, T.A., *Geometry in Ancient and Medieval India*, Motilal Banarsidass, New Delhi, 1999

Sen, S.N., & K.S. Shukla, (eds), *History of Astronomy in India*, Indian National Science Academy, New Delhi, 2nd edn, 2000

Sivaramamurti, C., *Indian Painting*, National Book Trust, India, New Delhi, 1996

The Cultural Heritage of India, The Ramakrishna Mission Institute of Culture, Calcutta, 6 vols, 2nd edn, 2001

3. Indian archaeology and history

Allchin, F.R., (ed.), *Archaeology of Early Historic South Asia: The Emergence of Cities and States*, Cambridge University Press, Cambridge, 1995

Allchin, Raymond & Bridget, *Origins of a Civilization: The Prehistory and Early Archaeology of South Asia*, Viking, New Delhi, 1997

Aurobindo, Sri, *Bande Mataram*, vol. 6–7 in *The Complete Works of Sri Aurobindo*, Sri Aurobindo Ashram, Pondicherry, 2002

Aurobindo, Sri, *Karmayogin*, vol. 8 in *The Complete Works of Sri Aurobindo*, Sri Aurobindo Ashram, Pondicherry, 1997

Chakrabarti, Dilip K., *The Oxford Companion to Indian Archaeology: The Archaeological Foundations of Ancient India*, Oxford University Press, New Delhi, 2006

Danino, Michel, *The Lost River: On the Trail of the Sarasvati*, Penguin Books, New Delhi, 2010

Goel, Sita Ram, *History of Hindu–Christian Encounters (AD 304 to 1996)*, Voice of India, New Delhi, 2nd ed., 1996

Goel, Sita Ram, (ed.), *Hindu Temples: What Happened to Them*, Voice of India, New Delhi, 2 vols, 1998, 1993

Kenoyer, Jonathan Mark, *Ancient Cities of the Indus Valley Civilization*, Oxford University Press & American Institute of Pakistan Studies, Karachi & Islamabad, 1998

Lahiri, Nayanjot, *Finding Forgotten Cities: How the Indus Civilization Was Discovered*, Permanent Black, New Delhi, 2005

Lal, B.B., *India 1947-1997: New Light on the Indus Civilization*, Aryan Books International, New Delhi, 1998

Lal, B.B., *The Sarasvatī Flows On: The Continuity of Indian Culture*, Aryan Books International, New Delhi, 2002

Lal, B.B., *How Deep Are the Roots of Indian Civilization? Archaeology Answers*, Aryan Books International, New Delhi, 2009

Majumdar, R.C., (ed.), *The History and Culture of the Indian People*, Bharatiya Vidya Bhavan, Bombay, 11 vols, 1951–1990

Majumdar, R.C., *History of the Freedom Movement in India*, Firma KLM, Calcutta, 1988, 3 vols.

Nivedita, Sister, *Footfalls of Indian History*, Advaita Ashrama, Calcutta, 1990

Possehl, Gregory L., *The Indus Civilization: A Contemporary Perspective*, Altamira Press, Oxford, 2002; Indian edn, Vistaar, New Delhi, 2003

Singh, Upinder, *The Discovery of Ancient India: Early Archaeologists and the Beginnings of Archaeology*, Permanent Black, New Delhi, 2004

Singh, Upinder, *A History of Ancient and Early Medieval India: From the Stone Age to the 12th Century*, Pearson, New Delhi, 2008

4. India and the world

Capra, Fritjof, *The Tao of Physics: An exploration of the parallels between modern physics and eastern mysticism*, 3rd edn, Flamingo, 1991

Capra, Fritjof, *Uncommon Wisdom: Conversations with Remarkable People*, Flamingo, London, 1989

Chandra, Lokesh, et al., *India's Contribution to World Thought and Culture*, Vivekananda Rock Memorial Committee, Madras, 1970

Kak, Subhash, *The Wishing Tree: The Presence and Promise of India*, Munshiram Manoharlal, New Delhi, 2001

Kumar, Shashiprabha, *Sanskrit across Cultures*, Special Centre for Sanskrit Studies, New Delhi, & D.K. Printworld, New Delhi, 2007

Londhe, Sushama, *A Tribute to Hinduism: Thoughts and Wisdom Spanning Continents and Time about India and Her Culture*, Pragun Publication, New Delhi, 2008

Ramaswamy, Krishnan, Antonio de Nicolas & Aditi Banerjee, *Invading the Sacred*, Rupa, New Delhi, 2007

Singhal, D.P., *India and World Civilization*, Sidgwick & Jackson, London, 1972, 2 vols.

Swarup, Ram, *Hindu View of Christianity and Islam*, Voice of India, New Delhi, 1992

Woodroffe, John, *Is India Civilized?*, Ganesh & Co., Madras 1918

Expressions of Christianity, with a Focus on India, Vivekananda Kendra Prakashan, Chennai, 2007

Index

The Index refers only to the main text (including Suggested Further Readings), not to the Notes. Italicized page numbers refer to footnotes.